ActionScript® 3.0 for
ADOBE® FLASH® CS4 PROFESSIONAL

CLASSROOM IN A BOOK®

The official training workbook from Adobe Systems

www.adobepress.com

Adobe

ActionScript® 3.0 for Adobe® Flash® CS4 Professional Classroom in a Book®

Adobe Press books are published by Peachpit, a division of Pearson Education located in Berkeley, California. For the latest on Adobe Press books, go to www.adobepress.com. To report errors, please send a note to errata@peachpit.com. For information on getting permission for reprints and excerpts, contact permissions@peachpit.com.

Writer: Chris Florio
Project Editor: Rebecca Freed
Development Editor: Robyn G. Thomas
Production Editor: Tracey Croom
Copyeditor: Wendy Katz
Technical Editor: Angela Nimer
Compositor: Kim Scott, Bumpy Design
Indexer: Jack Lewis
Proofreader: Robert Campbell
Cover design: Eddie Yuen
Interior design: Mimi Heft

Printed and bound in the United States of America

ISBN-13:   978-0-321-57921-8
ISBN-10:   0-321-57921-6

9 8 7 6 5 4 3 2 1

WHAT'S ON THE DISC

Here is an overview of the contents of the Classroom in a Book disc.

Lesson files ... and so much more

The *ActionScript 3.0 for Adobe Flash CS4 Professional Classroom in a Book* CD includes all the lesson files that you'll need to complete the exercises in this book, as well as other content to help you learn more about Flash CS4 and use it with greater efficiency and ease. The diagram below represents the contents of the CD, and should help you locate the files you need.

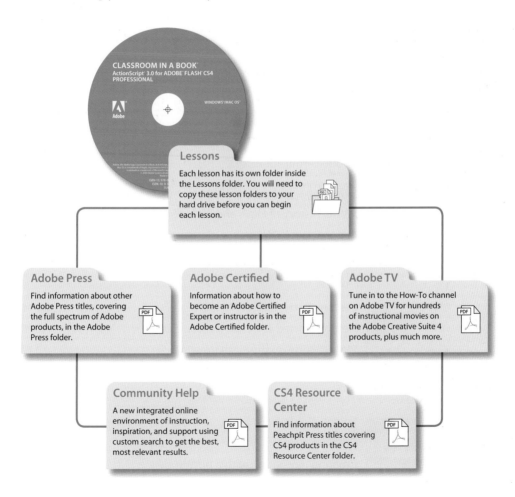

CLASSROOM IN A BOOK
ActionScript 3.0 for ADOBE FLASH CS4
PROFESSIONAL

WINDOWS/MAC OS

Lessons
Each lesson has its own folder inside the Lessons folder. You will need to copy these lesson folders to your hard drive before you can begin each lesson.

Adobe Press
Find information about other Adobe Press titles, covering the full spectrum of Adobe products, in the Adobe Press folder.

Adobe Certified
Information about how to become an Adobe Certified Expert or instructor is in the Adobe Certified folder.

Adobe TV
Tune in to the How-To channel on Adobe TV for hundreds of instructional movies on the Adobe Creative Suite 4 products, plus much more.

Community Help
A new integrated online environment of instruction, inspiration, and support using custom search to get the best, most relevant results.

CS4 Resource Center
Find information about Peachpit Press titles covering CS4 products in the CS4 Resource Center folder.

CONTENTS

GETTING STARTED

Adobe® Flash® CS4 Professional provides a comprehensive authoring environment with tools for working with 2D and 3D animation, sound, vector and bitmap graphics, text, and video. Adobe ActionScript® 3.0 is a sophisticated programming language that is totally integrated into Flash CS4 to develop rich interactive projects. The ActionScript techniques that you will learn in this book can be used with the great design and animation tools in the Flash interface to create rich interactive websites, games, e-learning content, e-commerce tools, and desktop applications for the Adobe AIR® platform.

About Classroom in a Book

ActionScript 3.0 for Adobe Flash CS4 Professional Classroom in a Book is part of the official training series for the Adobe Flash platform. The lessons are designed so that you can learn at your own pace. If you're new to ActionScript, you'll learn the fundamental concepts and features you'll need to accomplish a wide range of techniques covered in the book, but also gain enough understanding of the language to be able to learn additional techniques on your own. Each lesson in the book includes suggestions for continuing to develop your skills. Classroom in a Book teaches many advanced features, including tips and techniques for using the latest versions of ActionScript and Flash.

The lessons in this book include opportunities to use new features in Flash CS4, such as working with inverse kinematics, interacting with Adobe's new Pixel Bender Toolkit, and developing for the Adobe AIR platform.

Prerequisites

Before you begin to use *ActionScript 3.0 for Adobe Flash CS4 Professional Classroom in a Book*, make sure that your system is set up correctly and that you've installed the required software. You should know how to use the mouse and standard menus and commands, and also how to open, save, and close files. If you need to review these techniques, see the printed or online documentation included with your Microsoft Windows or Apple Mac OS software.

This book is geared toward Flash users who are already comfortable with the interface and basic design and animation features of Flash. If you are new to Flash entirely, you may want to go through the lessons in *Adobe Flash CS4 Professional Classroom in a Book*.

This book assumes no programming experience. If you are a designer wishing to learn ActionScript 3.0, but perhaps are a little daunted by code, this book is for you. It also is helpful for Flash users who may have worked with earlier versions of ActionScript but have not yet made the transition to ActionScript 3.0.

Installing Flash

You must purchase the Adobe Flash CS4 software either as a stand-alone application or as part of Adobe Creative Suite. Both products come with Flash Player 10, Adobe Media Encoder CS4, Adobe Extension Manager CS4, Adobe Device Central CS4, Adobe Bridge CS4, and the Pixel Bender Toolkit in addition to the actual Adobe Flash CS4 application. Flash CS4 requires Apple QuickTime 7.1.2 or later. For system requirements and complete instructions on installing the Flash software, see the Adobe Flash ReadMe.html file on the application DVD.

Install Flash from the Adobe Flash CS4 application DVD onto your hard disk. You cannot run the program from the DVD. Follow the onscreen instructions. Make sure that your serial number is accessible before installing the application. You can find the serial number on the registration card or on the back of the DVD case.

Optimizing performance

Flash CS4 Professional requires a minimum of 512 MB of RAM; 1 GB or more is recommended. The more RAM available to Flash, the faster the application will work for you.

Copying the lesson files

The lessons in this book all revolve around a Flash project contained in an FLA file. Most of the lessons use additional resources such as audio, video, image, and text files. To complete the lessons in this book, you must copy these files from the *ActionScript 3.0 for Adobe Flash CS4 Professional Classroom in a Book* CD (located inside the back cover of this book) to your computer.

Copy the Lessons folder (which contains folders named Lesson01, Lesson02, and so on) from the *ActionScript 3.0 for Adobe Flash CS4 Professional Classroom in a Book* CD onto your computer by dragging it to your hard drive.

When you begin each lesson, you will be instructed where to navigate within the Lessons folder to find all the assets you need to complete the lesson.

If you have limited storage space on your computer, you can copy each lesson folder individually as you need it, and delete it afterward if desired. As mentioned before, some lessons build on preceding lessons but even then, the assets in each lesson folder are self-contained and don't require materials from other lesson folders. You do not have to save any finished project if you don't want to or if you have limited hard disk space.

How to use these lessons

Each lesson in this book provides step-by-step instructions for creating a project that illustrates essential ActionScript techniques. Some lessons build on projects created in preceding lessons; others stand alone. All the lessons build on each other in terms of concepts and skills, so the best way to learn from this book is to proceed through the lessons in sequential order. Some techniques and processes are explained and described in detail only the first few times you perform them. Many of the most essential ActionScript processes are repeated throughout the exercises so that you can build a familiarity as well as a level of comfort with the basic tools in the language.

Each of the lesson folders contains a Start folder with the files that you will use to create the lesson as well as a Complete folder with a sample version of the completed lesson for reference; you can compare your work in progress against these samples of finished, working ActionScript. Some of the lessons also include other files and folders with media and resources needed to complete the lesson's project. Be sure to keep each folder's content together.

Standard elements in the book

Boldface text: Words that appear in **boldface** indicate text that you must type while working through the steps in the lessons.

Boldface code: Lines of code that appear in **boldface** within code blocks help you easily identify changes in the block that you are to make in a step.

```
function moveUp(e:Event):void {
  if (jt0.position.y>165) {
    var pt0:Point=new Point(jt0.position.x-5,jt0.position.y-5);
    mover0.moveTo(pt0);
  } else {
    stage.removeEventListener(Event.ENTER_FRAME, moveUp);
    snapshot_btn.visible = true;
  }
}
```

Code in text: `Code` or `keywords` appear slightly different from the rest of the text so you can identify them.

Code and wrapped code lines: To help you easily identify ActionScript, XML, and HTML code within the book, the code has been styled in a special font that's unique from the rest of the text. Single lines of code that are longer than the margins of the page allow, wrap to the next line. They are designated by an arrow at the beginning of the continuation of a broken line and are indented under the line from which they continue. For example:

```
var variables:URLVariables = new URLVariables();
var mailAddress:URLRequest=new
➥URLRequest("http://www.actionscript.tv/email.php");
```

Italicized text: Words that appear in *italics* are either for *emphasis* or are *new vocabulary*.

Italics are also used on placeholders, in which the exact entry may change depending on your situation. For example:

```
mailto:yourName@yourISP.com?subject=From Lesson 13 link&Body=
➥This message was sent from Flash
```

Menu commands and keyboard shortcuts: Menu commands are shown with angle brackets between the menu names and commands: Menu > Command > Subcommand. Keyboard shortcuts are shown with a plus sign between the names of keys to indicate that you should press the keys simultaneously; for example, Shift+Tab means that you should press the Shift and Tab keys at the same time.

Additional resources

ActionScript 3.0 for Flash CS4 Professional Classroom in a Book is not meant to replace documentation that comes with the program. This book explains the ActionScript concepts used in the lessons and covers most of the essentials, but there's much more to learn about ActionScript 3.0 and Flash CS4. The goal of Classroom in a Book is to give you confidence and skills so that you can start creating your own projects. For more comprehensive information about ActionScript 3.0 and Flash CS4 features, see:

* Adobe Flash CS4 Community Help, which you can view by choosing Help > Flash Help. Community Help is an integrated online environment of instruction, inspiration, and support. It includes custom search of expert-selected, relevant content on and off Adobe.com. Community Help combines content from Adobe Help, Support, Design Center, Developer Connection, and Forums—along with great online community content so that users can easily find the best and most up-to-date resources. Access tutorials, technical support,

---

▶ Tips: Alternative ways to perform tasks and suggestions to consider when applying the skills you are learning.

● Notes: Additional background information to expand your knowledge and advanced techniques you can explore to further develop your skills.

▶ Warnings: Information warning about situations you might encounter that could cause errors, problems, or unexpected results.

online product help, videos, articles, tips and techniques, blogs, examples, and much more. Of particular use in Flash Help is the "ActionScript 3.0 Language and Components Reference."

- Adobe Flash CS4 Support Center, where you can find and browse support and learning content on Adobe.com. Visit www.adobe.com/support/flash/.

- Adobe TV, where you will find programming on Adobe products, including a How To channel that contains hundreds of movies on Flash CS4 and other products across the Adobe Creative Suite 4 lineup. Visit http://tv.adobe.com/.

Also check out these useful links:

- The ActionScript Technology Center at www.adobe.com/devnet/actionscript/.

- The Flash CS4 product home page at www.adobe.com/products/flash/.

- Flash user forums at www.adobe.com/support/forums/ for peer-to-peer discussions of Adobe products.

- Flash Exchange at www.adobe.com/cfusion/exchange/ for extensions, functions, code, and more.

- Flash plug-ins at www.adobe.com/products/plugins/flash/.

- Adobe Developer Center (www.adobe.com/devnet/), where you'll find tutorials, articles, and sample applications. You can learn the industry trends you need to master Adobe development-oriented products and technologies.

Finding resources for using ActionScript

For complete and up-to-date information about using Flash CS4 panels, tools, and other application features, visit the Adobe website. Choose Help > Flash Help. You'll be connected to the Adobe Community Help website, where you can search Flash Help and support documents, as well as other websites relevant to Flash users. You can narrow your search results to view only Adobe help and support documents as well.

If you plan to work in Flash when you're not connected to the Internet, download the most current PDF version of Flash Help from www.adobe.com/go/documentation.

For additional resources, such as tips and techniques and the latest product information, check out the Adobe Community Help page at community.adobe.com/help/main.

⬤ **Note:** If Flash detects that you are not connected to the Internet when you start the application, choosing Help > Flash Help opens the Help HTML pages installed with Flash. For more up-to-date information, view the Help files online or download the current PDF for reference.

Checking for updates

● **Note:** To set your preferences for future updates, click Preferences in the Adobe Updater dialog box. Select how often you want Adobe Updater to check for updates, for which applications, and whether to download them automatically. Click OK to accept the new settings.

Adobe periodically provides updates to software. You can easily obtain these updates through Adobe Updater, as long as you have an active Internet connection.

1 In Flash CS4, choose Help > Updates. The Adobe Updater automatically checks for updates available for your Adobe software.

2 In the Adobe Updater dialog box, select the updates you want to install, and then click Download And Install Updates to install them.

Flash Player version

The lessons in this book (with the exception of Lesson 14 which uses Adobe AIR) are created to work with Flash Player 10 or higher. Many, but not all of the features in the lessons will work with Flash Player 9. Versions before Flash Player 9 do not support ActionScript 3.0. While most web users have a recent version of the Flash Player, it is always a good idea before beginning your own Flash-based projects to identify the target audience and determine which version of the Flash Player to develop for before starting the process. For information on Flash Player version penetration visit:

www.adobe.com/products/player_census/flashplayer/

For users of Flash CS3

The exercise files for the first six lessons will work equally well in Flash CS3 or Flash CS4. If you are using Flash CS4, the first time that you save one of the lesson files from these chapters you will be prompted to save the file in the CS4 format, which you should do.

While many of the techniques from the later lessons will work in Flash CS3, after Lesson 6, the exercise files will require Flash CS4. Remember that a free 30-day trial version of Flash CS4 is available from Adobe that you can use to complete these lessons.

Adobe certification

The Adobe Certified program is designed to help Adobe customers and trainers improve and promote their product-proficiency skills. There are four levels of certification:

- Adobe Certified Associate (ACA)
- Adobe Certified Expert (ACE)
- Adobe Certified Instructor (ACI)
- Adobe Authorized Training Center (AATC)

The Adobe Certified Associate (ACA) credential certifies that individuals have the entry-level skills to plan, design, build, and maintain effective communications using different forms of digital media.

The Adobe Certified Expert program is a way for expert users to upgrade their credentials. You can use Adobe certification as a catalyst for getting a raise, finding a job, or promoting your expertise.

If you are an ACE-level instructor, the Adobe Certified Instructor program takes your skills to the next level and gives you access to a wide range of Adobe resources.

Adobe Authorized Training Centers offer instructor-led courses and training on Adobe products, employing only Adobe Certified Instructors. A directory of AATCs is available at http://partners.adobe.com.

For information on the Adobe Certified program, visit www.adobe.com/support/certification/main.html.

INTRODUCTION TO ACTIONSCRIPT 3.0

Before you begin working through the lessons, it is worth taking a little time to understand the history of ActionScript and address a few topics that may clarify for you how Adobe ActionScript 3.0 works with Adobe Flash and the Flash platform.

A brief history of Flash and ActionScript

Flash and ActionScript have evolved together since Flash was originally released in 1996. Today, the combination of the design and animation tools in Flash CS4 with the advanced interactive capabilities of ActionScript 3.0 offer one of the most powerful, most versatile, and certainly most popular development environments available, but the origins of ActionScript as part of Flash were fairly humble.

In the first three versions of Flash, there were no programming tools available, and interactivity meant selecting from a few simple drag-and-drop options in the Actions panel. These actions allowed for navigation of the Flash timeline and creating links to URLs, but not much more.

Flash 4 was the first version that allowed typing code using a simple scripting language, which became informally known as *ActionScript.* In Flash 5, ActionScript evolved even more and became an *official* scripting language. With each version of Flash since that time, the capabilities of ActionScript have become richer, offering interactive control of animation, text, sound, video, data, and much more. In 2003, ActionScript 2.0 was introduced, and its capabilities were on par with object-oriented languages like Java and C#. You will learn more about object-oriented programming (OOP) starting in Lesson 4, "Creating ActionScript in External Files."

Serious programmers started becoming more interested in ActionScript as a development tool, but they found that even though ActionScript 2.0 rivaled the features of other languages, it did not rival their performance. This was because each version of ActionScript was built on the foundation of the previous one, going all the way back to its very simple beginnings. Flash Player was not originally designed for creating high-performance applications and games, but developers began using it for those purposes. It became clear that a new version of ActionScript needed to be written from the ground up.

In 2006, Adobe introduced ActionScript 3.0, which offered significant new functionality as well as dramatic performance increases. Flash CS3 was the first version of Flash to incorporate ActionScript 3.0, and Flash CS4 adds even more functionality to ActionScript 3.0, including new three-dimensional capabilities, new animation controls, and ActionScript classes for working with Adobe AIR (see Lesson 14, "Creating Adobe AIR Applications with Flash and ActionScript").

ActionScript 3.0 for new programmers

Having the power and sophistication of ActionScript 3.0 within Flash is wonderful, but with these capabilities comes more complexity and a steeper learning curve. Many designers and animators who use Flash regularly are daunted by the prospect of learning ActionScript 3.0, and the majority of books on the subject are written for those with programming experience. The truth is that with a little patience at the beginning, you can quickly learn enough ActionScript to be able to add lots of interactive features to your Flash work.

The lessons in this book are geared toward designers who have little or no programming experience. Some knowledge of ActionScript 1.0 or 2.0 is of course useful, but should not be necessary to successfully complete the lessons.

By working through these lessons, you will gain a comfort with the syntax of ActionScript 3.0. More importantly, you will gain a large repertoire of interactive tools to add to your existing Flash skills. You'll also build a foundation that will allow you to continue your ActionScript education using the material at the Adobe Flash Developer Center (adobe.com/devnet/flash) and the many other books and resources available.

For users of ActionScript 1.0 and 2.0

There are many changes to ActionScript 3.0 compared to ActionScript 1.0 and ActionScript 2.0; even some advanced ActionScript 1.0 and 2.0 programmers have been intimidated by the prospect of learning ActionScript 3.0. The next sections cover some points that may help you to make the transition and convince you that the benefits of ActionScript 3.0 will justify the effort.

First the bad news

There is no doubt that ActionScript 3.0 is more verbose than earlier versions of the language; this means that, especially in the beginning, you have to type more code to get the same results. The payoff becomes apparent fairly quickly, but at first glance, ActionScript 3.0 can be a little scary for new users.

Also, Flash applications written in ActionScript 3.0 cannot be simply integrated with Flash files created with earlier versions of ActionScript. This is because there are actually two ActionScript players inside Flash Player 9 and later.

Flash Player contains ActionScript Virtual Machine 1 (AVM1), which plays files created with ActionScript 1.0 and ActionScript 2.0, and Virtual Machine 2 (AVM2), which plays files created with ActionScript 3.0. While it is possible for files to communicate between the two virtual machines, it is not as simple as communicating with files created with the same version of AVM. In this book, we will focus exclusively on ActionScript 3.0, but if you plan on integrating new ActionScript 3.0 projects into older Flash websites or applications, you should make a thorough study of the resources in Flash Help on the subject of integrating ActionScript 3.0 with older files.

…and now the good news

ActionScript 1.0 and ActionScript 2.0 developers who have made the transition to ActionScript 3.0 very quickly appreciate the advantages of the latest version of the language, especially:

* Better performance. As mentioned, ActionScript 3.0 code executes much faster than earlier versions of the language—usually 2 to 10 times, but sometimes up to 100 times, faster. This makes Flash viable for creating high-performance games, simulations, three-dimensional interfaces, and data-driven applications.

* More consistent syntax. Because everything up to ActionScript 2.0 was built on top of the previous version, there were often many ways to do similar things. This could be extremely confusing. For example, in ActionScript 1.0 and 2.0 something as simple as responding to an event or creating a new object could be dramatically different, depending on what the event or object was. As you will see beginning in Lesson 2, "Working with Events and Functions," once you learn how to do something in ActionScript 3.0, the syntax will remain consistent throughout the language. For example, there is one way to listen for and respond to an event in ActionScript 3.0, regardless of the type of event.

* Better error checking and feedback. Everyone makes mistakes, so it is a blessing that ActionScript 3.0 offers much better feedback to help you identify and correct errors in your code.

* Lots of new features. ActionScript 3.0 has introduced dozens of new classes that offer functionality that was previously unavailable, including ways of working with sound, video, XML, 3D, and lots more. As you progress through the lessons you will become comfortable with many of these features.

- A more standardized OOP environment. ActionScript 3.0 is based on the ECMA standard and has many similarities to other languages including Java, C#, and C++. ActionScript is a true object-oriented language, which makes it very good for building larger and more complex projects. While this book does not put an emphasis on OOP, the later lessons will lay a foundation that will allow you to delve more deeply into OOP development in ActionScript 3.0 if you wish.

Formats for playing back Flash and ActionScript 3.0 files

Usually, creating a website or application in Flash means publishing your finished work as a SWF file that can be played using Flash Player, most typically in a web browser. This is the most common use of Flash for most developers.

Flash has also always provided the option of creating platform-specific projector versions of your projects. These are self-running executable files that can be created for either Macintosh or Windows.

Recently, Adobe introduced its Adobe AIR technology, which allows for the creation of true cross-platform desktop applications that run on Macintosh, Windows, or Linux. Adobe AIR applications can be made using Flash CS4, and in Lesson 15, you will learn to use ActionScript 3.0 to create desktop applications in Flash that can access the end user's operating system.

Flash and Flex

Many Flash users have heard of Adobe Flex but are not sure how or if it fits into their development process. Flash and Flex are both commercial applications from Adobe. You can use both Flash and Flex to create SWF files for Flash Player as well as standalone Adobe AIR applications. Flash and Flex both support the entire ActionScript 3.0 language, but Flex is more geared toward people with a programming background, while Flash includes tools and an interface adapted to the needs of designers and animators.

This book focuses on the use of ActionScript 3.0 in Flash, but all the concepts and nearly all the code would work equally well in Flex.

ActionScript in the Flash timeline vs. external ActionScript files

Traditionally, ActionScript in Flash has been placed on keyframes in the timeline. In earlier versions of Flash, ActionScript could also be placed directly on an object such as a button or a movie clip, but this is no longer the case with ActionScript 3.0.

An alternative to placing code on the timeline is to create dedicated ActionScript files that can be used in any Flash project. This is the foundation for OOP in Flash.

In the early lessons of this book, you will be placing all your code in the Flash timeline. Starting in Lesson 4, you will begin working with external ActionScript class files and begin to learn to take advantage of OOP principles.

That's enough background for now...

Let's get started in Lesson 1, "Navigating the Flash Timeline," by learning to use ActionScript 3.0 to navigate the Flash timeline.

1 NAVIGATING THE FLASH TIMELINE

Lesson overview

In this lesson, you'll learn to do the following:

- Add ActionScript to the timeline via the Actions panel.

- Add labels to frames on a timeline.

- Control playback with ActionScript you've added to the timeline.

- Preview your Flash project as a SWF file in the testing environment.

- Change the content of a dynamic text field in ActionScript.

- Use an ActionScript variable to keep track of a changing number.

- Use a conditional statement to respond to the looping of an animation.

 This lesson will take approximately 2 hours.

The Flash timeline is an extremely useful tool for creating animations. It is also a great environment for setting up a website or simple application that requires navigation between different sections of content. This lesson will introduce the techniques for adding code to the Flash timeline to control playback; it will also introduce a few essential ActionScript 3.0 programming concepts.

Coordinating the Flash Stage, Timeline, and Actions panel.

Getting started

To begin this lesson, from the Lessons > Lesson01 > Start folder, open the lesson01_start.fla file in Flash CS4. This file has layers, graphics, and animation. If you scrub (that is, click the playback head and drag to the left or right) through the Flash timeline, you'll see that the first 30 frames contain an animation and that frame 50 contains the background for an interactive interface.

● **Note:** If you are used to playing the Flash timeline by pressing Enter (Windows) or Return (Mac) or choosing Control > Play, then you should switch to Control > Test Movie or Ctrl+Enter (Windows) or Cmd+Return (Mac). When you preview in this manner, your files will play in the same way they will for your end users, with all of the ActionScript executing. From this point on, the instruction to test your movie refers to this method of previewing Flash files.

If you ran the movie at this point, it would just play through the whole timeline from start to end, showing a brief glimpse of the interface before returning to the beginning. We will add ActionScript to this file to alter the playback of the timeline.

Placing code on the Flash timeline

You can write ActionScript on any keyframe in the main timeline of a Flash movie. You can also write it on any keyframe inside a movie clip symbol. During playback, the code on each frame will execute when that frame plays.

All timeline code in Flash is written using the Actions panel, accessible in Flash from the Window menu or by pressing F9 (Windows) or Option+F9 (Mac).

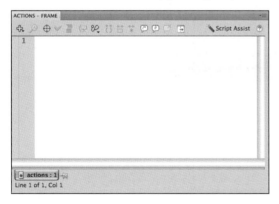

Later, you will see that you can write ActionScript in external ActionScript files, but for now, all code you will write will be in the Actions panel.

Working with labels

Before you start adding ActionScript, notice that among the layers in the timeline is one called *labels*. In this layer, frame 2 has a label called `loop` and frame 50 has a label called *home*. You can add labels to any keyframe on any timeline in Flash—labels can be very useful for identifying significant locations. ActionScript can even reference labels to control navigation. If you haven't worked with labels before, you may want to practice adding an additional label to the timeline on frame 30:

1   Select frame 30 in the `labels` layer of the timeline.

2   Add a keyframe to this frame by pressing F6 or choosing Insert > Timeline > Keyframe.

3   With the new keyframe selected, find the Label section in the upper left of the Properties panel, and in the Name field, type **endLoop**. (If the Properties panel is not visible, open it by choosing Window > Properties.)

4   Press Enter (or Return on the Mac). You will see the label name appear in the timeline on frame 30.

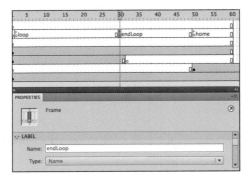

Looping playback with ActionScript

There are many situations when you may want to play a section of the timeline repeatedly. For example, an animation might loop while waiting for additional content to load or while the user is deciding which section of a website to go to next.

Creating looping animation

For our first foray into ActionScript, we will loop the animation that plays from frame 2 to frame 30. At first, you will write ActionScript that loops this section indefinitely, and then you will add code that will control how many times this section repeats before jumping to the home interface on frame 50.

1   Arrange your work area so that both the Timeline and the Actions panels (Window > Actions) are visible.

2   Select the top layer of the timeline and add a new layer above it (Insert > Timeline > Layer). Name the layer **actions**. We will place all the code for this file in this layer.

3   In the new `actions` layer, select frame 30, and press F6 to add a new keyframe in that layer.

4   Select the new keyframe in the `actions` layer in frame 30.

5   Click inside the Actions panel so that the insertion point appears in line 1 of the panel. If you do not see line numbers, you can turn them on by choosing Line Numbers from the Actions panel menu in the upper-right corner of the panel.

6   In the Actions panel, type the following code:

```
gotoAndPlay("loop");
```

7   Save your work and test your movie (Ctrl+Enter on Windows or Cmd+Enter on Mac). Notice that the movie no longer reaches the *home* frame but instead plays the opening animation over and over. This is because every time the playhead reaches frame 30, the action you just wrote sends it back to frame 2.

Keeping track of the number of loops

In the next section, you will program your file to jump to the *home* frame after a specific number of loops, but first let's add some code to keep track of the number of times that the animation has played. You will do this by storing the value for the number of loops in a variable.

Creating a count variable

The purpose of a variable is to store data. ActionScript 3.0 can store many different types of data in variables, and you will create many of these in the coming lessons. In this lesson, you will create a variable to store a numeric value to keep track of the number of times the animation in frames 2–30 repeats.

To create a variable in ActionScript 3.0, you type **var** and then the name you want to give to your new variable:

1 Select frame 1 on the `actions` layer, and click inside the Actions panel.

2 Type the following code:

```
var count:Number = 1;
```

Next, you will add some code that changes that value every time the animation loops.

Creating variables in ActionScript 3.0

You will be creating many variables in the lessons to come, so it is worth taking a closer look at the syntax used.

Consider this example:

```
var count:Number = 1;
```

The keyword `var` tells ActionScript that you are creating a new variable. The name of the variable is `count`. You can choose any name you want for your own variables, as long as you follow these three rules:

- Do not use spaces in your variable names; use underscores instead.

- Except for underscores or dashes, do not use special characters; stick to letters and numbers.

- Do not start your names with a number. So the variable name `2button` is not valid, but `button2` is fine.

The colon after the variable name indicates that the next piece of information will denote what type of data will be stored in the variable. In the example, the `count` variable stores a number. You will learn more about data typing in the coming lessons.

An equal sign (=) indicates that what follows is the value to be stored in the variable. It is not necessary to give a value to a variable when you create it. Often a variable is created so that it can store information at a later time. In our example, the variable `count` is assigned an initial value of 1.

Updating the count variable

To change the value of the count variable on each loop, you add some code to change the value each time the animation finishes:

1 Select the keyframe on frame 30 on the actions layer.

2 Click inside the Actions panel.

3 On a new line below the existing code, type the following code:

```
count++;
```

Using the characters ++ is a shorthand way in ActionScript to increase a value by one. The code you just wrote loosely translates to "take the current value of the count variable and add 1 to it." The result is that the second time the animation plays, count will equal 2, the third time it plays, count will equal 3, and so on.

Displaying the count in a text field

At this point, you have a variable keeping track of the number of loops, but when the movie runs, you have no visual feedback telling you how many times the animation has looped. Let's add that feedback in a text field:

1 Select the text field that is onstage in the text layer. Notice in the Properties panel that this text field is set to be dynamic. Also notice that it has been given the instance name info_txt. It is essential that all objects onstage that are intended to be controlled with ActionScript be given instance names.

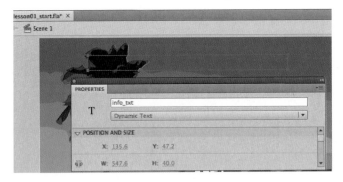

2 On the actions layer, select frame 2, and add a keyframe by pressing F6.

3 With the new keyframe selected in the timeline, click inside the Actions panel.

4 Type the following code:

```
info_txt.text = String(count);
```

About text fields and strings

When a text field is created with the Text tool in the Tools panel, it can be set to either Static, Dynamic, or Input Text in the Properties panel. Static text is for display only and cannot be manipulated with ActionScript.

Dynamic and input text fields can have many of their properties set using ActionScript. They can even be created from scratch with ActionScript. You will learn much more about working with text in ActionScript 3.0 in Lesson 8, "Creating a Radio Button Quiz in an ActionScript File."

Consider this example:

```
info_txt.text = String(count);
```

The text field named info_txt has had its `text` property set to equal the current value of the variable `count`. The text field will be updated with the value of `count` each time the timeline plays frame 2.

A text field can display only data that is stored as literal text. Literal text in ActionScript belongs to the data type String. Because the `count` variable is set to store the data type Number, the last bit of code in the example,

```
String(count);
```

tells ActionScript to convert (or *recast*) the `count` number to a text string so that it can be displayed in a text field.

If this is a little confusing, don't worry about it for now. You will have plenty of practice with text and data typing in the coming lessons.

5   Save your work and test your movie. The text field should start by displaying the number 1, and increase by one each time the animation loops.

Using a conditional statement to control the timeline

A project that just plays its introduction over and over is not ideal, so let's limit the number of times the introduction loops before jumping to the *home* frame. For a web project, you might want to set up an introduction that plays over and over until the next section is fully downloaded. You will learn how to create this type of preloader in Lesson 5, "Using ActionScript and Components to Load Content." In this lesson, you will limit the number of times that the introduction plays by making the timeline jump to the frame with the label *home* (frame 50) when the count variable reaches a certain number.

You will accomplish this by adding a conditional statement to your code. A conditional statement in ActionScript checks to see if a condition is true. In this case, if the count variable is more than 4, then code will execute that goes to the *home* frame.

1   Make sure that both the Timeline and the Actions panels are visible, and select frame 30 on the actions layer.

2   With frame 30 selected, switch to the Actions panel. Place the insertion point before the code that is already in this window, and press Enter.

3   Select and delete the line of code that reads:

```
gotoAndPlay("loop");
```

then add the following code (above the line that says count++;):

```
if(count>4) {
    gotoAndStop("home");
} else {
    gotoAndPlay("loop");
}
```

The result is that each time the animation finishes, the conditional statement checks to see if count has become greater than 4. On the first four loops, when the condition was not true, the playhead goes back to frame 2 and replays the animation. After the fifth time the animation plays, the condition is true, so it goes to, and stops on, the *home* frame.

(continues on the next page)

Conditional statements

Conditional statements are a big part of the interactive power of ActionScript. They allow your Flash projects to react differently under different circumstances.

Conditional statements are available in most programming languages and work similarly to the way they do in ActionScript 3.0. Even if you have no experience with programming languages, you are probably familiar with the concept of a conditional statement. You hear an almost-perfect example of one every time you interact with a voice mail system!

For example, you call your friend's house and hear a voice mail system that says:

If you want John, press one,

or,

if you want Mary, press two,

or,

leave a message after the beep.

In ActionScript, the same interaction would look like this:

```
If (wantJohn) {
    pressOne();
} else if(wantMary) {
    pressTwo();
} else {
    leaveMessage()
}
```

Examples of conditions you might want to respond to with ActionScript include:

- If a file has successfully downloaded, then display something.
- If a question on a quiz has been answered correctly, then go to the next question.
- If a level of a game has been completed, then update the score and go to the next level.
- If a product has been dragged to the shopping cart, then add its cost to the total purchased, and ship the product.

You will be working with conditional statements quite a bit in the lessons to come.

4 Save your work and test your movie. The count should increase to 5 in the text field, and then the timeline should jump to the home frame.

Updating the text on the home frame

Lastly, you will change the text on the home frame. Since the user is no longer watching the animation loop on this frame, there is not a reason to still display the count number. Instead, you will add a message to welcome them to the home frame.

1 Make sure that both the Timeline and the Actions panel are visible, and select frame 50 on the `actions` layer.

2 Add a keyframe to frame 50 in the `actions` layer by pressing F6.

3 Add the following code to the Actions panel for this frame:

```
info_txt.text = "Welcome to the home frame";
```

This uses the same dynamic text field as you used before, but instead of using the `count` variable to populate the text field, you use the literal words "Welcome to the home frame". When you want to set the `text` property of a text field to literal words, the characters you want to use are placed inside quotation marks.

4 Test your movie once more; you should see the updated text on the home frame.

Although the application you just created is very simple, a number of essential ActionScript concepts have been introduced. Storing and passing data with variables and responding to changing circumstances by using conditional statements are both critical parts of creating rich interactivity with ActionScript 3.0. You will be working with these techniques quite a bit more in the lessons to come.

In the next lesson, you will learn how to respond to events in ActionScript 3.0 using buttons to add some functionality to the file you created in this lesson.

Some suggestions to try on your own

To get comfortable with the techniques introduced in this chapter you may want to try some of the following techniques:

- Change the number of times that the opening animation repeats by altering the conditional statement.

- Change the code on frame 50 to display different text in the info_txt field.

- Add a new dynamic text field to the stage. Give it an instance name and try to write some ActionScript that will place text into that field.

Review questions

1 What ActionScript code would you use to navigate to a specific frame of the timeline?

2 What is the keyword that you use to create a new ActionScript variable?

3 What is the purpose of a conditional statement in ActionScript?

Review answers

1 To navigate to a specific frame of the timeline you would use `gotoAndPlay()` or `gotoAndStop()`. The value between the parentheses describes the specific frame to which you want to navigate. For example:

```
gotoAndPlay(1);
gotoAndPlay("home");
```

2 A line of ActionScript that creates a variable begins with the keyword `var`.

3 A conditional statement lets you check to see if a condition or conditions are true and if so execute blocks of code. If the condition is false, you can execute an alternate block of code.

2 WORKING WITH EVENTS AND FUNCTIONS

Lesson overview

In this lesson, you will learn to do the following:

- Use event listeners to listen for mouse events.

- Write event handling functions that respond to mouse events.

- Navigate the Flash Timeline in response to button clicks.

- Open a URL in a browser using ActionScript triggered by a button click.

- Combine strings of text with variable values to populate a text field.

- Create and call a function that sets the language in a text field.

- Use buttons to change the value of a variable.

 This lesson will take approximately 2 hours.

Understanding the event model in ActionScript 3.0 is probably the biggest step in mastering the basics of the language and being able to create rich interactive applications.

In the previous lesson, you wrote code directly on frames of the timeline that executed automatically when the frame on which the code was written played.

In ActionScript 3.0, a large number of built-in events and an infinite number of actions can occur when an event takes place, but most events do not trigger code automatically; instead, you need to tell ActionScript to specifically listen for and respond to the events.

The good news is that the basic syntax to listen and respond to events is the same across all of ActionScript 3.0.

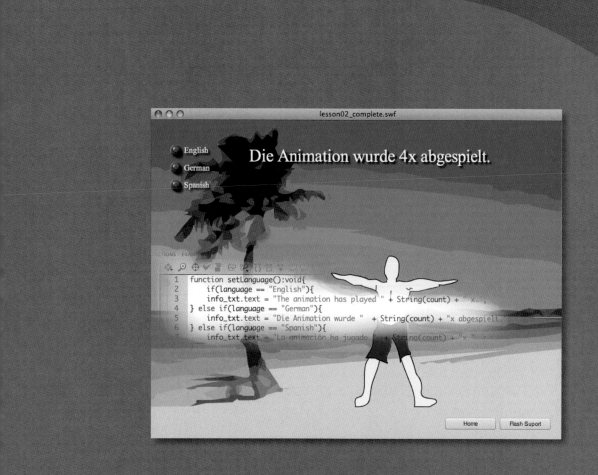

ActionScript events and functions create more
interactive possibilities for you and your users.

Creating event listeners and event handling functions

Listening to and responding to an event in ActionScript takes place in two parts. One piece of code, called an `addEventListener()` method, listens for a specific event from a particular object. Another piece of code, called an *event handler* function, responds when that event takes place.

For example, if you have a button onstage, you might want it to do three separate things:

- Display a menu when the user rolls over the button.
- Hide the menu when the user rolls off the button.
- Stop the timeline when the user clicks the button.

In this example there is only one button, but three separate events to listen for (ROLL_OVER, ROLL_OUT, and CLICK), and three separate sets of actions that may occur, depending on which event took place.

For the first event in our example, if the instance name of the button were button1, then you would tell ActionScript to listen for the ROLL_OVER event like this:

`button1.addEventListener(MouseEvent.ROLL_OVER, showMenu);`

There would be a similar line of code for the ROLL_OUT and CLICK events.

An `addEventListener` method is always the way to tell ActionScript 3.0 to begin listening for a specific event. Once `addEventListener` is called, it continues to listen until it is removed. The first element inside the parentheses indicates which event to listen for. In this case, from the category MouseEvent, we are specifically listening for ROLL_OVER. Notice that the actual event names are all uppercase with underscores between words. The convention of using the uppercase constants for event names may give you a little extra to remember when you are beginning, but it also helps identify errors when compiling the files and is worth the effort to memorize.

After the event name, and separated by a comma and a space, is the name of the function that happens when the ROLL_OVER takes place. A *function* is just a block of code that performs one or more, usually related, tasks. An *event handler function* is one that responds to an event.

Functions can be created and given any name that you like, following the same three rules that we saw for naming variables in Lesson 1, "Navigating the Flash Timeline." In the example, the function name is showMenu. It is a good idea to name functions so that they describe what they are supposed to do.

Reviewing the naming rules in ActionScript

Remember when you are naming variables, functions, classes, and instances in ActionScript, you should follow these three rules:

- Use only letters, numbers, underscores, and dashes in your names; avoid other special characters.

- Do not begin a name with a number.

- Avoid spaces in your names; use underscores rather than spaces.

The basic syntax for our function looks like this:

```
function showMenu(e:MouseEvent):void {
//all the ActionScript to show the menu would go here between the
//left and right curly braces.
}
```

When creating a function in ActionScript 3.0, always start with the lowercase (ActionScript is always case sensitive) word `function` and then the name you choose to give your function. After that, a set of parentheses contains what are called *parameters*. You will work with parameters more in the coming lessons; for now, it is enough to know that the required parameter for an event handling function describes the event that triggered the function. After the parentheses, a colon precedes information about the type of data that the function returns. In this case, `void` means that the function does not return data.

After that, a pair of curly braces contains all the code that will take place each time an event triggers the function.

If all this is not absolutely clear, don't worry. After a few times, it begins to make more and more sense, and pretty soon the process will be second nature. And the payoff will be worth it. As already mentioned, becoming comfortable working with event listeners and event handling functions is probably the biggest step in learning ActionScript 3.0, and the technique is consistent through the entire language. So what you learn in this lesson will be your entryway into many of the interactive possibilities with ActionScript 3.0.

Creating navigation with a button click

This lesson will continue using the file from Lesson 1. You can start this exercise with your completed version of that file; otherwise, in Flash CS4, open the lesson02_start.fla file in Lessons > Lesson02 > Start folder.

Creating button instances for controlling navigation

For many simple Flash web projects, the bulk of the interactive functionality consists of navigation triggered by button clicks. The ability to write ActionScript that responds to a button Click event is also the foundation for understanding much of the rest of the ActionScript language, since all other ActionScript events work in similar ways. You will begin this lesson by adding a new buttons layer to the project.

1 Insert a new layer to the timeline above the text layer and name it **buttons**.

2 In the new buttons layer, add a keyframe (F6) to frame 2.

3 Open the Components panel (Window > Components).

4 From the User Interface list in the Components panel, drag two instances of the Button component, and place them next to each other in the lower right of the stage, in frame 2 of the `buttons` layer.

5 Select the first of these two buttons, and, in the Component Inspector (Window > Component Inspector), select the `label` property.

6 In the field to the right of the `label` property, type **Home** and press Enter (or Return on a Mac). You should see the label on the button update to say Home. You will use this button to allow the user to navigate to the home frame.

7 Select the second button, and repeat the technique in Steps 5 and 6, adding the label name **Flash Support**. You will use this button to allow the user to open the Adobe Flash support page in a browser.

Now, you'll give your buttons instance names.

8   Select the Home button, and, in the Properties panel, place the cursor in the
    field that says <Instance Name>. Give the button the instance name **home_btn**.
    Instance names follow the naming rules already discussed for variables and
    functions.

The importance of instance names

It is essential to give an instance name to all onstage buttons, MovieClips, or other
objects that you wish to control with ActionScript. One of the most common mistakes for new ActionScript programmers is to write their code correctly but to forget
to give their objects instance names. Checking your instance names is often a good
place to start when troubleshooting code that is not working the way you expect.

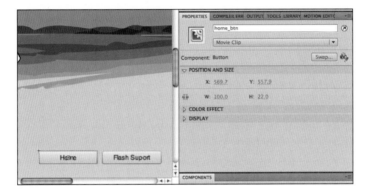

9   Select the Flash Support button, and in the Properties panel give it the instance
    name **help_btn**.

Adding functions to respond to button clicks

Now that you have two buttons onstage, let's add some code to make them work.

1   Select frame 2 of the `actions` layer and then, in the Actions panel (Window >
    Actions), insert a new line below the existing code.

2   Add event listeners for your two buttons by adding the following code:

```
home_btn.addEventListener(MouseEvent.CLICK, goHome);
help_btn.addEventListener(MouseEvent.CLICK, goHelp);
```

Be careful to match the capitalization exactly, and notice that
`addEventListener` and `MouseEvent.CLICK` turn blue when typed correctly.
The color coding of ActionScript as you type provides useful feedback to let you
know you are typing things correctly. Keywords and most ActionScript syntax
turn blue by default. If you type something that is part of the ActionScript

language and it appears as black text, double-check your spelling and capitalization.

After these listeners are added, when the Home button is clicked it will try to call a function named goHome, and when the Flash Support button is clicked, it will try to call a function called goHelp. So, let's add those two functions and give your buttons their functionality.

3 In frame 2, below the lines of code you just added, insert the following code:

```
function goHome(e:MouseEvent):void {
  gotoAndStop("home");
}
```

Remember that when a function is called, all the code between the curly braces is executed. In this case, that means that when the user clicks the Home button, the goHome() function will send the timeline to the home frame. The goto action is the same as we used in Lesson 1. The only difference is that now it is triggered by a button event.

4 Now let's add the function for the Flash Support button. Add the following code under the goHome() function:

```
function goHelp(e:MouseEvent):void {
  navigateToURL(new URLRequest("http://www.adobe.com/support/
  ➥flash"));
}
```

The basic syntax for the function is the same as for the Home button; the only difference is what happens between the curly braces. In this case, an ActionScript method called navigateToURL() is called. As the name implies, this method is used to navigate to a URL using the user's default browser. A reference to a URL in ActionScript 3.0 is stored in an object called a URLRequest. We will be working with URLRequests quite a bit in the coming lessons.

5 Save your work and test your movie (Control > Test Movie). When you click the Home button, the timeline should skip directly to the home frame. When you click the Flash Support button, your browser should navigate to the Flash support page.

If everything is working, congratulations! You are well on your way to being comfortable with ActionScript 3.0. If you had problems with your code, compare it carefully with the example code. If there are errors in the code, the Output panel should appear with descriptions of the errors and on which lines they appear. Notice which line numbers contained the errors, and check your spelling and the color-coding of your ActionScript on those lines. Especially make note of capitalization, and be sure that the instance names of your buttons match the names in your event listeners.

● **Note:** It doesn't matter how many empty lines you place between sections of your code. Many programmers like to leave space between sections of code for clarity; others like to keep things concise by starting new blocks of code on every line. As you start to get comfortable with ActionScript, you will find a style that you prefer.

Here is the completed code for frame 2 so far:

```
info_txt.text = String(count);

home_btn.addEventListener(MouseEvent.CLICK, goHome);
help_btn.addEventListener(MouseEvent.CLICK, goHelp);

function goHome(e:MouseEvent):void {
 gotoAndStop("home");
}

function goHelp(e:MouseEvent):void {
 navigateToURL(new URLRequest("http://www.adobe.com/support/
 ➥flash"));
}
```

Adding a restart button

Now let's add some functionality on the home page to make it possible for the user to restart the animation.

1   Add a keyframe (F6) to the buttons layer on the home frame.

2   Select the Home button on the stage.

3   With the Home button selected, open the Component Inspector (Window > Component Inspector) and change the label name from Home to **Restart**.

4   With the Restart button still selected, switch to the Properties window and change the button's instance name from home_btn to restart_btn.

5   With the Actions panel visible, select the home frame of the actions layer.

6   Add the following code in the Actions panel below the existing code:

```
restart_btn.addEventListener(MouseEvent.CLICK, goStart);
function goStart(e:MouseEvent):void {
 gotoAndPlay("loop");
 count=1;
}
```

This code adds a listener that listens for a click from the Restart button and a function that responds to that click by going back to the beginning of the animation and resetting the count to 1. Remember that count is the variable that keeps track of how many times the opening animation has played, so by setting count to 1, you are restarting the movie with its initial setting.

7   Save your work and test your movie.

When you reach the home frame in the testing environment, the button that previously said "Home" should now say "Restart". The Restart button should respond to the code you added by replaying the opening animation, with the button again reading "Home". Notice that the Flash Support button works the same throughout. Because you did not change its instance name, it always responds to the listener and function that you created for it on frame 2.

Adding to the dynamic text field

Right now, when your movie loops over the opening animation, the text field is instructed to display the number representing the times the animation has played. The number is accurate, but it is not elegant user feedback. Let's make the information in the text field more useful by adding some prose to the field to make a complete sentence.

1 With the Actions panel and the timeline visible, select the loop frame (frame 2) in the `actions` layer of the timeline.

2 In the Actions panel, change the code that currently reads:

```
info_txt.text = String(count);
```

so that it reads:

```
info_txt.text = "The animation has played " + String(count) +
➥"x.";
```

The plus signs are used to concatenate (or join) the literal text (in quotes) with the value of the `count` variable to form a sentence.

3   Save your work and test the movie once more. The text field should now read: "The animation has played 1x (2x, 3x, and so on)."

Adding buttons to control language

To solidify what you've covered so far, add a few more buttons to the stage to let the user control the language that is displayed in the text field. You will begin by adding a variable that keeps track of the user's language choice and sets a default language to the first frame of the movie.

1   With the Actions panel and timeline visible, select frame 1 of the `actions` layer.

2   Add the following code below the existing code:

```
var language:String = "English";
```

Now, add code that checks the value of the `language` variable before adding text to the text field.

3   With the Actions panel and timeline visible, select frame 2 of the `actions` layer.

4   In the Actions panel on frame 2, select the line of code that reads:

```
info_txt.text = "The animation has played " + String(count) +
➥"x.";
```

and cut it (Edit > Cut) to the clipboard.

5   Place the cursor in the Actions panel below the final line of existing code.

6 Create a new function to check which language has been set by adding the following code in the Actions panel:

```
function setLanguage():void {
 if(language == "English") {


 }
}
```

7 In the line above the first right curly brace (}), paste the code that you cut, so that the function now reads:

```
function setLanguage():void {
 if(language == "English") {
 info_txt.text = "The animation has played " + String(count) +
 ➥"x.";


 }
}
```

When the function is called, it will now check to see if the language variable is set to "English" (which is the default because of the code you added in Step 2). If the language is English, then the text field will display your message.

Soon you will add buttons that will let the user choose German or Spanish as well as English, so let's put those two additional possibilities into the conditional statement.

8 Add to the setLanguage() function so that it reads:

```
function setLanguage():void {
 if(language == "English") {
  info_txt.text = "The animation has played " + String(count)
   ➥ + "x.";
 } else if(language == "German") {
  info_txt.text = "Die Animation wurde "  + String(count) + "x
   ➥ abgespielt." ;
 } else if(language == "Spanish") {
  info_txt.text = "La animación ha jugado "  + String(count) +
   ➥ "x." ;
 }
}
```

Unlike the functions that we created earlier, the setLanguage() function is not an event handler function, meaning it is not intended to respond to a specific type of event. This is because this function needs to run at the very start of the application as well as any time the user changes the language selection.

● **Note:** The conditional statement in the setLanguage() function checks to see if the language has been set to English. Note that it does this comparison by using two equal signs (==).

In ActionScript 3.0, you check to see if one value matches another value with two equal signs. In this case you are checking to see if language is equal to "English".

It is especially important to remember to use two equal signs when comparing values because a single equal sign (=) is what is used to set one value to equal another. In other words a single equal sign in this example would be used to set language to English, not check to see if language is English.

To call this type of freestanding function, you just refer to it by name and add a pair of parentheses after the name. If there were any parameters to pass to the function, they would go between the parentheses. This particular function does not have any parameters.

9 In the Actions panel, select the line after the `setLanguage()` function.

10 Call the `setLanguage()` function, so it sets the `language` variable at the beginning of the animation loop, by typing the following code:

```
setLanguage();
```

Finally, you will add buttons that let the user change the language.

11 In the Library panel (Window > Library), you will see three buttons named English Button, German Button, and Spanish Button. Drag one instance of each button to the upper left of the stage. These are just stock buttons with some text added to them.

12 In the Properties panel, name the instances of the new buttons **english_btn**, **german_btn**, and **spanish_btn**, respectively.

13 Continuing in frame 2 of the `actions` layer, add a listener to each button by typing the following code below the last line that you added:

```
english_btn.addEventListener(MouseEvent.CLICK, setEnglish);
german_btn.addEventListener(MouseEvent.CLICK, setGerman);
spanish_btn.addEventListener(MouseEvent.CLICK, setSpanish);
```

When one of these three buttons is clicked, it needs to do two things:

- Set the `language` variable to the language that was chosen.

- Call the `setLanguage()` function, which will change the contents of the text field.

Remember, the conditional statement in the `setLanguage()` function uses the value of the `language` variable to determine what gets written in the text field.

14 On the line below the listeners you just created, add the following code:

```
function setEnglish(e:MouseEvent):void {
  language = "English"
  setLanguage();
}
function setGerman(e:MouseEvent):void {
  language = "German"
  setLanguage();
}
function setSpanish(e:MouseEvent):void {
  language = "Spanish"
  setLanguage();
}
```

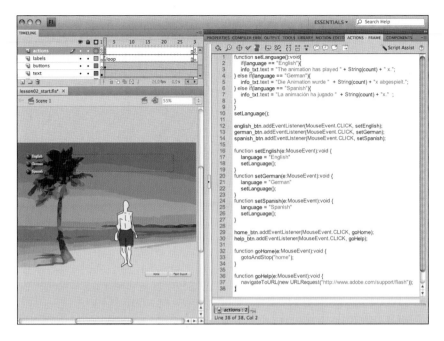

15 Save your work and test your movie. The text field will always display English first. While the opening animation is playing, you should be able to switch the contents of the text field between English, German, and Spanish. If you click the Restart button, the currently selected language should be retained until it is changed (by clicking a different button).

Some suggestions to try on your own

If you made it all the way through this chapter, congratulations! You can now consider yourself a serious student of ActionScript, and you may be amazed at what you can accomplish using just the techniques you have covered in these first two lessons.

In order to practice and become more comfortable with the techniques covered in this lesson, you can try to add a few more features to the lesson02_start.fla file. For example:

- Add additional languages. This will involve adding new buttons, as well as new listeners and functions, to the existing ActionScript. Use any languages that you happen to know, use a translation site such as http://www.freetranslation.com, or just make up your own translation.

- Translate the text on the home frame. Right now you have translated only the content of the text field during the opening animation, but you could write a similar function for the text on the home frame to translate that text based on the language the user chooses.

- Using ActionScript similar to what you added on the Flash Support button, add additional buttons with links to other URLs.

- Using ActionScript similar to what you added on the Home button, add buttons that go to and stop at specific frames or go to and play specific frames of the animation.

Review questions

1 Describe how the addEventListener() method is used in ActionScript 3.0.

2 What is one way to describe a mouse click in the addEventListener() method?

3 In ActionScript 3.0, what is one way to open a URL in a browser window?

4 Which character is used in ActionScript 3.0 to join or concatenate strings of text and variable names?

5 What is the syntax to check to see if one value is equal to another? What is the syntax to set a variable to a given value?

Review answers

1 The addEventListener() method is used to listen for a specific event on a specific object and to respond to that event by calling an event handling function.

2 In an addEventListener() method, a mouse click could be described as MouseEvent.CLICK, as in:

```
Button1.addEventListener(MouseEvent.CLICK, doSomething);
```

3 The navigateToURL() method is used to open a URL in a browser window.

```
navigateToURL(new URLRequest("http://www.anyurl.com"));
```

4 The plus sign (+) is used to concatenate text with evaluated code. This is commonly used to set the text property of a dynamic text field. For example:

```
someTextField.text = "Hello" + userName;
```

5 Two equal signs are used to compare values to see if they are the same, as in:

```
if(password == 3456789) {
 enterSafely();
}
```

A single equal sign is used to set the value of a variable, as in:

```
var firstUSPresident:String = "Washington";
```

3 CREATING ANIMATION WITH ACTIONSCRIPT

Lesson overview

In this lesson, you will learn to do the following:

- Change the properties of a movie clip using ActionScript.

- Use the ENTER_FRAME event to animate MovieClip properties.

- Use a conditional statement to detect stage boundaries.

- Use a variable to store a reference to a movie clip.

- Use buttons to control property changes.

- Use the Tween class to animate MovieClip properties.

- Use easing to create animation effects.

 This lesson will take approximately 2 hours.

Flash has always been a great animation tool, and Flash CS4 includes many new animation capabilities, including 3D animation, built-in inverse kinematics, and the Motion Editor. When you are creating a cartoon or some other type of linear animation, then the Flash timeline and interface offer great and easy-to-use animation features. However, by learning to control animation with ActionScript, you can create animation that is very interactive and responsive. This is essential in most game development but also in training applications, simulations, and creative interface design.

The previous lesson introduced event listeners and event handling functions. This lesson assumes you are familiar with the technique for adding listeners and functions to respond to mouse clicks. To review these techniques, see Lesson 2, "Working with Events and Functions."

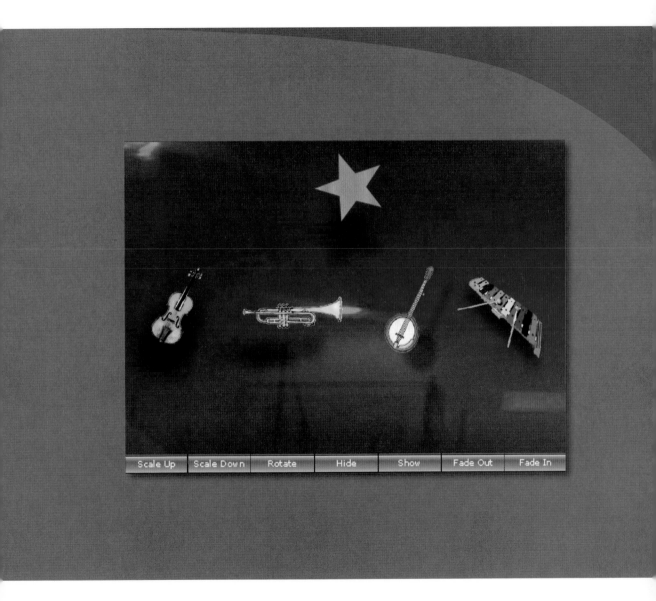

Lesson 3 project interface.

Reviewing the starting file

This lesson will use the lesson03_start.fla file from the Lessons > Lesson03 > Start folder.

Open the file and go over the contents. Onstage there are four MovieClips that contain static graphics of musical instruments. Notice that these MovieClips have instance names of *violin*, *trumpet*, *banjo*, and *glock*. There is also a MovieClip of a star with the instance name of *star_mc*.

In addition, the `text` layer has a single dynamic text field with the instance name of instrument_txt, and the `buttons` layer has a row of buttons, each with a descriptive instance name.

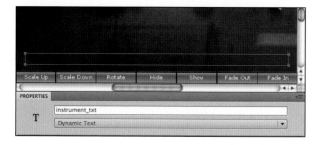

Right now, there is no ActionScript in this file, but not for long. On frame 1 of the `actions` layer, you will add ActionScript to bring some animation into this project.

Controlling MovieClip properties with ActionScript

Most Flash designers are used to working with movie clip symbols in the Flash interface. Nearly all the features that can be accomplished with movie clips in the Flash interface can also be controlled with ActionScript. You can even create new movie clips from scratch in ActionScript. By using ActionScript in addition to or instead of the Flash interface, you can create many more interactive possibilities in your projects.

For example, it is very easy to control the properties of a movie clip or any display object (more on display objects soon) with ActionScript.

The basic syntax to change any property of a MovieClip is to type the clip's instance name, then a dot, followed by the property name that you want to change, and then an equal sign (=), followed by the new value:

```
movieClipInstanceName.propertyName = value;
```

For example, if you have a MovieClip with an instance name of *clip1* and you want to rotate it 90 degrees, the code would read:

```
clip1.rotation = 90;
```

If you know the possible properties that you can control and their range of values, then this simple technique can accomplish quite a bit. For the full range of properties and values, see Flash CS4 Help. The following table contains a few of the most common properties and their ranges.

Common properties and their ranges

PROPERTY	VALUES	DESCRIPTION
x	–infinity to +infinity	Horizontal position
y	–infinity to +infinity	Vertical position
rotation	–180 to 180 (degrees)*	Rotation
alpha	0 to 1 (0 = transparent, 1 = opaque)	Transparency
scaleX	–infinity to +infinity	Horizontal Scale
scaleY	–infinity to +infinity	Vertical Scale
visible	true (visible) or false (invisible)	Visibility

*For the `rotation` property, you can use any numbers, but ActionScript will convert them to the range between –180 and +180 degrees.

Changing a property value

Try changing the horizontal position of the *star_mc* MovieClip.

1. With the timeline and Actions panel both visible, select frame 1 of the `actions` layer.

2. Click the insertion point inside the Actions panel, and type the following code:

   ```
   star_mc.x = 275;
   ```

3. Save and test the movie. The star clip should appear in the center of the stage horizontally.

   Now we'll change a few other properties of the star.

● **Note:** The Flash stage is measured from the upper-left corner. A movie clip with an x position of 0 means that the registration point of the clip is on the exact left of the stage. A position of 0 for the *y* value means that the clip is at the top of the stage. Values greater than zero for *x* and *y* refer to positions to the right and down, respectively. Negative *x* and *y* values indicate positions offstage to the left and above the stage.

4   Add the following below the code you just inserted:

```
star_mc.rotation = 90;
star_mc.alpha = .5;
```

5   Save and test the movie. The star should appear rotated and 50 percent transparent.

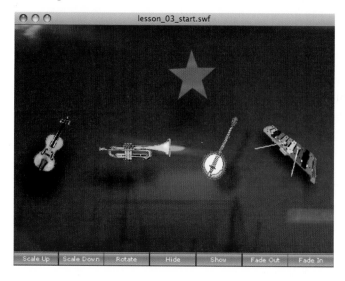

Increasing or decreasing a property's value

Rather than setting a property to a specific value, you can add to or subtract from its current value. For example, rather than rotating the star by 90 degrees, you could write code that would take the current amount of rotation and add or subtract from it.

Let's create some code that adds five degrees to the star's rotation every time it's clicked.

1   Select and delete all the code that you typed in the Actions panel, and replace it with the following:

```
star_mc.addEventListener(MouseEvent.CLICK, rotateStar);

function rotateStar(e:MouseEvent):void {
  star_mc.rotation += 5;
}
```

2   Save and test the movie. Each time you click the star, it should rotate an additional five degrees.

● **Note:** Using += is a shorthand way of saying "take the current value of the object on the left and add the value on the right to it." The longhand way to do the same would be:

```
star_mc.rotation = star_mc.rotation + 5;
```

Using an ENTER_FRAME event to animate a MovieClip property

Now that you know how to increment a MovieClip property, all you need to do to create animation is to increment the property repeatedly at a speed fast enough to make the eye believe that the object is moving.

Because the Flash timeline moves at a frame rate that is meant to move graphics fast enough to fool the eye, code that repeats at the current frame rate is an easy way to create animation.

The ENTER_FRAME event is ideal for this purpose. The ENTER_FRAME event takes place repeatedly, while a Flash movie is playing, even when there is only a single frame in the timeline.

Creating an ENTER_FRAME event listener and function is similar to what you have already done with a mouse event.

Try using the ENTER_FRAME event to animate the horizontal position of the star clip using its x property.

1 Below the existing code in the actions layer, add the following code:

```
addEventListener(Event.ENTER_FRAME, starMove);

function starMove(e:Event):void {
 star_mc.x += 2;
}
```

2 Save and test the movie. The star should now move slowly from left to right. It should also still rotate five degrees each time it is clicked.

At this point, when your movie runs, the star will continue to move to the right off into infinite virtual space. Once it is offstage, it is no longer visible, so let's add some code to keep the star within the stage bounds. You will do this with a conditional statement that checks to see if the star has gone offstage to the right.

3 Modify the code from Step 1 so that it reads:

```
addEventListener(Event.ENTER_FRAME, starMove);

function starMove(e:Event):void {
 if (star_mc.x < stage.stageWidth) {
   star_mc.x += 2;
 } else {
   star_mc.x = 0;
 }
}
```

Now, as long as the star is still within the bounds of the stage, it will continue to move to the right, but if the conditional statement detects that the star's horizontal position is greater than the `stageWidth`, then it will move the star back to the far left to begin again. This will keep the animation visible and playing forever.

Notice the syntax that describes the width of the stage: `stage.stageWidth`. The stage height can be described similarly, with the syntax `stage.stageHeight`. Both `stageWidth` and `stageHeight` are properties of the stage.

Creating a variable to store a MovieClip reference

In this section, you will create code to have the buttons at the bottom of the stage change the properties of the four instruments. Which instrument the user selects will determine which MovieClip the buttons will affect. You will achieve this by creating a variable to keep track of which instrument the user clicked most recently.

1   On a new line below the existing code in frame 1 of the `actions` layer, add a new variable called `instrument`:

```
var instrument:MovieClip = banjo;
```

When creating a variable, the data type is set by typing a colon after the variable's name and then indicating the type of data that will be stored in this variable. Notice that the data type of this variable is set to MovieClip. This means that the value of `instrument` will always be a reference to a MovieClip.

This code sets the default value to banjo. If you prefer a different default instrument (who wouldn't choose banjo?), feel free to set the value of the variable to the instance name of one of the other instruments.

Next, give the user some feedback in the text field to show which instrument is selected.

2   Below the existing code in the Actions panel, supply some information to the user by setting the `text` property of the dynamic text field whose instance name is instrument_txt.

```
instrument_txt.text = "The Banjo has been selected.";
```

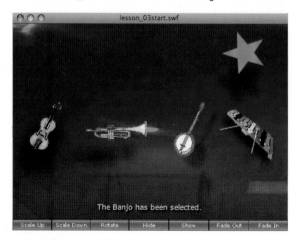

Now, add listeners and functions to the four instrument clips to let the user choose their own instrument.

3   In the line below the existing code, add the following listeners and functions:

```
violin.addEventListener(MouseEvent.CLICK,onViolin);
banjo.addEventListener(MouseEvent.CLICK,onBanjo);
trumpet.addEventListener(MouseEvent.CLICK,onTrumpet);
glock.addEventListener(MouseEvent.CLICK,onGlock);

function onViolin(e:MouseEvent):void {
 instrument = violin;
 instrument_txt.text = "The Violin has been selected.";
}

function onBanjo(e:MouseEvent):void {
 instrument = banjo;
 instrument_txt.text = "The Banjo has been selected.";
}

function onTrumpet(e:MouseEvent):void {
 instrument = trumpet;
 instrument_txt.text = "The Trumpet has been selected.";
}

function onGlock(e:MouseEvent):void {
 instrument = glock;
 instrument_txt.text = "The Glockenspiel has been selected.";
}
```

4   Save and test the movie. When you click any of the instruments, you should see the text change onstage to indicate your selection.

Now, we will use the value of the `instrument` variable to control which MovieClip the buttons at the bottom of the stage will control.

Changing MovieClip properties with buttons

The code in this exercise, which changes the values of the instrument properties, should be starting to look familiar to you.

First, for each of the blue buttons at the bottom of the stage add an event listener to listen for a CLICK event.

1 In the Actions panel below the existing code for frame 1, add a listener for each button, using the following code:

```
grow_btn.addEventListener(MouseEvent.CLICK, grow);
shrink_btn.addEventListener(MouseEvent.CLICK, shrink);
rotate_btn.addEventListener(MouseEvent.CLICK, rotate);
hide_btn.addEventListener(MouseEvent.CLICK, hideClip);
show_btn.addEventListener(MouseEvent.CLICK,showClip);
fadeOut_btn.addEventListener(MouseEvent.CLICK,fadeOut);
fadeIn_btn.addEventListener(MouseEvent.CLICK,fadeIn);
```

Now add a function to correspond to each button's listener.

2 Add the grow function, which makes the selected instrument grow by 10 percent each time the Scale Up button is clicked:

```
function grow(e:MouseEvent):void {
  instrument.scaleX += .1
  instrument.scaleY += .1;
}
```

3 Add the shrink function, to decrease the size of the selected instrument by 10 percent when the Scale Down button is clicked :

```
function shrink(e:MouseEvent):void {
  instrument.scaleX -= .1;
  instrument.scaleY -= .1;
}
```

4 Add the rotate function to rotate the selected instrument by five degrees each time the Rotate button is clicked:

```
function rotate(e:MouseEvent):void {
  instrument.rotation += 5;
}
```

5 Add the hideClip function to hide the selected instrument by setting its visible property to false when the Hide button is clicked:

```
function hideClip(e:MouseEvent):void {
  instrument.visible = false;
}
```

6 Add the showClip function to show the selected instrument by setting its visible property to true when the Show button is clicked:

```
function showClip(e:MouseEvent):void {
  instrument.visible = true;
}
```

7   Add the `fadeOut` function to set the selected instrument's opacity level to 50 percent when the Fade Out button is clicked:

```
function fadeOut(e:MouseEvent):void {
  instrument.alpha = .5
}
```

8   Add the `fadeIn` function to set the selected instrument's opacity level to 100 percent when the Fade In button is clicked:

```
function fadeIn(e:MouseEvent):void {
  instrument.alpha = 1
}
```

9   Save and test your movie. Try selecting different instruments and then seeing the results of changing their properties by clicking various buttons.

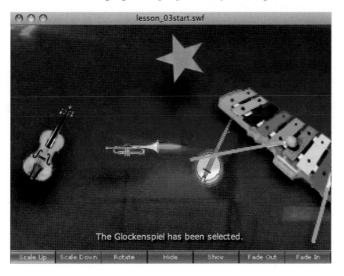

Creating animation using ActionScript tweens

Just as you can create animation using tweens on the timeline, you can also create tweens in ActionScript (for a review of creating tweens in the timeline or an overview of the new tweening features in Flash CS4 see the Flash Help files or *Adobe Flash CS4 Classroom in a Book* by Adobe Press). As is often the case when comparing a task in ActionScript to a similar task done in the Flash interface, the main benefit of creating tweens in code rather than on the timeline is that the resulting animation can be more versatile and more interactive. It also means that tweens can be created on a single frame of the timeline, or even without any frames at all.

ActionScript tweens have a number of similarities to those created in the interface. In both cases, you are changing the properties of an object over a span of time. In both cases, you select the property that you want to change, and then set an initial and a final setting for that property's animation. Also in both cases, you have the option of setting the amount and type of easing that you want.

Easing classes in ActionScript 3.0

Easing is a technique for accelerating or decelerating the velocity of the start or end of an animation. In Flash CS4, this can be controlled in the interface or with ActionScript. There are quite a few built-in easing classes in ActionScript that do a wide variety of easing effects, including a `CustomEase` class that lets you create your own easing effects.

For more information see the Flash CS4 ActionScript 3.0 language reference in the Flash Help files.

Note: The keyword new is used in ActionScript anytime that you wish to make a new instance of an ActionScript class. You will be seeing a lot more about ActionScript classes and creating new instances in the coming lessons.

A reference to a new tween instance in ActionScript is typically stored in a variable. The syntax is similar to other variables you have created:

```
var tweenName:Tween = new Tween(objectToBeTweened,
    ➥"propertyToBeAnimated", EasingType, startingValue,
    ➥endingValue, time, trueForSeconds);
```

When a new tween variable is created in this way, all the parameters that control the tween go between parentheses and are separated by commas. The first parameter is the instance name of the object to be tweened. The second parameter indicates which property will be animated. This is referenced as a string—meaning it goes between quotation marks. The property names are the same as the ones you have already been working with. The third parameter is the easing type, which can control the way the animation begins or ends. The next two parameters are the numeric values that start and end the animation. Next is the length of time that it will take for the animation to change from the first property value to the second. By default, the length of time is set in milliseconds, but if the optional final parameter is set to `true`, then the time of the tween can instead be set in seconds.

As an example, if you had a MovieClip onstage with an instance name of *rocket* and you wanted to send it from the top of the stage (y = 0) to the bottom of the stage (y = 400) over five seconds, you could create a tween like this:

```
var rocketTween:Tween = new Tween(rocket, "y", None.easeOut, 0,
    ➥400, 5, true)
```

The only non-intuitive parameter is the third one, for the easing type. You can look up all the possibilities for the easing types in Flash Help, but for now, let's try a couple of examples by updating a few of your button functions.

Importing the Tween and easing classes

All the ActionScript that you have used so far has been part of the built-in Flash classes. These classes have not had to be imported in order to use them on the Flash timeline (although it is considered a good practice). However, the Tween and easing classes must be imported into your project using an import statement before they can be used by the ActionScript in a Flash file..

You will learn much more about class files and importing starting in Lesson 4. For now we will add code to import the Tween and easing classes.

1   With frame 1 of the timeline and the Actions panel visible, place the cursor before the first code in the Actions panel and press Enter (or Return on a Mac).

2   Starting on the first line in the Actions panel before any of the existing code add the two lines:

```
import fl.transitions.Tween;
import fl.transitions.easing.*;
```

The Tween class and all of the easing classes are now available for use in this file. Now you will add your first ActionScript tween.

Adding ActionScript tweens

Now, let's add some ActionScript tweens.

1   In the Actions panel, with frame 1 of the actions layer selected, scroll down to find the function you created called fadeOut. It should now read:

```
function fadeOut(e:MouseEvent):void {
 instrument.alpha = .5
}
```

2   Change the code in the fadeOut function to read:

Now, the fadeOut function gradually fades the selected instrument from

```
function fadeOut(e:MouseEvent):void {
    var tweenfadeOut:Tween = new Tween(instrument, "alpha", None.easeOut, 1, 0, 3, true);
}
```

completely opaque (1) to completely transparent (0) over three seconds. There is no easing added in the third parameter of this tween.

3   Locate the function called fadeIn. It should read:

```
function fadeIn(e:MouseEvent):void {
 instrument.alpha = 1
}
```

4   Change this function to a tween by updating the code to read:

```actionscript
function fadeIn(e:MouseEvent):void {
 var tweenfadeIn:Tween = new Tween(instrument, "alpha",
   ➥None.easeIn, 0, 1, 3, true);
}
```

The new tween fades the selected instrument from 0 to 1 over three seconds.

5   Locate the `rotate` function, which should read:

```actionscript
function rotate(e:MouseEvent):void {
 instrument.rotation += 5;
 }
```

6   Change this function by replacing the `rotation` property change with a tween:

```actionscript
function rotate(e:MouseEvent):void {
 var spin:Tween = new Tween(instrument, "rotation",
   ➥Elastic.easeOut, 0, 360, 5, true)
}
```

The spin tween animates the selected instrument in one complete rotation over five seconds. Notice that the easing type is now set to `Elastic`. This will create a bouncing, rubbery effect at the end of the tween.

7   Save and test the movie. Select different instruments and try out the updated versions of your buttons. You should now have an application that includes quite a lot of interactive animation.

Here is the completed code for this lesson:

```actionscript
import fl.transitions.Tween;
import fl.transitions.easing.*;

star_mc.addEventListener(MouseEvent.CLICK,rotateStar);

function rotateStar(e:MouseEvent):void{
  star_mc.rotation += 5;
}

addEventListener(Event.ENTER_FRAME, starMove);

function starMove(e:Event):void {
 if (star_mc.x < stage.stageWidth) {
  star_mc.x += 2;
 } else {
  star_mc.x = 0;
 }
}
```

```
var instrument:MovieClip = banjo;
instrument_txt.text = "The Banjo has been selected.";

violin.addEventListener(MouseEvent.CLICK,onViolin);
banjo.addEventListener(MouseEvent.CLICK,onBanjo);
trumpet.addEventListener(MouseEvent.CLICK,onTrumpet);
glock.addEventListener(MouseEvent.CLICK,onGlock);

function onViolin(e:MouseEvent):void {
 instrument = violin;
 instrument_txt.text = "The Violin has been selected.";
}


function onTrumpet(e:MouseEvent):void {
 instrument = trumpet;
 instrument_txt.text = "The Trumpet has been selected.";
}


function onBanjo(e:MouseEvent):void {
 instrument = banjo;
 instrument_txt.text = "The Banjo has been selected.";
}

function onGlock(e:MouseEvent):void {
 instrument = glock;
 instrument_txt.text = "The Glockenspiel has been selected.";
}

grow_btn.addEventListener(MouseEvent.CLICK, grow);
shrink_btn.addEventListener(MouseEvent.CLICK, shrink);
rotate_btn.addEventListener(MouseEvent.CLICK, rotate);
hide_btn.addEventListener(MouseEvent.CLICK, hideClip);
show_btn.addEventListener(MouseEvent.CLICK,showClip);
fadeOut_btn.addEventListener(MouseEvent.CLICK,fadeOut);
fadeIn_btn.addEventListener(MouseEvent.CLICK,fadeIn);

function grow(e:MouseEvent):void {
 instrument.scaleX += .1;
 instrument.scaleY += .1;
}

function shrink(e:MouseEvent):void {
 instrument.scaleX -= .1
```

(code continues on the next page)

(continued)

● **Note:** It is not at all uncommon—even for experienced programmers—for things to not work the first time you test them. If you test your movie and things are not working, check the feedback in the Output panel. Often, the errors listed in the Output panel can be the result of a single spelling mistake early in the code. If the error messages include line numbers, compare those lines carefully to the example code (line number visibility in the Actions panel can be turned on or off in the Actions panel preferences). Again, remember to look at color-coding, capitalization, and spelling. More often than not, the errors are small spelling mistakes rather than major syntax errors. You can compare your code with the completed version of the lesson file found in Lessons > Lesson03 > Complete > lesson03_complete.fla.

```
  instrument.scaleY -= .1;
}

function rotate(e:MouseEvent):void {
 var spin:Tween = new Tween(instrument, "rotation",
  ➥Elastic.easeOut, 0, 360, 5, true)
}

function hideClip(e:MouseEvent):void {
 instrument.visible = false;
}

function showClip(e:MouseEvent):void {
 instrument.visible = true;
}

function fadeOut(e:MouseEvent):void {
 var tweenfadeOut:Tween = new Tween(instrument, "alpha",
  ➥None.easeOut, 1, 0, 3, true);
}

function fadeIn(e:MouseEvent):void {
 var tweenfadeIn:Tween = new Tween(instrument, "alpha",
  ➥None.easeIn, instrument.alpha, 1, 3, true);
}
```

Some suggestions to try on your own

You now have a large repertoire of techniques to play with. You can probably come up with an infinite number of variations on the techniques in this lesson to experiment with. Here are a few suggestions to get you started:

- Try creating a MovieClip that bounces off two or even four sides of the stage.

- Look in the Flash Help files and experiment with some of the other properties available for a MovieClip.

- Try displaying the changing values of an animating property in a text field.

- Try creating tweens for some other properties of a MovieClip.

- Look in the Flash Help files and experiment with some of the other easing types.

You are starting to get comfortable with the basics of animating with ActionScript. In the next lesson, you will learn to create ActionScript in an external ActionScript file. This is the foundation of object-oriented programming and will open many more possibilities for making rich interactive applications.

Review questions

1 Name four properties of a MovieClip that can be controlled with ActionScript.

2 What is an event in ActionScript that you could use to have code repeat at the current frame rate?

3 What is the keyword that is used to create a new instance of an ActionScript class?

4 What is the syntax in ActionScript 3.0 to indicate what type of data will be stored in a variable?

5 When creating an instance of the Tween class, what are the parameters (values between the parentheses that are used to determine how the tween behaves)?

Review answers

1 There are many properties of a MovieClip that can be controlled with ActionScript. Your answers could include:

- `rotation`
- `x` (horizontal position)
- `y` (vertical position)
- `alpha` (transparency)
- `scaleX` (horizontal size)
- `scaleY` (vertical size)

For a full list of MovieClip properties, see the ActionScript 3.0 language reference in the Flash Help files.

2 The ENTER_FRAME event is used in ActionScript 3.0 to have code repeat at the current frame rate. For example to have a MovieClip named *logo_mc* rotate five degrees on every frame, you could write:

```
addEventListener(Event.ENTER_FRAME,rotateLogo);

function rotateLogo(e:Event):void {
  logo_mc.rotation += 5;
}
```

3 To create a new instance of an ActionScript class, you use the keyword new. For example, to make a new instance of the Sound class, you could write:

```
var song:Sound = new Sound();
```

The Sound class is covered in Lesson 9, "Controlling Sound with ActionScript."

4 When a variable is created, the type of data it will store is indicated by typing a colon after the variable name followed by the data type. For example, to indicate that a variable named totalPrice will contain the data type Number, you could write:

```
var totalPrice:Number;
```

5 There are six required parameters for an instance of the Tween class. The first parameter indicates the object that will have the tween applied to it. The second parameter indicates the property of that object that will be animated. The third parameter indicates the type of easing used. The fourth parameter is the starting value of the property to be animated, and the fifth parameter is the ending value that that property will animate to. The sixth parameter is the length of time that the tween will take place. By default, the sixth parameter is measured in milliseconds, but if an optional seventh parameter is set to true, then the sixth parameter is measured in seconds.

In this example, an instance of the Tween class named spin is set to animate the rotation of an object named instrument. The type of easing is Elastic.easeout, and the object will animate from 0 degrees to 360 degrees over the course of 5 seconds.

```
var spin:Tween = new Tween(instrument, "rotation", Elastic.easeOut,
➥0, 360, 5, true)
```

4 CREATING ACTIONSCRIPT IN EXTERNAL FILES

Lesson overview

In this lesson, you will learn to do the following:

- Create an ActionScript file using the tools in Flash CS4.

- Create an ActionScript class that extends the MovieClip class.

- Create a constructor function.

- Add methods and properties to a class file.

- Define parameters for class methods.

- Use ActionScript code to create vector shapes.

- Use code to create instances of a custom class file in the Flash timeline.

- Use the MOUSE_MOVE event.

- Turn off an event listener.

- Generate random colors.

 This lesson will take approximately 2 hours.

Creating external ActionScript files can be a convenience for reusing code, or it can be the foundation for building large applications that use object-oriented programming practices (OOP).

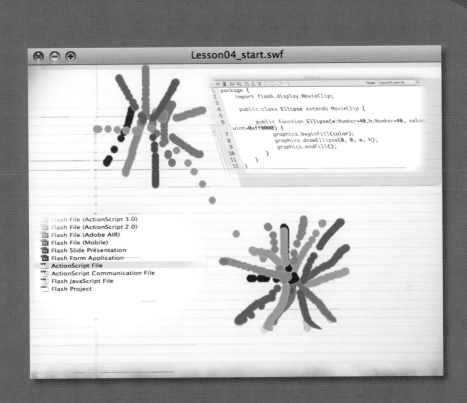

Each mouse movement in the Lesson 4 project produces a trail of ellipses with a different random color.

Up until this point, all the lessons have created ActionScript in frames of the Flash timeline. This is a very useful way to work, and many Flash developers create all their projects exclusively using this method. For simpler projects, this has the benefit of keeping all the graphics and media in the same file as the ActionScript. However, for Flash projects that are more complex, it is often cumbersome to have hundreds or even thousands of lines of code in the timeline.

The alternative is to store the ActionScript for a project in one or more external files that just contain code. These ActionScript files can then be integrated with graphics, animation, and other Flash content to create the final project. External ActionScript files are plain text files saved with an .as suffix.

There are many benefits to developing larger projects in this manner. Most importantly, it means that the functionality of your applications can be divided into reusable chunks of code.

One characteristic that makes for a successful ActionScript file is that it's often written to be as versatile as possible. For example, you could create an ActionScript file called Scoring.as that contains code to keep track of a user's score. By writing the code such that some of its properties could be individually modified, the code could be used in a game where the user gets 10 points for shooting space aliens and needs 1000 points to win or in a history quiz where the user gets 1 point for each correct answer and proceeds to the next lesson when the score reaches 20 points.

In this lesson, you will get some experience creating an external ActionScript file designed to generate a simple graphic. You will then use this external .as file in a very simple Flash painting application, to determine the shape of the brushstrokes.

Creating an ActionScript file

As mentioned, an ActionScript file is just a plain text file. Therefore, ActionScript files can be created with any software that can create text files, including TextEdit and Notepad. Of course it is preferable to create ActionScript files in tools that offer features like color-coding and error checking. Adobe tools like Flex Builder and Dreamweaver offer full support for creating ActionScript files, as do a number of third-party tools, some of which are free. So you've got a lot of options, and over time you'll find the ones that are right for you.

Creating a basic ActionScript file in Flash

Since Flash has great tools for creating ActionScript files, so those are what we will be using.

1 In Flash, choose File > New.

2 In the General tab of the New Document dialog box, choose ActionScript File, and then click OK. The new file that is created should look very similar to the Flash Actions panel. The default name of a new ActionScript file is Script-1.

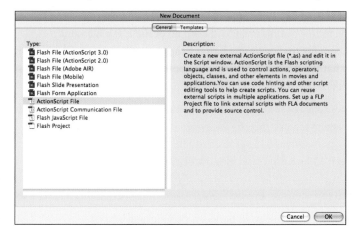

3 Choose File > Save, and name your new file **Ellipse.as**.

4 Save the new file to your Lesson04 > Start folder of your lessons folder.

Basic structure of an ActionScript 3.0 class file

The ActionScript 3.0 language is largely just a collection of classes.

A class file is a collection of code that usually relates to all or part of a single task or related tasks.

If you have worked in Flash at all, then you have already worked with classes. For example, the MovieClip class is a built-in ActionScript class that describes the functionality that is unique to MovieClips in Flash. In the previous lesson, you were able to manipulate many MovieClip properties such as rotation and alpha, because the MovieClip class contains code that describes those properties. Similarly, there are built-in ActionScript classes for working with text, sound, video, and other features available in Flash Player.

Many beginners find that once they become comfortable with the way classes work in ActionScript 3.0, then the entire language begins to make a lot more sense.

ActionScript that you type in an .as file is nearly identical to ActionScript that you type in the timeline. Once you learn the basic structure of an ActionScript file, most of what you already know about ActionScript will apply to external files.

In your new Ellipse.as file, let's add the basic structure common to most .as files.

1   In the first line of the Ellipse.as file, type the following:

```
package{
```

All ActionScript files begin with the `package` keyword. You can think of the package as describing the path to your ActionScript file. For example, if the Ellipse.as file were inside a folder named scripts, and the scripts folder was in a folder named com, then the first line of code in the file would read:

```
package com.scripts {
```

For simplicity, in this example you will keep all of the Flash files and ActionScript files for the lesson together in the same directory. When this is the case, then no path needs to be described after the `package` keyword. However, the package reference still needs to be there.

2   Skip a few lines to leave some space for the code you will soon create and add a right curly brace:

```
package {


}
```

All the code for this file will go in between the package braces.

3   In an ActionScript file, you must import all the external classes that the file will use. Because this file uses the `MovieClip` class, it must be imported. Add the following code on a line below the left curly brace:

```
import flash.display.MovieClip;
```

Now you will create a new ActionScript class.

4   Skip a line, and add the following code to create a new class:

```
public class Ellipse extends MovieClip {

}
```

Your file now reads:

```
package {

  import flash.display.MovieClip;

  public class Ellipse extends MovieClip {

  }

}
```

All the code for this class will go between the inner set of curly braces. Most ActionScript files contain a single class and are often referred to as class files.

The name of the class created in an ActionScript file must match the name of the file. Thus, in this case the class is named `Ellipse` and the file is named Ellipse.as. This name structure is what allows class files to be referenced by other files.

A little bit about ActionScript classes

In this lesson, you are creating a custom ActionScript class file to do a specific set of tasks. By making an external class file, you make it possible to use the code in this file from within other Flash and ActionScript files.

Actually, this is the way the entire ActionScript language works. You can think of ActionScript as a large collection of classes that together offer the wide range of functionality available in the language. When you work with a movie clip in ActionScript, you are using the `MovieClip` class. When you work with a text field, you are using the `TextField` class; when working with video, you use the `Video` class; and so on.

The functions that are contained in an ActionScript class file are referred to as *methods* of that class, and the variables that are in a class file are referred to as *properties* of the class.

By creating custom ActionScript classes, as you are doing in this lesson, you are expanding the collection of classes that are available to you in your Flash projects.

There are two terms in the code you just added to create the `Ellipse` class that you may not have encountered before: `public` and `extends`.

In the line:

public class Ellipse extends MovieClip {

the term *public* is what is known as an *access modifier*. By setting the class to public, you are indicating that this class can be accessed from any other file.

There are three other access modifiers:

- `private`—methods and properties that are labeled private are only available from within the class file
- `protected`—methods and properties that are labeled protected are only available from within the class file and its descendents (the `extends` keyword is described in a short while)
- `internal`—methods and properties that are labeled internal are available from within the class file and to all other files within the same package

For simplicity's sake, these lessons will mostly use only the public and private modifiers, but in other class files, you may often see other access modifiers used on methods (functions) and properties (variables) within the class. As you get more comfortable with ActionScript, it is a good idea to make a deeper study of how to use these modifiers in your applications. For more information, see the ActionScript 3.0 Help files or Colin Moock's excellent book *Essential ActionScript 3.0* from O'Reilly Media.

The other new code (you thought we forgot!) is the term *extends*.

```
public class Ellipse extends MovieClip {
```

When one class extends another class, it means that the new class has all the capabilities of the original parent class in addition to whatever new capabilities are added in the new class file.

In this case, the purpose of the Ellipse class is to draw a simple ellipse. By making the Ellipse class a descendent or child of the MovieClip class, we know that instances of the Ellipse class will be able do all the things that can be done with movie clips, such as have their position, scale, and rotation set.

All the code for an ActionScript class goes between the curly braces that contain that class. In this case, the code to create an ellipse will require only one function.

5   Inside the inner curly braces, add the following code:

```
public function Ellipse(w:Number=40,h:Number=40,
➥color:Number=0xff0000) {
  graphics.beginFill(color);
  graphics.drawEllipse(0, 0, w, h);
  graphics.endFill();
}
```

About constructor functions

Although a class file will often contain many functions, each class will have only one *constructor function*. which is very specific type of function.

The constructor function in a class file has the same name as the class itself (in this case, both are named Ellipse). The constructor function is automatically called every time an instance of the class is created. You will put this into practice soon.

Notice that what you've added between the parentheses are three parameters. These will be used to set the width, height, and color of a new ellipse that will be created when the Ellipse function is called. The parameters for width (w) and height (h) are given default values of 40, and the color parameter is given a default value of red.

Required vs. optional parameters

If a function has parameters that are given default values, as in the example in Step 5, then when the function is called, references to those parameters do not need to be included. These are called *optional* parameters. If references to these parameters are included with new values, they will override the default values. You will see this in action soon.

If a function has parameters that are not given initial values, it is necessary to assign these values when calling the function. These are called *required* parameters.

The three lines of code inside the brackets of the `Ellipse()` function are used to create an ellipse. These lines call methods that are part of the extensive and powerful ActionScript toolset for creating and manipulating vector graphics. In the `Ellipse()` function, the first of these lines indicates that the vector graphics that are about to be created will have a specific fill color:

`graphics.beginFill(color);`

The `color` parameter determines the color of the Ellipse. Remember that this parameter was set to a default of red when you created the function, but can be overridden when called.

The second line of code draws an ellipse using a built-in function called `drawEllipse()`.

`graphics.drawEllipse(0, 0, w, h);`

This function or *method* takes four parameters. The first two parameters set the position of the ellipse, in this case to 0 horizontally and 0 vertically (the upper-left corner). The next two use the w and h parameters of the `Ellipse()` function to set the width and height of the ellipse.

The third line inside the `Ellipse()` function ends the fill and completes the drawing.

`graphics.endFill();`

6   Save your file. Your entire `Ellipse` class file should now read:

```
package {
    import flash.display.MovieClip;

    public class Ellipse extends MovieClip {

        public function Ellipse(w:Number=40,h:Number=40,
color:uint=0xff0000) {
            graphics.beginFill(color);
            graphics.drawEllipse(0, 0, w, h);
            graphics.endFill();
        }
    }
}
```

You'll soon get to test your handiwork.

ActionScript 3.0 and hexadecimal color

ActionScript 3.0 can describe colors in a variety of ways, but the most common is as numeric hexadecimal values. This system is very easy once you are used to it. The characters "0x" before a color description tell ActionScript that a hexadecimal value is to follow. Then there is a six-digit number that describes the amount of red, green, and blue in the color. (Optionally, an eight-digit number would also include transparency information.)

If you have worked with hexadecimal colors in web design, you know that each digit can range from 0 to 15 with the letters A, B, C, D, E, and F representing the numbers 10, 11, 12, 13, 14, and 15, respectively. In this example, the color red is described as 0xFF0000, which has the greatest possible amount of red (FF) and no green (00) or blue (00). The hex color 0x0000FF would be a color with no red (00) or green (00) and the full amount of blue (FF).

To find the hexadecimal value of a specific color in Flash, you can open the Color panel (Window > Color). You can select a color in a variety of ways in this panel. The hexadecimal value of the selected color will be displayed in the lower right of the panel. If you are using a value from the Color panel in your ActionScript, replace the initial pound symbol (#) shown in the color panel with "0x" before typing the hexadecimal value in your code.

For more information on hexadecimal colors, see Flash Help or any basic web design book.

Creating instances of a class file in Flash

Without further ado, let's put our new class file to work.

1 Open the Lesson04_start.fla file from the Lessons > Lesson04 > Start folder. This should be the same location where your ActionScript file is saved.

2 Notice that this file is simply made up of a background layer with a full-screen bitmap image and an empty `actions` layer with no code added (yet).

3 With frame 1 of the `actions` layer selected, open the Actions panel and select the first line, where you'll begin adding code.

4 To create a single instance of your `Ellipse` class, add the following code:

```
var ellipse:Ellipse = new Ellipse();
```

Using the new keyword to create instances

To create a new instance from any ActionScript class, you use the keyword new. This is consistent across the entire ActionScript 3.0 language, whether you are creating instances of built-in classes as in:

```
var myClip:MovieClip = new MovieClip();
```

and

```
var userForm:TextField = new TextField();
```

or, as in this lesson, you are making a new instance of a custom class as in:

```
var ellipse:Ellipse = new Ellipse();
```

Many newcomers to ActionScript find that this consistency makes ActionScript much easier than they expected once they get comfortable with learning the foundations of the language.

5 To add the ellipse to the stage, on a new line type the following code:

```
addChild(ellipse);
```

About addChild() and the display list

In the background of every Flash file, every visual object that is onstage is tracked in what is called the *display list*. This is true whether a visual object was placed onstage using the tools in the Flash interface, imported to the stage as an external file, or created from scratch using ActionScript.

All visual objects in a Flash project, including movie clips, shapes, buttons, text fields, bitmaps, and video, are considered *display objects* and are added to the display list when made viewable.

When a visual object is created with ActionScript, it may exist in code but that does not mean it will automatically be visible onstage. To place something into the display list, and therefore onstage, you call the method addChild(). A common mistake for beginners to ActionScript is to forget to use addChild() and then wonder why they are not seeing their expected graphics onstage. You will be delving deeper into display objects and the display list in later lessons.

6 Save and test your movie. You should see a single red ellipse in the upper-left corner of the stage.

A single red ellipse is not too exciting, so next you will add a few things to make more interesting use of the Ellipse class.

First, instead of generating a single instance of the Ellipse automatically, the user will generate multiple instances whenever they move their mouse.

7 Select all the existing code in the Actions panel, and cut it to the clipboard.

8 On the first line of the now empty Actions panel, add an event listener for an event called MOUSE_MOVE. This event takes place whenever the user moves the mouse. This movement will call a function called makeShapes().

```
stage.addEventListener(MouseEvent.MOUSE_MOVE, makeShapes);
```

9 On a new line, create the makeShapes() function:

```
function makeShapes(e:MouseEvent):void {

}
```

10 Paste the code from the clipboard in between the curly braces of the makeShapes() function so that the function now reads:

```
function makeShapes(e:MouseEvent):void {
    var ellipse:Ellipse = new Ellipse();
    addChild(ellipse);
}
```

If you tested your movie now, every time the mouse was moved a new ellipse would be added to the stage—but they would all be in the exact same spot in the upper left. In order to give each new ellipse a unique location, you will set each new ellipse to be placed at the current mouse location using the mouseX and mouseY properties.

11 Add two new lines to the makeShapes() function so that it now reads:

```
function makeShapes(e:MouseEvent):void {
  var ellipse:Ellipse = new Ellipse();
  addChild(ellipse);
  ellipse.x = mouseX;
  ellipse.y = mouseY;
}
```

12 Save and test your movie. Move the mouse around. A trail of red circles should be created that follow your mouse path. Congratulations, you have created a "virtual paintbrush" that uses big red ellipses (which are circles because the w and h parameter default values were set equal). More importantly, you have succeeded in creating and using a custom ActionScript class in a Flash file!

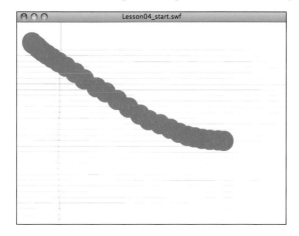

13 Close the lesson04_start.swf file to exit the testing environment.

Overriding the parameters of each Ellipse instance

At this point, your Flash file is creating nothing but big red ellipses from your class file...but remember, they are big and red because those are the defaults you placed in the constructor function. Each time a new ellipse is created, those defaults can be overridden by passing new parameters. Let's change the parameters to make smaller green ellipses.

1 In the makeShapes() function, change the line of code that currently reads:

```
var ellipse:Ellipse = new Ellipse();
```

So that it reads:

```
var ellipse:Ellipse = new Ellipse(10, 10, 0x00FF00);
```

2 Save and test your movie. Now, moving the mouse should produce a trail of 10-pixel by 10-pixel green circles. If you want, you can experiment by trying different sizes and colors and test the results.

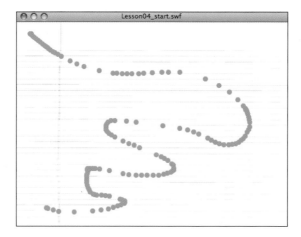

Turning the makeShapes() function on and off

Even software that does nothing but paint green trails should give users control over when they choose to paint. So far you have added event listeners using the addEventListener() method, you can also remove a listener using a similar method called removeEventListener(). Here, you'll alter your code so that the listener for mouse movement is added when the user clicks onstage and removed when the mouse is released.

1 In the Actions panel, click to place the mouse pointer before the first line of code, and press the Enter key a few times to insert a few lines of space before the beginning of the code.

2 On the first line of the Actions panel, above the existing code, add two new addEventListener() methods to listen for the MOUSE_UP and MOUSE_DOWN events by typing the following code:

```
stage.addEventListener(MouseEvent.MOUSE_DOWN, startDrawing);
stage.addEventListener(MouseEvent.MOUSE_UP, stopDrawing);
```

The MOUSE_DOWN event will call a function named startDrawing(), and the MOUSE_UP event will call a function named stopDrawing(), so next add those two new functions.

3 On the lines below the event listeners, add this code:

```
function startDrawing(e:MouseEvent):void {

}
```

```
function stopDrawing(e:MouseEvent):void {

}
```

4   Next, find and select the line in your code that reads:

```
stage.addEventListener(MouseEvent.MOUSE_MOVE, makeShapes);
```

5   Cut this line of code (Edit > Cut) to place it on the clipboard.

6   Place the mouse pointer between the curly braces of the new startDrawing function, and paste the code from the clipboard. The function should now read:

```
function startDrawing(e:MouseEvent):void {
  stage.addEventListener(MouseEvent.MOUSE_MOVE, makeShapes);
}
```

7   Place the mouse pointer between the curly braces of the stopDrawing function, and paste the same code from the clipboard.

8   In your newly pasted code in the stopDrawing() function, change addEventListener to removeEventListener. The function should now read:

```
function stopDrawing(e:MouseEvent):void {
  stage.removeEventListener(MouseEvent.MOUSE_MOVE, makeShapes);
}
```

The result of these changes is that the function that draws the ellipses on mouse movement will occur only when the user clicks the mouse and will stop occurring when the mouse is released.

9   Save and test your movie. Click on the stage and move the mouse around. Ellipses should be created that follow the mouse. Release the mouse, and the ellipses should stop being generated.

Randomizing the color of the ellipses

To generate a random number in ActionScript 3.0, you use the random method of the Math class. The syntax for that is:

```
Math.random();
```

This code will return a random number between 0 and 1, usually with multiple decimal places. To control the range that Math.random generates, you perform some math on the resulting random number. For example, if you wanted to generate a random number between 0 and 50, you would multiply the Math.random result by 50:

```
Math.random() * 50;
```

If you wanted to generate a random number from among the full range of possible hexadecimal colors, you would write:

```
Math.random() * 0xFFFFFF;
```

Note: An asterisk is the ActionScript character for the multiplication operation.

Now you'll use this technique to add random colors to the ellipses.

1 Add a variable to your file to store a numeric color value: At the top of the Actions panel, above the existing code, add a new line, and create a new variable with this code:

```
var color:Number;
```

2 Next, locate the startDrawing() function, and add to the code so that it now reads:

```
function startDrawing(e:MouseEvent):void {
  stage.addEventListener(MouseEvent.MOUSE_MOVE, makeShapes);
  color = Math.random() * 0xFFFFFF;
}
```

Now each time the user clicks to begin drawing, a new random color will be chosen.

To assign that color to the ellipses, you will use the new color variable as the parameter that is passed to the Ellipse() constructor function.

3 Locate the makeShapes() function, and change the line that currently reads:

```
var ellipse:Ellipse = new Ellipse(10,10,0x00FF00);
```

so that it reads:

```
var ellipse:Ellipse = new Ellipse(10,10,color);
```

4 Save and test your movie. Each mouse movement produces a trail of ellipses with a different random color.

The completed code in Flash should now read:

```
var color:Number;

stage.addEventListener(MouseEvent.MOUSE_DOWN, startDrawing);
stage.addEventListener(MouseEvent.MOUSE_UP, stopDrawing);
```

```
function startDrawing(e:MouseEvent):void {
 stage.addEventListener(MouseEvent.MOUSE_MOVE, makeShapes);
 color = Math.random() * 0xFFFFFF;
}

function stopDrawing(e:MouseEvent):void {
 stage.removeEventListener(MouseEvent.MOUSE_MOVE, makeShapes)
}

function makeShapes(e:MouseEvent):void {
 var ellipse:Ellipse = new Ellipse(10, 10, color);
 addChild(ellipse);
 ellipse.x = mouseX;
 ellipse.y = mouseY;
}
```

By learning to create external ActionScript files and integrate them into your Flash projects, you can begin to make your rich interactive applications much more modular. It can take some time to get comfortable with this way of working, but the efforts will be very rewarding.

In the coming lessons, you will get more practice working with ActionScript classes.

Give your brain a rest between each lesson, and go back to earlier lessons for review as many times as you need to. You may be surprised how much more sense ActionScript concepts make after you are exposed to them a few times.

Some suggestions to try on your own

There are an infinite number of ways to enhance the application you created in this lesson using techniques that you have already covered.

The Lesson04 folder has an Addendum folder containing a tutorial that goes through the process of creating a class that is a simple variation of the Ellipse class, but that makes rectangles instead of ellipses. Use the Lesson 4 Addendum, "Creating Animation with ActionScript—Addendum" in the Lesson04 > Addendum folder to create the second class file, and then try experimenting with some of the following techniques:

* Change your Flash file so that mouse movements paint rectangles instead of ellipses.

* Create buttons that allow users to switch between painting ellipses and painting rectangles.

* Create buttons that let users set the size of the shapes that they paint.

- Create buttons that let users choose the color they paint.

- Look in the Flash Help files and explore some of the other possible shapes you can create with the drawing capabilities in ActionScript. See if you can create additional ActionScript files that create new shapes, and incorporate them into your Flash file. You will learn more about generating visual elements with ActionScript in upcoming lessons.

In the next lesson, you will learn to import external content into a Flash application at runtime using ActionScript and Flash components.

Review questions

1 When creating an ActionScript class file, how should the file be named?

2 How is the constructor function in an ActionScript class file named?

3 Define an ActionScript method and an ActionScript property.

4 What is the difference between a required parameter and an optional parameter in an ActionScript method?

5 How do you create an instance of an external class in ActionScript?

6 How is a display object added to the display list in ActionScript?

7 What is one way to generate a random color in ActionScript?

Review answers

1 An ActionScript class file must have the same name as the class that it contains followed by the suffix .as. For example if a file contained an ActionScript class called ScoringSystem, then the filename would need to be ScoringSystem.as.

2 The constructor function in an ActionScript class file is the function in that file with the same name as the class. For example in a class named ScoringSystem the constructor function would look like this:

```
public function ScoringSystem(parameters){
//code that does something goes here
}
```

3 A method in ActionScript 3.0 is a function that is contained in a class. A property in ActionScript 3.0 is a variable contained in a class.

4 When a function is created in an ActionScript class file, it can be given any number of parameters. If those parameters are given initial default values when they are created, then they are considered optional parameters and it is not necessary to pass parameters to the function when calling it. If a parameter does not have a default value, then a value must be passed when the function is called. These are required parameters. For example, in the following example, the finalScore parameter has no initial value, so it is a required parameter. However, the startingScore parameter has an initial value of 0, so it is an optional parameter.

```
public function ScoringSystem(finalScore:Number,
➥startingScore:Number = 0,){
 //code that does something goes here
}
```

5   To create an instance of an external class in ActionScript, you can use the keyword new followed by the class name. For example, to create a new instance of the Rocket class in a variable named rocket1, you could write:

```
var rocket1:Rocket = new Rocket();
```

6   To add an object to the display list with ActionScript and make it appear onstage, you use the addChild() method. For example, to add an instance named rocket1 to the Flash stage, you could write:

```
addChild(rocket1);
```

or

```
stage.addChild(rocket1);
```

7   You can generate a random color value by calling the Math.random() method and multiplying the result by the full range of hexadecimal colors, as in:

```
var color:Number = Math.random() * 0xFFFFFF;
```

5 USING ACTIONSCRIPT AND COMPONENTS TO LOAD CONTENT

Lesson overview

In this lesson, you will learn to do the following:

- Work with Flash CS4 User Interface components.

- Create instances of the List component and customize their parameters.

- Trigger an ActionScript event listener when the selected item in a List component instance changes.

- Use the UILoader component to control loading and displaying SWF files and bitmap images.

- Change the source file of the UILoader component with ActionScript.

- Work with the URLLoader class to load text data from an external file into a Flash movie.

- Add an event listener to respond to the successful completion of loaded data.

- Set properties of a text field with ActionScript.

- Use the UIScrollBar component to create a scrolling text field.

 This lesson will take approximately 2.5 hours.

If you have been proceeding through the lessons sequentially, you now have a collection of ActionScript 3.0 techniques in your repertoire to add functionality to your Flash files. Most large Flash projects, however, are not made up of just a single Flash file, but instead consist of a number of SWF files in addition to supporting content and data that is loaded at runtime.

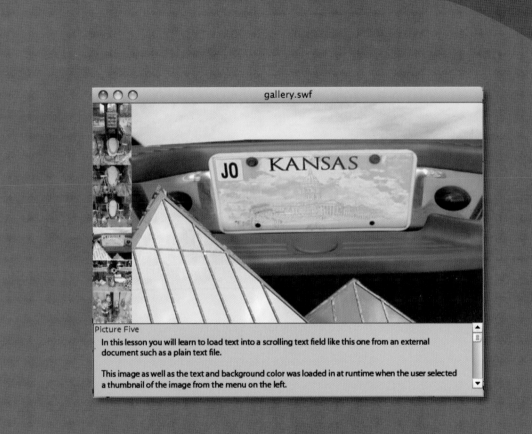

In this lesson, you will create a simple image gallery
and integrate it into a larger Flash project.

Since one of the main goals of this lesson is to integrate multiple files into a single Flash project, the materials for this lesson are more varied than in previous lessons.

Take a minute to examine the contents of the Lessons > Lesson05 folder. In this folder is an Images folder with JPG files and a Text folder with plain text files, all of which you will load into your Flash project using ActionScript.

The Start folder has a lesson05_start.fla file that you will work with in this lesson. It also has an instruments.swf file and a paint.swf file. These files are completed versions of the Lesson 3 and Lesson 4 projects respectively. You will begin the lesson by learning to load these two SWF files into the lesson05_start.fla file using an instance of the List component. After that, you will create a new gallery file that lets the user select from a list of thumbnails to display larger loaded images. Each image will have a text caption. The captions will each be loaded from separate text files. The finished gallery file will then be added to the list of files that can be loaded into the lesson05_start file.

Creating an instance of the List component and setting its parameters

The List component that ships with Flash CS4 makes it easy to create lists of objects for the users to choose from. The List component has parameters that can be set in the Flash interface or in ActionScript for adding labels and associating data with the items in the list. The component also has built-in events that automatically take place when the user makes a selection from the list.

Begin the lesson by opening the lesson05_start.fla file from the Lessons > Lesson05 > Start folder. Notice that this is the project you created in Lesson 1, "Navigating the Flash Timeline," and Lesson 2, "Working with Events and Functions." In this lesson, you will begin to create a working interface for the project.

1 In the timeline, above the buttons layer, add a new layer, and name it **components**.

2 Select frame 50 (labeled *home*) of the new layer, and add a keyframe (F6).

3 Open the Components panel (Window > Components).

4 In the Components panel, open the User Interface group and select the List component.

5 With frame 50 of the new `components` layer selected, drag an instance of the List component to the stage. You will use this component to create a list of files that the user can select and load into this project.

6 With the Properties panel visible (Window > Properties), select the new List component instance onstage.

7 In the Properties panel, give the List instance the name **loadList**.

8 Also in the Properties panel, set the X property for the `loadList` to **30** (X = 30) and its Y property to **150** (Y = 150).

9 Set the Width and Height Properties of the `loadList` to W = **140** and H = **60**.

10 With the `loadList` instance selected, open the Component Inspector panel (Window > Component Inspector).

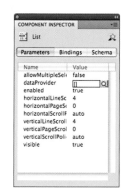

11 Select the `dataProvider` parameter, and then click the magnifying glass that appears to the right of the parameter. This opens a window where you can populate the list with labeled items and associate data with each item.

12 Add three items to the list by clicking the Plus button (+) three times.

13 Select the `label` parameter of the first item, and in the field on the right, type **Instruments**.

This will be the label for the first item in the list.

14 Select the `data` parameter for the first item, and give it the value **instruments.swf**.

You will use the data associated with each item in the list to store the name of the file that you wish to load when that item in the list is selected.

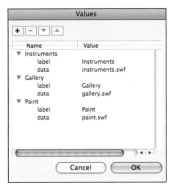

15 Give the second item in the list the label **Gallery** and the data value **gallery.swf**. You will create the gallery file later in the lesson.

16 Give the third item the label **Paint** and the data value **paint.swf**. You will add code to the file so that selecting this item in the list loads a finished version of the painting application that was created in Lesson 4, "Creating ActionScript in External Files."

17 Click OK to exit the Values dialog box.

Adding an instance of the UILoader component

Later in this lesson, you will learn to load content into Flash using just ActionScript. But if you want to load SWF, JPG, PNG, or GIF files, then using the UILoader component can save you several steps. Here you will use the UILoader component to load SWF files into the lesson05_start file. Later in your project, you will use the same component to load JPG images into a gallery file. Finally, you will load text into the gallery file using ActionScript only, since text files cannot be loaded with the UILoader component.

You'll start by adding an instance of the UILoader to the stage.

1 With frame 50 (*home*) of the components layer selected and the Components panel visible, from the User Interface folder, select the UILoader component.

2 Drag an instance of the UILoader component to the stage.

3 With the UILoader instance selected onstage, give it an instance name of **loadWindow** in the Properties panel.

4   Also in the Properties panel, set the following values for the `loadWindow` instance: X = **200**, Y = **135**, W = **550**, H = **400**. You will be loading a series of SWF files that have a stage size of 550×400 into this UILoader.

Adding a CHANGE event listener to the List component

When the user selects an item in an instance of the List component, an event called CHANGE automatically fires. Responding to the CHANGE event with ActionScript is very similar to the way you have responded to other events in earlier lessons.

1   With the Actions panel visible (Window > Actions), on the timeline, select frame 50 (*home*) of the `actions` layer.

2   Place the cursor on the line below the existing code, and add the following code:

```
loadList.addEventListener(Event.CHANGE, loadFile);

function loadFile(e:Event):void {

}
```

This syntax should be starting to look familiar to you. The listener for the CHANGE event is added in the same way listeners were added for Mouse events and Frame events in earlier lessons.

Your `loadFile()` function will be called any time the user makes a selection from the list. Next, you will add code so that each selection from the list loads a different SWF file into the UILoader instance.

Loading SWF files into a UILoader component

You can load any SWF, JPG, PNG, or GIF file into the UILoader component with ActionScript by setting the `source` property of the UILoader. The basic syntax for this is:

```
UILoaderInstanceName.source = "Path file to be loaded goes here";
```

For example, if you wanted to load the instruments.swf file into the `loadWindow` component, the code would read:

```
loadWindow.source = "instruments.swf";
```

In this exercise, you want to write a single function that determines which file to load by using the data that you stored in each item of the list. Remember setting the `dataProvider` parameters a little while ago? You will use those parameters each time the user selects an item from the list. For example, if the user selects the item labeled Paint in the list, then the paint.swf file will load into the UILoader instance. This is because paint.swf is what you set as data for that particular item.

1 In the loadFile() function that you just created, add code between the curly braces so that the function now reads:

```
function loadFile(e:Event):void {
  loadWindow.source = e.target.selectedItem.data;
}
```

The target (e.target) is the list, the selectedItem property is the item that the user chose from the list, and the data property is the data that you added to that particular item in the list.

Your completed code on frame 50 should look like this:

```
 1  info_txt.text = "Welcome to the home frame";
 2
 3  restart_btn.addEventListener(MouseEvent.CLICK, goStart);
 4
 5  function goStart(e:MouseEvent):void {
 6      gotoAndPlay("loop");
 7      count = 1;
 8  }
 9
10  loadList.addEventListener(Event.CHANGE, loadFile);
11
12  function loadFile(e:Event):void {
13      loadWindow.source = e.target.selectedItem.data;
14  }
```

2 Save and test the movie.

3 In the testing environment, select the Paint item in the list. The paint.swf file will seamlessly load into the interface.

4 Select the Instruments item in the list. The instruments.swf file will load.

5 Select the Gallery item in the list. This will cause an error, because the gallery.swf file has not yet been created. You will create that file next. In Lesson 10, "Manipulating Video with ActionScript," you will learn how to respond to error events at runtime so that the user does not have a confusing experience if there is a problem when a file should be loading.

Creating the gallery file

Now you will create the gallery file that you referred to in the List component. This file will let the user select from a set of thumbnails to load and display JPG images in a UILoader instance. When a thumbail image is selected, text from an external text file, which describes the selected image, will load and display in a text field on the Flash stage. The starting point for this file is provided for you as gallery.fla in the Lesson05 > Start folder. You will add quite a bit of ActionScript to this file to create its functionality, but first take a look at the content already in the file.

Examining the gallery.fla file

The basic layout and graphics for the gallery file have been prepared for you. You will add ActionScript to the file to control loading text and images.

1 From the Lessons > Lesson05 > Start folder, open the gallery.fla file.

There are four layers on the timeline and three items on the stage. There are no actions yet. You will add code to the `actions` layer soon. In the `loader` layer is an instance of the UILoader component.

2 With the Properties panel visible, select the UILoader component instance. It has been given the instance name `ldr`.

3 In the `text` layer, select the dynamic text field. It has been given the instance name `info`.

4 In the `thumbs` layer, select the movie clip containing a series of thumbnail images. You will see in the Properties panel that it has been given the instance name *thumbs_mc*.

5 Double-click the *thumbs_mc* movie clip.

The seven thumbnails are each individual buttons. If you select these buttons, you'll see they have the instance names btn1 through btn7. Because these buttons are inside a movie clip named *thumbs_mc*, you would describe the path from the main timeline to these buttons in ActionScript as thumbs_mc.btn1, thumbs_mc.btn2, and so on.

6 Go back to the main timeline by choosing Edit > Edit Document.

Adding event listeners to the thumbnails

In earlier lessons, you use the addEventListener() method to create buttons that respond to user clicks. Now, you will do the same to the seven buttons inside the *thumbs_mc* clip. In this situation, however, you will need to indicate the path for each of the buttons so that your ActionScript targets objects that are inside the *thumbs_mc* clip.

1 With frame 1 of the actions layer selected and the Actions panel visible, place the insertion point in the first line of the Actions panel.

2 Keeping in mind the path to the seven thumbnail buttons, add the following code to create an addEventListener method for each button:

```
thumbs_mc.btn1.addEventListener(MouseEvent.CLICK, ldr1);
thumbs_mc.btn2.addEventListener(MouseEvent.CLICK, ldr2);
thumbs_mc.btn3.addEventListener(MouseEvent.CLICK, ldr3);
thumbs_mc.btn4.addEventListener(MouseEvent.CLICK, ldr4);
thumbs_mc.btn5.addEventListener(MouseEvent.CLICK, ldr5);
thumbs_mc.btn6.addEventListener(MouseEvent.CLICK, ldr6);
thumbs_mc.btn7.addEventListener(MouseEvent.CLICK, ldr7);
```

The buttons will now call functions named ldr1, ldr2, and so on. Next, you will create these functions.

3 In a line below the addEventListener calls, create the ldr1() function to respond to the first button:

```
function ldr1(e:Event) {
 ldr.source = "../images/image1.jpg";
}
```

When the first button is clicked, it will load an image called image1.jpg into the UILoader instance onstage. Notice the syntax for describing the path to the JPG file. The characters "../" tell ActionScript to go up one level from the location of the current Flash file and then to look in a folder named images for a file named image1.jpg. If this method of describing a path is unfamiliar to you, compare the syntax to the location of the files in the Lessons > Lesson05 folder.

4 Add one more line to this function so that it reads:

```
function ldr1(e:Event) {
 ldr.source = "../images/image1.jpg";
 textLoad("../text/picture1.txt", 0xAAFFAA);
}
```

When each button is clicked, it will load an image into the UILoader. The line you just added calls a function named textLoad() that will load text files into the text field onstage. This function does not exist yet; if you test the movie before you create the function, you will get an error message. Notice that the call to the `textLoad()` function includes two parameters. The first one passes the path to a text file. The second passes a numeric color value that will be used to set the background color of the text field. You will create the `textLoad()` function soon, but first, you'll add the functions for the remaining buttons.

5 Create functions similar to the `ldr1()` function for the other six buttons.

Note that in earlier lessons, each `addEventListener()` method you created was followed by its corresponding function. In this exercise, all the `addEventListener()` calls are grouped together, followed by all the functions. The order in which you arrange the listeners is up to you.

Your Actions panel should look like this:

```
ACTIONS - FRAME

1   thumbs_mc.btn1.addEventListener(MouseEvent.CLICK, ldr1);
2   thumbs_mc.btn2.addEventListener(MouseEvent.CLICK, ldr2);
3   thumbs_mc.btn3.addEventListener(MouseEvent.CLICK, ldr3);
4   thumbs_mc.btn4.addEventListener(MouseEvent.CLICK, ldr4);
5   thumbs_mc.btn5.addEventListener(MouseEvent.CLICK, ldr5);
6   thumbs_mc.btn6.addEventListener(MouseEvent.CLICK, ldr6);
7   thumbs_mc.btn7.addEventListener(MouseEvent.CLICK, ldr7);
8
9   function ldr1(e:Event) {
10      ldr.source = "../images/image1.jpg";
11      textLoad("../text/picture1.txt", 0xAAFFAA);
12  }
13  function ldr2(e:Event) {
14      ldr.source = "../images/image2.jpg";
15      textLoad("../text/picture2.txt", 0xCCCCEE);
16  }
17  function ldr3(e:Event) {
18      ldr.source = "../images/image3.jpg";
19      textLoad("../text/picture3.txt", 0xCCEECC);
20  }
21  function ldr4(e:Event) {
22      ldr.source = "../images/image4.jpg";
23      textLoad("../text/picture4.txt", 0xFFCCCC);
24  }
25  function ldr5(e:Event) {
26      ldr.source = "../images/image5.jpg";
27      textLoad("../text/picture5.txt", 0xCCDDAA);
28  }
29  function ldr6(e:Event) {
30      ldr.source = "../images/image6.jpg";
31      textLoad("../text/picture6.txt", 0xBBFFCC);
32  }
33  function ldr7(e:Event) {
34      ldr.source = "../images/image7.jpg";
35      textLoad("../text/picture7.txt", 0xCDEFED);
36  }
37

actions : 1
Line 12 of 49, Col 2
```

Loading text from an external file

Now you will create the code to load a different text file into the info text field for each button. The UIComponent that you have been using to load SWF and image files makes use of an ActionScript class called the `Loader`. Because the UILoader component was used, you didn't need to write ActionScript to load any files—the component took care of this in the background. To load text or data into Flash, you use a class called the `URLLoader`. Because you will not be using a component to help with loading the text, you will write ActionScript to make an instance of the `URLLoader` class to load text.

1 In the Actions panel, below the existing code, add a new URLLoader instance:

```
var loader:URLLoader = new URLLoader();
```

Next, you will create the textLoad() function to load text from an external file. This is the function that the button listeners refer to that you created earlier.

2 Add the following below the code in the Actions panel:

```
function textLoad(file:String, color:uint) {
 loader.load(new URLRequest(file));
 info.backgroundColor = color;
}
```

The textLoad() function performs two tasks. First it calls the load() method of the URLLoader class. This is what does the loading of the text file. Remember that this function is being called when any of the seven thumbnail buttons are clicked. If you review those functions, you'll see that when the textLoad() function is called, it is passed two parameters. Each button function passes the textLoad() function a string that describes a path to a text file and a numeric color value. The first parameter is called file; the second is called color.

The file parameter is used to determine the path to the file that the load() method will load. The color parameter is used to set the background color of the text field onstage named info.

When this function is called, it loads the text file into Flash and changes the color of the text field, but at this point it will not yet display the text. Actually displaying the text is just a matter of taking the data that has been loaded and setting it to be the text property of the text field.

To display data that is loaded from the external text files in a text field is very simple, but before that step is made, you should always confirm that the data that you asked to load has actually arrived.

Using the COMPLETE event to confirm loading external text

The COMPLETE event works using the listener model, just like the other events you have used. Let's add the COMPLETE event to listen for when the content is successfully loaded.

1 Below the existing code in the Actions panel, add the following lines:

```
loader.addEventListener(Event.COMPLETE, displayText);

function displayText(e:Event) {
 info.text = (loader.data);
}
```

When the loader object successfully completes the loading of one of the text files, it will display the text from that file in the info text field instance.

Now you can tweak the text field's formatting. You'll give the text field a visible background and border, and set the border color.

Confirming the loading of external content

One line of code is all it will take to display the text you loaded into the loader object in text field named info. That line would read:

```
info.text = (loader.data);
```

Instinctively you might be inclined to add this line to the `textLoad()` function as in:

```
function textLoad(file:String, color:uint) {
  loader.load(new URLRequest(file));
  info.backgroundColor = color;
  info.text = (loader.data);
}
```

The problem is that while this would work reliably locally, it would be likely to cause problems when the loaded text files are downloaded from a server. Remember that each line of ActionScript is usually executed in a small fraction of a second. If on one line of code you instruct Flash Player to load a text file from a server, and a few lines later you give instructions to display the text, the odds are good that computers with slow or moderate connection speeds will not have had time to download the text file needed for display. This will cause a runtime error.

Any time you use ActionScript to load content from a remote location, it's a good practice to confirm that the load has completed before using the loaded content.

Fortunately, ActionScript makes this relatively easy, because both the Loader class and the URLLoader class have a built-in event called COMPLETE, which automatically fires when a request for loaded content is completed successfully.

2 Add the bold code within the `displayText()` function:

```
function displayText(e:Event) {
  info.text = (loader.data);
  info.background = true;
  info.border = true;
  info.borderColor = 0x333333;
}
```

Note: You will learn much more about formatting text with ActionScript in Lesson 8, "Creating a Radio Button Quiz in an ActionScript File."

Adding a scroll bar to the text field

There is more text in the text files that you will be loading than will fit visibly in the onstage text field. Fortunately, a built-in component called UIScrollBar makes it easy to create a working scroll bar for that field.

Scrolling text is an important feature in many interfaces when space is limited. Fortunately it is easy to add a working scrollbar to a text field using the built-in UIScrollbar component. Because the info text field onstage is not large enough to display all the text in the text files that may be loaded into it, you will create a scrollbar for that field.

1 Select the info text field onstage.

2 From the Text menu, choose Scrollable.

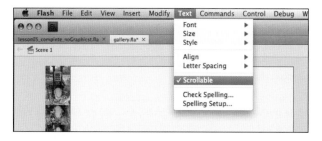

3 With the Components panel open (Window > Components), select the UIScrollbar component from the list of User Interface components.

4 Drag a UIScrollbar instance to the stage so that it lines up with the upper-right corner of the info text field.

5 With the new UIScrollbar instance selected onstage, make the Component Inspector panel visible (Window > Component Inspector).

6 Select the `scrollTargetName` parameter.

7 Set the `scrollTargetName` to **info**.

8 Save and test the movie. When you click any of the thumbnail buttons, a new image loads and displays in the UILoader, and text appears in the info field, with its background color changed. A working scrollbar is available for the text field.

9 Save this file, and return to the lesson05_start.fla file.

10 Test the lesson05_start.fla file. Pressing the Gallery item in the list will now open your new gallery file in the file's UILoader instance. The gallery's buttons should still perform their funtions in the movie's interface.

Some suggestions to try on your own

Experimenting on your own will help you solidify your knowledge of the techniques in this lesson. Here are a few suggestions to get you started:

- Create a new Flash movie, and add another item to the list in the lesson05_start.fla file to load your new movie.

- Replace the JPG files in the gallery.fla file with your own JPG files. Try getting files to load from a different path.

- Experiment with some of the other User Interface components that ship with Flash CS4. Refer to Flash Help for information on their parameters.

In the next lesson, you will learn how to create preloaders to monitor the loading progress of your Flash files.

Review questions

1 Name the file types that you can load into a Flash project with the UILoader component.

2 Name an event that is available for the List component that can react when the user makes a selection from a List instance.

3 Name an event associated with the URLLoader class that you can use to confirm that data has finished loading.

Review answers

1 The UILoader component can be used to load SWF, JPG, PNG, and GIF files into a Flash file.

2 You can use the CHANGE event to keep track of when a user makes a new selection from a List component instance.

3 You can use the COMPLETE event to confirm the successful loading of data into a URLLoader instance.

6 CREATING PRELOADERS IN ACTIONSCRIPT 3.0

Lesson overview

In this lesson, you will learn to do the following:

- Check your Flash files to determine if you need to use a preloader.

- Use the testing and simulation tools in Flash to experience your projects at different connection speeds.

- Use the methods of the UILoader class to track the progress of loading media.

- Use the ProgressBar component to give the user feedback on loading media.

- Calculate the percentage of requested content that has loaded, and display that percentage in a text field for the user.

- Use the COMPLETE event to hide the preloader and display content when it is completely loaded.

- Use the percentage of a file that is loaded to trigger the playback of frames in a MovieClip.

 This lesson will take approximately 2.5 hours.

The lessons so far have supplied you with enough ActionScript to add quite a bit of functionality to your Flash projects, and the lesson files you have completed should all work seamlessly on your local machine. However, a large percentage of Flash projects are intended

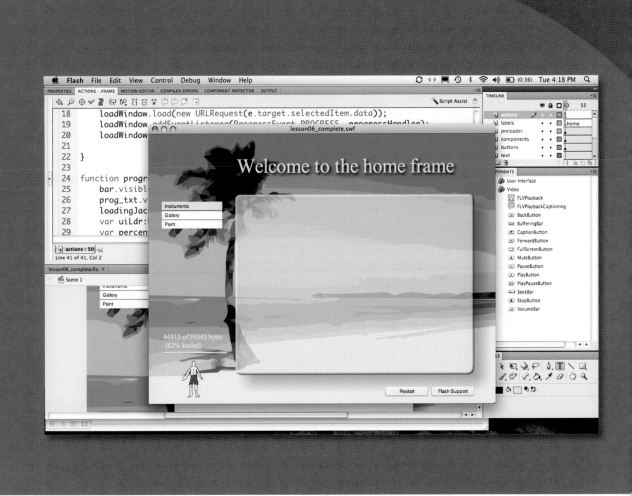

In this lesson, you will learn to monitor and give your
users feedback on loading content.

as online applications. When you are creating a Flash project for the web, it's essential that you take into account that all the content in your project has to be downloaded to your end users' machines before they can view it. The term *preloader* is frequently used to describe the techniques used to track the loading of content into Flash Player, to give the user feedback, when needed, on that loading, and to respond to the results of the loading.

Nearly everyone who has surfed the web has encountered preloaders. The classic example of a preloader occurs when loading content into a web page. While the content is loading, a progress bar appears, which expands gradually to the right as a text message tells you what percentage of the content has loaded. When the content is fully loaded, both the progress bar and text disappear and are replaced by the loaded content. In this lesson, you will create this archetypal preloader.

While creating a basic preloader may not be the most intriguing ActionScript technique, the knowledge of how to ensure that your user has a good experience downloading your content is a critical part of good Flash development. As you become more comfortable with the concepts of preloaders, you will be able to implement creative variations on the techniques that serve the purpose of a preloader but offer the user something more interesting to do than watch the movement of a progress bar. The final steps in the lesson will show you some possibilities for alternative preloading techniques.

The file for this lesson is called lesson06_start.fla and can be found in the Lessons folder (Lessons > Lesson06 > Start > lesson06_start.fla). It is the completed file from Lesson 5, "Using ActionScript and Components to Load Content." Up until this point we have not been preparing this file for successful web streaming. Now, let's take a look at some of the tools in Flash that will help you to see how this file would perform online.

Tools in the testing environment

Flash ships with a number of extremely helpful tools for troubleshooting potential problems with your projects and testing their performance under various user conditions. Each time you test a Flash web-based project by choosing Control > Test Movie, you are taken to the testing environment in Flash. In this testing environment, the Flash menu system changes, offering a number of very useful features that help ensure your Flash projects will perform as desired. Two important features in the testing environment are the Bandwidth Profiler and Simulate Download. You may already be using these tools in Flash; if not, you are about to discover how they can be part of a good user experience.

Bandwidth Profiler

The Bandwidth Profiler offers very helpful visual feedback for estimating the download times for the content of your Flash projects. It works in conjunction with the Download Settings menu to compare the size of the content in the frames of your Flash files to the time it will take to download them at the estimated connection speed of your audience.

1 Open the Lesson06_start.fla file (Lessons > Lesson06 > Start > lesson06_start.fla).

2 Test the file (Control > Test Movie).

The feedback that's viewable in the Bandwidth Profiler, as well as that offered by some of the other testing tools, is based on what you tell Flash is the minimum connection speed of your intended audience. For this lesson, we will assume that all the audience has at least a 32 KB-per-second (KB/s) connection. Remember, this is not always the case; be sure on real projects to discuss the intended audience with the team or the client.

3 While still in the testing environment, choose View > Download Settings > DSL (32.6 KB/s).

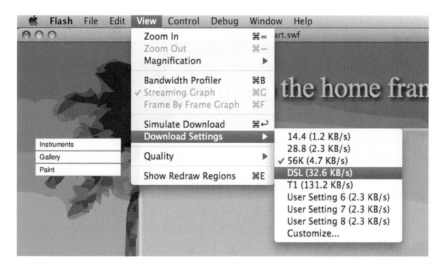

Now the testing tools will give you feedback on how your movie will perform at this data rate.

4   Choose View > Bandwidth Profiler.

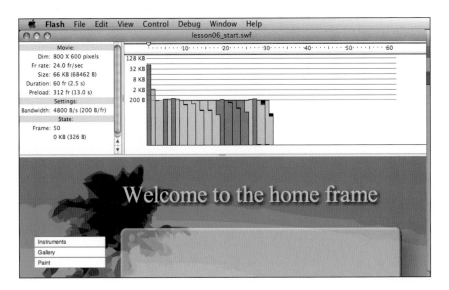

The Bandwidth Profiler contains a lot of useful information. Let's focus on the main streaming graph on the right-hand part of the Bandwidth Profiler. The timeline in this graph represents the main Timeline of the Flash file that you are testing. The movie we are working with is set to a frame rate of 24 fps. This means each frame in the graph represents 1/24th of a second.

If a SWF file is streaming from the web, the content in each frame of the Flash Timeline is downloaded sequentially, starting with frame 1. If the content in a frame is not fully downloaded when Flash Player reaches that frame, then the entire movie freezes until the frame's content is fully loaded; playback then resumes. Obviously, having frames that are not fully loaded when the viewer needs to see them is a situation to be avoided.

The Bandwidth Profiler gives visual feedback that clearly shows where potential problems may lie. The red line across the graph represents the data rate that you have set for your download setting, and the vertical bars represent frames of content that need to be downloaded. When the bars are on or below the red line, the frames they represent have content whose total size will download in real time under typical circumstances at your selected download setting. Bars that extend above the line represent frames whose total content is too large to download in real time.

In this file, frame 1 is the only frame that is significantly above the line. As the streaming graph shows, frame 1 needs to download nearly 64 KB of content before it can play, and that will take more than the 1/24th of a second it would take to play that frame. However, at our selected rate of 32 KB/s, the user would need to wait only approximately two seconds before the file would begin to play—and most users would not mind, or even notice, a wait of two seconds before a file begins.

Frame 2 has significantly less content and will load in close-to-real time. On a real project, you would probably consider trying to optimize the file to reduce the content in frame 2, but for this project we'll call it close enough. The bigger problem with this file will occur when the user tries to load the external SWF files in the UILoader that you created in Lesson 5, "Using ActionScript and Components to Load Content." These files are not huge—they range only from about 12 K to about 64 K—but they are large enough that your intended audience will not receive the files instantly. If members of your audience tried to view this file from the web in its current state, each time they selected a file to load from the menu on the *home* frame, they would receive no feedback about the status of the load in progress. The purpose of this lesson is to create the feedback that will keep users aware of what is happening, so they'll stay around long enough to view your content. But before we do that, let's look at one more very useful tool in the testing environment, which lets you experience the loading of your file as your audience would.

It is a good habit to take advantage of this tool in all your own Flash projects, so that you can always know which frames in your files need to be adjusted or compensated for with a preloader. For now, however, deselect the Bandwidth Profiler in the View menu and then you will look at another extremely useful tool that allows you to experience the downloading of your Flash files as your users might.

Simulate Download

Simulate Download plays your file as if it were being downloaded at whatever connection speed was chosen in the Download Settings menu (View > Download Settings). Remember that these settings are just approximations of average connections and that every user's experience on the Internet can vary dramatically from moment to moment regardless of what their connection speed should be. All the testing tools should be used as conservative points of reference.

1 While still in the testing environment, play your file (lesson06_start.fla) as if it were downloading from a typical DSL connection by choosing View > Simulate Download.

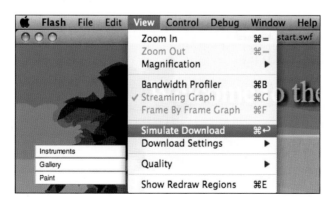

The Simulate Download command works in conjunction with the current Download setting. The current test will run at 32.6 KB/s, since that's what you set in an earlier step.

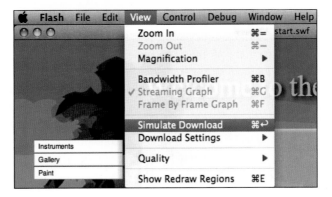

The file should take a few seconds longer to start than in previous tests, but then should play normally.

2 Navigate to the *home* frame of the project by clicking the Home button in the bottom-right of the stage, or wait until the animation completes to be automatically taken to the *home* frame.

3 From the list on the left, choose Paint. The paint.swf file should load relatively quickly, because it's fairly small.

4 Choose either Gallery or Instruments from the list, and notice that the wait is much longer than for the Paint file. Most users would consider it unacceptable to have to wait this long for content, with no interim feedback letting them know that something is happening. You will add feedback that reports to the user what percent of the requested data is loaded.

5 Close the window containing the lesson06_start.swf file to leave the testing environment and return to the Flash authoring environment.

Creating a text field and progress bar to track loading

As mentioned earlier, the classic example of a preloader is a progress bar that shows both the loading progress and a text field displaying the percent of the loading that has taken place. Now you will begin to add those elements to the project.

1 Add a new layer to your timeline above the existing components layer, and name it **preloader content**.

2 In the new layer, add a keyframe (F6) on frame 50. This is where you will place the progress bar and text field for your preloader.

3 From the Tools panel, select the Text tool, and create a new text field onstage.

4 In the Properties panel, select Dynamic Text from the drop-down list on the left.

5 Also in the Properties panel, give the new text field the instance name **prog_txt**.

6 In the Properties panel, under Position And Size, give the text field these settings: X = **30**, Y = **440**, W = **150**, H = **50**.

7 Choose any font you like in the Family field, and select a color that contrasts with the background. (In a coming lesson, you will learn to create and format text entirely with code.)

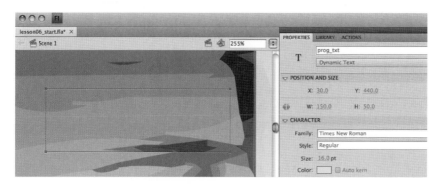

Next, you will add a ProgressBar component.

8 Open the Components panel (Window > Components), and from the User Interface components list, select the ProgressBar component.

9   Drag an instance of the ProgressBar component to frame 50 of the `preloader content` layer, and place it directly below the prog_txt field.

10 With the new instance selected and the Properties panel visible, give your ProgressBar the instance name **bar**.

11 With the new ProgressBar instance still selected make the Component Inspector panel visible (Window > Component Inspector).

12 In the Component Inpector set the ProgresBar's `source` parameter to be `loadWindow`. The ProgressBar instance will now be used to track progress of files loaded into the onstage UILoader instance.

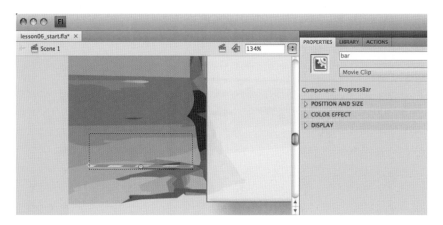

Inserting ActionScript to track progress of the UILoader component

If you completed Lesson 5, you will remember using a UILoader component to load image and SWF files. The UILoader component has ActionScript events, properties, and methods that make it relatively easy for you to monitor the progress of files being loaded into it. The text field and ProgressBar instances that you just created will use these UILoader methods and properties to give accurate feedback to the user on loading progress.

1   With the Actions panel visible, select frame 50 of the `actions` layer.

    Since the ProgressBar component you added does not need to be visible until the user chooses to load a file, let's hide it by setting its `visible` property to `false`.

2   On the line below the existing code, add the following:

```
bar.visible = false;
```

    The Actions panel should now read as follows:

```
ACTIONS - FRAME  MOTION EDITOR  COMPILER ERRORS  COMPONENT INSPECTOR  OUTPUT
                                                                          Script Assist
 1  info_txt.text = "Welcome to the home frame";
 2
 3  restart_btn.addEventListener(MouseEvent.CLICK, goStart);
 4
 5  function goStart(e:MouseEvent):void {
 6      gotoAndPlay("loop");
 7      count = 1;
 8  }
 9
10  loadList.addEventListener(Event.CHANGE, loadFile);
11
12  function loadFile(e:Event):void {
13      loadWindow.load(new URLRequest(e.target.selectedItem.data));
14  }
15
16  bar.visible = false;
```

You may remember from Lesson 5 that content is being loaded into a UILoader instance onstage that has an instance name of loadWindow. The loading takes place any time the user makes a selection from the onstage list component that has an instance name of loadList.

The code on line 14 uses the source property of the UILoader component to load each selected file. This technique works fine for choosing which file will load into the UILoader component, but does not offer many options for tracking the loading progress. The load method of the UILoader component is an alternative way of loading content into the component that offers much more control.

3 Change the line that now reads:

    loadWindow.source = e.target.selectedItem.data;

so that it reads:

    loadWindow.load(new URLRequest(e.target.selectedItem.data));

If you tested the file now, the results would be exactly the same as before. Each selection from the list would load the file that was associated with that selection. However, now that this is being accomplished by the load method, you can access events that are associated with the loading.

Repeatedly while a requested file is loading, an event takes place called PROGRESS. Each time this event occurs, it reports on what percentage of the file has loaded. When the file has successfully finished loading, another event, called COMPLETE, automatically takes place. These are the events you will use for your preloader.

Adding event listeners for PROGRESS and COMPLETE

Adding event listeners for the PROGRESS and COMPLETE events is nearly identical to the way you have already added event listeners for mouse and frame events in previous lessons. First you will create addEventListener() methods for these two events, and then you will write event handling functions to respond when the events take place.

1   With the Actions panel visible, select frame 50 of the actions layer.

2   In the existing code, locate the loadFile() function. It should now read:

```
function loadFile(e:Event):void {
  loadWindow.load(new URLRequest(e.target.selectedItem.data));
}
```

3   In the body of the function, add two addEventListener() methods to the loadWindow component so that the function now reads:

```
function loadFile(e:Event):void {
  loadWindow.load(new URLRequest(e.target.selectedItem.data));
  loadWindow.addEventListener(ProgressEvent.PROGRESS,
    ➥progressHandler);
  loadWindow.addEventListener(Event.COMPLETE, completeHandler);
}
```

The PROGRESS event will fire repeatedly any time a file is loading into the UILoader component. When the PROGRESS event occurs, it will call a function named progressHandler(). You will create this function soon, and it will contain much of the preloader functionality.

The COMPLETE event will be triggered once each time a file has loaded into the UILoader component successfully. When the COMPLETE event occurs, it will call a function named completeHandler(). This will be used to hide all the preloader elements and to remove the event listeners once they are no longer needed. You will create this function soon as well.

Creating the progressHandler() function

This function will repeat regularly while the requested file is loading (exactly how often will vary). This function will be user to monitor and report on the progress of the loading.

In the Actions panel, below the existing code, add the following function:

```
24  function progressHandler(e:ProgressEvent):void {
25      bar.visible = true;
26      prog_txt.visible = true;
27      var percent:int = loadWindow.percentLoaded;
28      prog_txt.text = String(loadWindow.bytesLoaded) + " of " + String(loadWindow.bytesTotal)
    + " bytes" + "\n" + " (" + percent +"% loaded)";
29      bar.setProgress(e.bytesLoaded, e.bytesTotal);
30  }
```

Notice that the parameter for the `progressHandler()` function has the data type of ProgressEvent. The ProgressEvent works very similarly to the events and mouse events you have already used.

Lines 25 and 26 (your line numbers may vary) set both the ProgressBar component and the text field you created to `visible` when the ProgressEvent takes place.

Line 27 creates a new variable called `percent` and stores the `percentLoaded` property of the UILoader component. This property should change every time the ProgressEvent takes place. The `percent` variable keeps track of the percentage of the requested file that has been loaded. Notice that the data type of the `percent` variable is set to int. Previously, when you have stored a numeric value in a variable, you have set the data type to Number. The reason that int was chosen in this case is that unlike the `Number` data type, which can return any number including fractions, int will always return an integer—in this case between 0 and 100. It will be much easier for your user to read that 49 percent of the file is loaded rather than 49.34572194858 percent.

Line 28 is where the text feedback is created for the user. First, two additional very useful properties of the `UILoader` class are used. The `bytesLoaded` property, not surprisingly, returns the number of bytes of the file loaded; equally intuitively, the `bytesTotal` property returns the total number of bytes for the entire file. These two properties are converted to strings so they can be added to a sentence that informs the user how many bytes of the total have loaded. The characters `\n` force a new line in the text field, and then the current value of the variable `percent` is displayed, along with some literal characters to make it more readable.

Note: Notice that in the previous figure, line 28 wraps over two lines. Depending on the size of your Actions panel, this line may or may not wrap on your machine. When typing your version of the code, do not press Enter before the entire line is complete.

Finally, line 29 uses the `setProgress` method of the ProgressBar component to give graphical feedback of the loading progress. The `setProgress` method takes two parameters: The first value describes the progress that has been made so far, in this case the number of bytes that are currently loaded. The second parameter is the maximum possible progress, which in this case is the total size (in bytes) of the loading file. As the value of `bytesLoaded` approaches that of `bytesTotal`, the ProgressBar expands to the right.

Before you test your movie, there is one more function to add for the COMPLETE event.

Adding the completeHandler() function

Now we'll add the function that will respond to the COMPLETE event.

1 Below the exisiting code in the Actions panel, add the following:

```
35  function completeHandler(event:Event):void {
36      bar.visible = false;
37      prog_txt.visible = false;
38      loadWindow.removeEventListener(ProgressEvent.PROGRESS, progressHandler);
39      loadWindow.removeEventListener(Event.COMPLETE, completeHandler);
40  }
```

This code is a little simpler than the progressHandler() function. Lines 33 and 34 hide both the ProgressBar and the text field that display the loading progress. Remember that since the requested load is now completed, these items are no longer necessary. The event listeners themselves are also no longer needed, so lines 35 and 36 remove both the PROGRESS and COMPLETE listeners. If the user decides to load a file later by selecting another item from the list, the listeners will be added once again.

Your completed code in frame 50 should now read:

```
info_txt.text = "Welcome to the home frame";

restart_btn.addEventListener(MouseEvent.CLICK, goStart);

function goStart(e:MouseEvent):void {
 gotoAndPlay("loop");
 count = 1;
}

loadList.addEventListener(Event.CHANGE, loadFile);

function loadFile(e:Event):void {
 loadWindow.load(new URLRequest(e.target.selectedItem.data));
  ➡loadWindow.addEventListener(ProgressEvent.PROGRESS,
  ➡progressHandler);
 loadWindow.addEventListener(Event.COMPLETE, completeHandler);

}

bar.visible = false;

function progressHandler(e:ProgressEvent):void {
 bar.visible = true;
 prog_txt.visible = true;
 var percent:int = loadWindow.percentLoaded;
```

```
prog_txt.text = String(loadWindow.bytesLoaded) + " of "
  ➥+ String(loadWindow.bytesTotal) + " bytes" + "\n"
  ➥+ " ("+ percent +"% loaded)";
bar.setProgress(e.bytesLoaded, e.bytesTotal);
}

function completeHandler(event:Event):void {
bar.visible = false;
prog_txt.visible = false;
loadWindow.removeEventListener(ProgressEvent.PROGRESS,
  ➥progressHandler);
loadWindow.removeEventListener(Event.COMPLETE,
  ➥completeHandler);
}
```

2 Test your movie.

3 In the testing environment, select View > Simulate Download.

4 Navigate to the *home* frame of your movie.

5 From the list, choose Instruments. The ProgressBar and the text field should give accurate information about loading of the file.

6 Try the other two items in the list, and watch their load progress. Notice that when the load is complete, the preloader items (text field and ProgressBar) disappear.

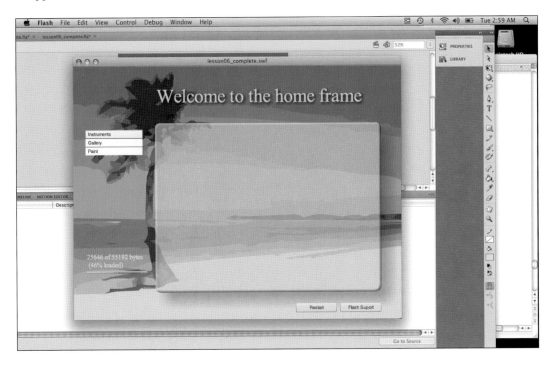

Controlling the frames of a MovieClip to reflect loading progress

The ProgressBar component is a very easy and useful way to give the user clear feedback on loading progress. Anyone who has used a computer will understand the purpose of the ProgressBar. However, it is not the most interesting thing to stare at for very long. Fortunately, the same techniques that you just used to track loading progress can be used in an infinite variety of ways to give the user a more interesting waiting period. For example, if your user has a very slow connection and a lot of content to load, you may want to display new text in a text field every time a certain percent of the content has loaded. Using this technique, the user could be reading lots of instructional or entertaining information while they are waiting.

Another useful technique is to have the percent of loaded content determine which frame of a MovieClip onstage is displayed. The data rate of the download would determine the frame rate of the MovieClip.

Let's add an example to the project of a stepping through the frames of a MovieClip triggered by loading progress. You don't want to give the user a new large MovieClip to load, since this technique is just to maintain interest while other content is loading, so we will reuse the animated MovieClip that the user has already loaded.

1   Open the Library, if it's not visible (Window > Library).

2   Locate the JumpingJack symbol, and double-click it to view its timeline. Notice that the timeline of the symbol has 34 frames.

You will write code that uses the loading percent of the UILoader to determine which frame of this movie clip is displayed.

3   In the upper-left corner of the stage, click the tab that says Scene 1 to return to the main Timeline.

4   With frame 50 of the `preloader content` layer selected, drag an instance of the JumpingJack symbol to the stage.

5   With the symbol selected onstage, go to the Properties panel, and, in the drop-down list in the top-left, switch the symbol type from Graphic to MovieClip.

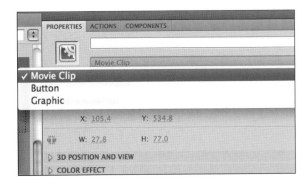

6 With the symbol still selected, give it the instance name **loadAnimation**.

7 In the Position and Size section of the Properties panel, give the *loadAnimation* clip the following properties: X = **105**, Y = **530**, W = **30**, H = **80**.

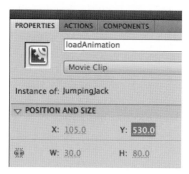

This will give you a small instance of the animation that appears below your other preloader content.

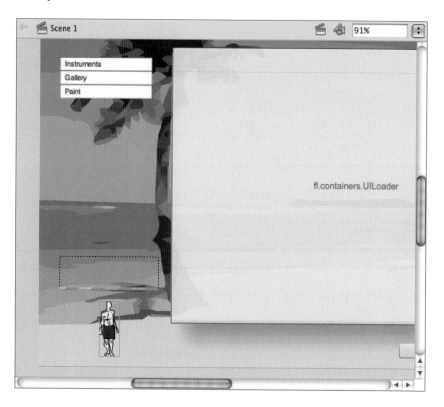

Adding ActionScript for the loadAnimation clip

If you tested the movie now, the *loadAnimation* clip would play continuously for the duration it was on the stage. By adding a few lines of code, you can make the *loadAnimation* clip appear only when new content is loading, and play once through as the load progresses.

1 With the Actions panel visible, select frame 50 of the `actions` layer.

2 Locate the line of code that reads:

```
bar.visible = false;
```

3 On a new line below this code, add code to stop the timeline of the *loadAnimation* clip:

```
bar.visible = false;
loadAnimation.stop();
```

4 Now add a line to make the *loadAnimation* clip invisible at the start of the movie:

```
bar.visible=false;
loadAnimation.stop();
loadAnimation.visible = false;
```

5 On the next line, give the animation a little transparency:

```
bar.visible=false;
loadAnimation.stop();
loadAnimation.visible = false;
loadAnimation.alpha = .8;
```

The time that the *loadAnimation* clip should appear is while the progress of a loading file is being tracked. You will add some code to the existing `progressHandler()` function to do this. Currently, the function should read:

```
function progressHandler(e:ProgressEvent):void {
 bar.visible = true;
 prog_txt.visible = true;
 var percent:int = loadWindow.percentLoaded;
 prog_txt.text = String(loadWindow.bytesLoaded) + " of
    ➡" + String(loadWindow.bytesTotal) + " bytes" + "\n"+
    ➡" (" + percent + "% loaded)";
 bar.setProgress(e.bytesLoaded, e.bytesTotal);
 }
```

6 Click at the end of the line that reads:

```
prog_txt.visible = true;
```

and press Enter to add a new line.

7   Add this code on the new line to make the *loadAnimation* clip visible:

```
loadAnimation.visible = true;
```

Now for the code that ties the frames of the *loadAnimation* clip to the loading progress.

8   In the `progressHandler` function, locate the line that creates the percent variable:

```
var percent:int = loadWindow.percentLoaded;
```

9   On a new line below the `percent` variable insert the following code:

```
loadAnimation.gotoAndStop(percent);
```

Recall that the variable percent represents the percentage of the file that is loaded.

By using a variable to stand in for the frame number, you can create a `goto` action whose frame changes as the variable value changes. In this case, as the percentage of the file loaded increases, the MovieClip progressively plays through its frames. As it stands now, each one percent of loading progress would advance the *loadAnimation* clip one frame.

Since the *loadAnimation* clip has 34 frames, this would work fine up until 34 percent of the file was loaded, but then there are no more frames in the MovieClip to display. A little math to divide the percent variable by three would give a range that more closely matches the animation so that each frame will be displayed for approximately three percent of the load time.

10 Modify the line that you just typed to read:

```
loadAnimation.gotoAndStop(percent / 3);
```

The only remaining potential problem with this code is that it might send a request to navigate to frame 0 when zero percent of the file is loaded. To avoid this, we will use a method of the Math class called `ceil`, which rounds any number up to the nearest whole number.

11 Make one final adjustment to the line so that it reads:

```
loadAnimation.gotoAndStop(Math.ceil(percent / 3));
```

The full function should now read:

```
function progressHandler(e:ProgressEvent):void {
  bar.visible = true;
  prog_txt.visible = true;
  loadAnimation.visible = true;
  var percent:int = loadWindow.percentLoaded;
  loadAnimation.gotoAndStop(Math.ceil(percent / 3));
```

```
prog_txt.text = String(loadWindow.bytesLoaded) + " of
➥" + String(loadWindow.bytesTotal) + " bytes"+"\n" + "
➥(" + percent + "% loaded)";
bar.setProgress(e.bytesLoaded, e.bytesTotal);
}
```

When the load is complete, you want the animation to disappear with the rest of the preloader content.

12 Locate the `completeHandler()` function.

13 Add a line to set the *loadAnimation* clip `visible` property to `false`. The completed function should now read:

```
function completeHandler(event:Event):void {
bar.visible = false;
prog_txt.visible = false;
loadAnimation.visible = false;
loadWindow.removeEventListener(ProgressEvent.PROGRESS,
➥progressHandler);
loadWindow.removeEventListener(Event.COMPLETE,
➥completeHandler);
}
```

The completed code on frame 50 of the `actions` layer should now read:

```
info_txt.text = "Welcome to the home frame";


restart_btn.addEventListener(MouseEvent.CLICK, goStart);


function goStart(e:MouseEvent):void {
gotoAndPlay("loop");
count = 1;
}


loadList.addEventListener(Event.CHANGE, loadFile);


function loadFile(e:Event):void {
loadWindow.load(new URLRequest(e.target.selectedItem.data));
loadWindow.addEventListener(ProgressEvent.PROGRESS,
➥progressHandler);
loadWindow.addEventListener(Event.COMPLETE, completeHandler);

}

bar.visible = false;
loadAnimation.visible = false;
loadAnimation.stop();
loadAnimation.alpha = .8;
```

(code continues on the next page)

(continued)

```
function progressHandler(e:ProgressEvent):void {
 bar.visible = true;
 prog_txt.visible = true;
 loadAnimation.visible = true;
 var percent:int = loadWindow.percentLoaded;
 loadAnimation.gotoAndStop(Math.ceil(percent / 3));
 prog_txt.text = String(loadWindow.bytesLoaded) + " of
  ➥" + String(loadWindow.bytesTotal) + " bytes" + "\n"+"
  ➥(" + percent + "% loaded)";
 bar.setProgress(e.bytesLoaded, e.bytesTotal);
}

function completeHandler(event:Event):void {
 bar.visible = false;
 prog_txt.visible = false;
 loadAnimation.visible = false;
 loadWindow.removeEventListener(ProgressEvent.PROGRESS,
  ➥progressHandler);
 loadWindow.removeEventListener(Event.COMPLETE,
completeHandler);
}
```

14 Test your movie. In the testing environment, select View > Simulate Download.

15 Navigate to the *home* frame of your movie.

16 From the file list, choose Instruments. In addition to the previous feedback, the animation should now appear and play exactly once through while the file is downloading. When the load is complete, the animation should disappear.

Remember, the *loadAnimation* clip could have any graphical content at all, and it would work the same way. This offers many creative possibilities. Be careful, however, to watch the file size of MovieClips that you are using for this purpose. Making the content of a MovieClip too large would defeat the purpose of using it as a preloader.

In this lesson, these preloader techniques were used for loading content into a UILoader component, but the same or similar techniques could be used for loading any media or data into Flash Player. They could also be used to monitor loading of the main movie.

Get in the habit of using preloaders whenever necessary, and search the Flash Help files and other Flash community resources for variations on the preloading techniques covered here.

As your projects get larger and more sophisticated, it becomes increasingly important to stay aware of the user's potential experience when streaming and loading your files. The creativity you apply to the otherwise mundane task of creating preloaders can become a significant and interesting part of your Flash project's identity.

Some suggestions to try on your own

You now have an ever expanding repertoire of techniques to play with. You can probably come up with even more variations on the techniques in this lesson. Here are a few suggestions to get you started:

- Create your own MovieClip, and use it as feedback of loading progress. It will be easier if the number of frames in your clip is a multiple of 100, so that it can more easily be associated with the integer for the percent of a file that is loaded.

- Add a new item to the loadList component, and use it to load in a much larger file. Try to make preloader content that will hold the user's interest that much longer.

- Create a new dynamic text field, and have the `text` property of the field change as the percent of the file increases. For example, you could use a conditional statement to have the text change every time the `percent` variable increased by 20. Tell a story that unfolds while a large file downloads.

Review questions

1 Name two features in the Flash testing environment that can help to determine the user's experience when downloading your Flash projects.

2 What are the two ActionScript properties that keep track of the total number of bytes in a file and the current number of bytes loaded?

3 What are two events of the UILoader component class that can be used to track loading?

Review answers

1 In the Flash testing environment, the Bandwidth Profiler (View > Bandwidth Profiler) can be used to determine which frames will load in real time at a given data rate, and the Simulate Download (View > Simulate Download) command can be used to play a Flash project as if it were being downloaded via a connection of a specific bandwidth. Both of these tools test your project based on the download settings (View > Download Settings) chosen in the testing environment.

2 The UILoader's PROGRESS event has two properties that can keep track of loading content. The number of bytes of requested content that have loaded can be retrieved as the bytesLoaded property, and the total number of bytes can be found with the bytesTotal property.

3 The PROGRESS event of the UILoader class takes place regularly while a file is being loaded into the component, and the COMPLETE event takes place when the file has successfully finished loading.

7 USING ARRAYS AND LOOPS IN ACTIONSCRIPT 3.0

Lesson overview

In this lesson, you will learn to do the following:

- Create `for` loops to control the repetition of ActionScript.

- Create ActionScript arrays to store, manipulate, and reference lists of data from a single variable.

- Place instances of symbols from the Library on the stage using ActionScript.

- Create new properties for MovieClip instances with ActionScript.

- Use Boolean variables to keep track of `true/false` values.

- Create arrays to keep track of lists of objects.

- Use methods of the `Array` class to store references to MovieClip instances and their properties.

- Use a `for` loop to cycle through an array and check the properties of its elements.

 This lesson will take approximately 2 hours.

This lesson introduces two very important ActionScript tools: the array and the `for` loop. These are common techniques in many programming languages; once you have gained a level of comfort with them, you'll find they make a great many tasks possible.

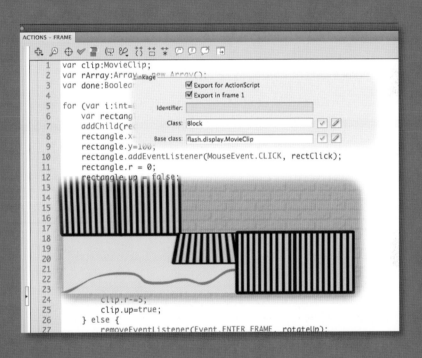

ActionScript that places Library items onstage and makes them interactive.

As with many other programming concepts, the initial syntax of these techniques can be confusing, but rest assured that with a little experience, the actual techniques are very easy. You'll probably find that what seemed perplexing at first will soon seem straightforward, and quickly become a very useful part of your ActionScript repertoire.

In the exercise for this lesson, you'll begin to create a project that you will continue to develop over the next few lessons.

Examining the completed file

In order to have a sense of what you are building in this file, it may be helpful to vew the completed version. You can do this by opening the Lessons > Lesson07 > Complete > lesson07_complete.fla file.

1 With the lesson07_complete.fla file open, choose Control > Test Movie to test the file as a SWF.

2 Click one of the square blocks in the center of the stage. It "opens" to reveal part of the graphic underneath.

3 One at a time, click the remaining blocks. When all five have been clicked open, the animation underneath plays to reveal the text message "Hurray!" (You will add much more to this project in coming lessons.)

4 Close the lesson07_complete.fla file.

Examining the starting file

In this lesson, we'll learn how to add MovieClips to the stage—but first, let's get a little bit more familiar with the functions and behaviors of movie clips in general. To begin this project, open the Lessons > Lesson07 > Start > lesson07_start.fla file.

The main timeline of the lesson07_start.fla file has three layers. The bottom `background` layer contains a static background graphic, the middle `animation` layer contains a MovieClip symbol, and the top `actions` layer is empty. You will place all the code for this lesson in frame 1 of this top layer. Before that, however, let's take a closer look at the MovieClip in the `animation` layer.

1 With the Properties panel visible, select the MovieClip in the `animation` layer (the wavy blue line). Notice that the clip has an instance name of *wave_mc*.

2 Double-click the *wave_mc* clip on the stage to view the clip's timeline. Notice that the clip's timeline has two layers and 45 frames. The `animation` layer contains a 45-frame shape tween. Scrub the playback head across the timeline to view the shape tween.

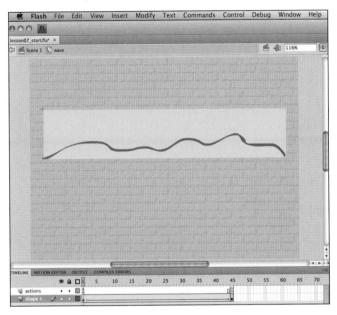

3 The `actions` layer has keyframes on the first and last frames. With the Actions panel visible, select frame 1 of the clip's `actions` layer. Notice that there is a `stop()` action on frame 1, and another on frame 45. This means that when the Flash project is played, this MovieClip will not play its animation until instructed to do so by ActionScript. When the animation does play, it will automatically stop on the final frame. You will make use of the way this clip is set up later in the lesson.

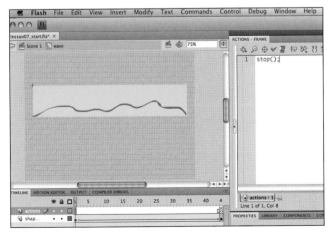

4 In the upper-left corner above the stage, click the tab labeled Scene 1 to return to the main timeline. The remaining graphics and functionality for this project will be added using ActionScript in frame 1 of the main timeline.

Adding MovieClip instances to the stage from the Library

One of the great benefits of Flash is that it gives you a strong set of design tools that you can control with a powerful programming language. One excellent way of using the hybrid of design and programming tools in Flash is to create graphical elements that can be stored in the Flash Library and added or removed from the stage at runtime using ActionScript.

Setting the linkage properties of a MovieClip

If you plan on placing instances of a MovieClip from the library onto the stage using ActionScript, it is necessary to first set the linkage properties of that clip in the library.

The Library is a convenient tool for storing and managing multiple elements. Objects in the library are not, by default, included in published SWF files (which is generally a good thing, since including them would make SWF files unnecessarily large).

When an object is added to the Flash stage from the library, it is automatically identified to be included in compiled .swf files. However, when a MovieClip in the library is not placed onstage in the Flash interface, but instead will be added to the stage at runtime with ActionScript, it needs to be explicitly set to be included in the SWF files. This is done in the clip's linkage settings that can be found in the Properties dialog box for each MovieClip symbol in the library.

You will set these properties for the *Block* clip in the library so that instances of this clip are available from ActionScript.

1 Open the Library for the lesson07_start.fla file (Window > Library).

2 In the Library, select the *Block* MovieClip symbol.

3 With the *Block* clip selected, choose Properties from the Library panel menu.

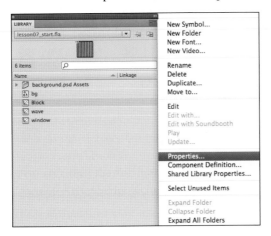

4 If you don't see the Linkage section of the Symbol Properties dialog box, click the Advanced button in the bottom-right corner.

5 In the Linkage section, select the Export for ActionScript check box.

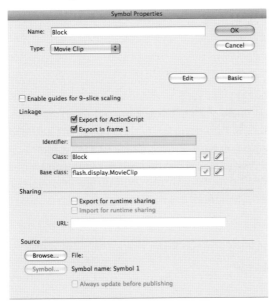

6 Leave the Class field and all other settings as they are, and click OK.

When Export for ActionScript is selected, a new ActionScript class is created that references this MovieClip. The name in the Class field is automatically set to the same name as the symbol (in this case Block). Of course you have the option to change the class name, but for this example, the default is fine.

About the base class and inheritance

Notice in the Symbol Properties dialog box that the new Block class will have a base class of flash.display.MovieClip. Another way of saying this is that the Block class extends the MovieClip class. This means that in addition to its own particular characteristics, the Block class will be able to do anything that the MovieClip class can do, and can function as a MovieClip. You will see a number of ways to take advantage of inheritance in coming lessons, and it is a large part of object-oriented programming (OOP).

7 A dialog box will likely appear that indicates that a definition for the class cannot be found. This is normal and is telling you that Flash is creating a new class for your MovieClip. Click OK, and Flash will create a new Block class.

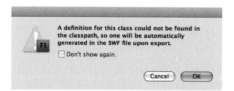

Using linkage properties to create new classes

When you set a MovieClip symbol in the library to be exported for ActionScript, Flash will create a new class in the background that contains the information on the symbol. By default, the new class will extend the MovieClip class, but you can change this in the Symbol Properties dialog box.

Now that this MovieClip is available for ActionScript control, you will add an instance of it to the stage using code.

Adding a new instance of the Block class to the stage

Since the *Block* symbol in the library can now be considered to represent the `Block` class, making instances of it and controlling it with ActionScript will be very similar to the way you have worked with other classes in earlier lessons. Start by adding a single instance of the `Block` class to the stage.

1   With the Actions panel visible and frame 1 of the `actions` layer selected, add the following code to the top of the Actions panel:

```
var rectangle = new Block();
addChild(rectangle);
```

This creates a variable named `rectangle` that stores a new instance of the `Block` class and adds it to the stage.

2   Test your movie. A single instance of the `Block` class should appear in the top-left of the stage.

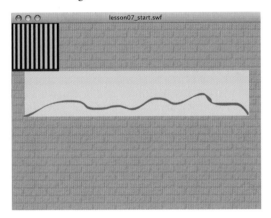

Your goal for this step, however, is not to generate a single Block instance, but to create a row of five blocks that cover the light blue area of the stage. To do that, you will use a `for` loop.

Generating multiple instances with a for loop

There are a number of ways to have ActionScript repeat code a specific number of times. Probably the most convenient and commonly used is the `for` loop. The basic syntax of a `for` loop typically looks like this:

```
for(var i:int = 0; i < someCondition; i++) {
  repeatSomething();
}
```

The first statement between the parentheses after the keyword `for` creates a variable with an initial value; the second statement sets the condition that will be checked each time the code loops; and the third statement increases or decreases the value each time the loop is repeated. Code between the curly braces is executed each time the loop repeats.

About trace statements

The trace statement in this example is a very useful technique in ActionScript, providing you temporary feedback on your projects and helping troubleshoot problems.

The basic syntax for a trace statement is the lowercase word "trace" followed by a pair of parentheses. Whatever is between the parentheses is evaluated and displayed in the Output panel when the code executes. trace statements are primarily used for feedback while developing, and not for use in the finished application. You can turn off trace statements before you publish your finished applications by selecting the Omit Trace Actions option in the Flash tab of the Publish Settings dialog box (File > Publish Settings).

Creating the for loop

In this section you create a for loop that repeats five times, adding a new Block instance each time.

1 To display the numbers 1 through 10 in the Output panel, you could add a for loop below the exiting code in the timeline:

```
for(var i:int = 1; i < 11; i++) {
  trace(i);
}
```

2 Test the movie. The for loop should execute the code in between the braces 10 times, and display the numbers 1–10 in the Output panel.

3 With frame 1 of the timeline still selected and the Actions panel still visible, select the code that reads:

```
var rectangle = new Block();
addChild(rectangle);
```

and cut it to the clipboard (Edit > Cut).

4 In between the curly braces of the for statement, paste the code that you just cut so the code now reads:

```
for (var i:int = 1; i < 11; i++) {
  var rectangle:Block = new Block();
  addChild(rectangle);
  trace(i);
}
```

Since you need only five instances of the block, change the `for` statement so that it runs while i < 5 instead of i < 11. Also, for reasons that you will soon see, it will be useful to set the variable i to an initial value of 0 instead of 1.

5 Change the `for` statement so that it reads:

```
for (var i:int = 0; i < 5; i++) {
 var rectangle:Block = new Block();
 addChild(rectangle);
 trace(i);
}
```

6 The `trace` statement has served its purpose, so you can delete it:

```
for (var i:int = 0; i < 5; i++) {
 var rectangle:Block = new Block();
 addChild(rectangle);
}
```

7 Test the movie.

The code you've just written created five Block instances and added them to the stage, but the SWF file should not look any different than it did before, and only one Block instance should be visible. Why? The code performed perfectly—placing five instances onstage—but they were all placed at exactly the same location, so that only the final and topmost one is visible. Now you will modify the code so that each Block instance is in a different location.

Modifying a for loop's behavior with variables

You will frequently find that the easiest way to modify the behavior of a `for` loop is to work with the variable whose value changes each time the loop repeats. In our example file, that variable is i, and its value increases by one on each repeat. If we want each of our Blocks to be 100 pixels to the right of the previous one, we set the x position of each Block instance to be the value of i times 100 (the ActionScript operator to indicate multiplication is the asterisk (*)).

In a previous step, you set the initial value of i to zero. If we set the `rectangle` variable's x property to i * 100, then the first block will have an x value of zero (0 * 100). The second block will have an x value of 100 (1 * 100), the third an x value of 200 (2 * 100), and so on.

1 With frame 1 of the `actions` layer still selected, add a new line to your `for` loop to create a row of Blocks:

```
for (var i:int = 0; i < 5; i++) {
 var rectangle = new Block();
 addChild(rectangle);
 rectangle.x = i * 100;
}
```

Note: The technique of looping through a series of increasing values is very helpful for many types of projects. For example, you could loop through a group of items in a List, or through a series of clips with names that were ended in an increasing number (*clip1*, *clip2*, *clip3*, and so on) or a series of values in a database. You will use *for* loops for this purpose a number of times in upcoming lessons.

2 Test the movie. You should now have a row of Blocks. Now you want to have them line up onstage with the blue background. That will be your next step.

3 Close the lesson07_start.swf file to return to Flash.

4 Make the rulers visible in Flash (View > Rulers). You will see that the blue area of the background begins 100 pixels from the top of the stage and 25 pixels from the left.

5 With frame 1 of the action layer selected, change the for loop in the Actions so that it reads:

```
for (var i:int = 0; i < 5; i++) {
  var rectangle = new Block();
  addChild(rectangle);
  rectangle.x = i*100;
  rectangle.y = 100;
}
```

This gives all the rectangle instances a y value of 100, which will line them up vertically with the blue background.

6 Offset all the blocks by 25 pixels horizontally by changing the rectangle.x line so that it reads:

```
rectangle.x = i * 100 + 25;
```

The full code at this point should read:

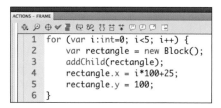

7 Test your movie. The row of Blocks should now perfectly cover the blue area of the background.

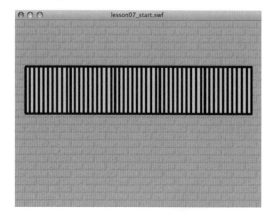

8 Close the lesson07_start.swf file to leave the testing environment and return to Flash.

In the next sections, you will add code so that each block, when clicked, opens to reveal the animation underneath.

Adding event listeners to the Block instances

When creating objects in a `for` loop, you can simultaneously create `addEventListener()` methods for those objects. These listeners will be applied to each Block instance when it is created so that they can respond when the user clicks them. The process of adding Listeners is the same as you have seen in previous lessons.

1 With frame 1 of the `actions` layer selected and the Actions panel still visible, add the following line above the closing brace of the `for` loop:

```
rectangle.addEventListener(MouseEvent.CLICK, rectClick);
```

The full loop should now read:

```
for (var i:int = 0; i < 5; i++) {
  var rectangle = new Block();
  addChild(rectangle);
  rectangle.x = i * 100 + 25;
  rectangle.y = 100;
  rectangle.addEventListener(MouseEvent.CLICK, rectClick);
}
```

When any one of the rectangles is clicked, the `rectClick()` function is called. This function doesn't exist yet, so next you'll add the shell for that function.

2 Below all the existing code in the Actions panel, add the following:

```
function rectClick(e:MouseEvent):void {

}
```

You will soon add to this function to rotate each rectangle open like a window when it is clicked, but first, in the `for` loop, let's add a couple of properties to each rectangle as it's created, so that when the file runs, each rectangle can keep track of how much it has been rotated (r) and whether or not it is has already been clicked open (up).

3 Within the curly braces of the `for` loop, add the following two lines:

```
rectangle.r = 0;
rectangle.up = false;
```

The r property will be used to track of how much each clip has rotated. The plan is to rotate each rectangle up −180 degrees when clicked. Soon you will add a rotateUp() function that will use the r value to track the amount each rectangle is open.

When a rectangle is clicked, its up property will be set to true. When all the rectangles have been clicked and rotated, the user's task will be complete, and the final animation will play.

About dynamic classes and creating MovieClip properties

The up and r properties that you just added to each rectangle are not built-in properties; they were created for this project, to specifically serve the needs of the project. Properties, as well as functions, can be dynamically created and added to instances of the MovieClip class (and other classes that extend it, like the Block class). This is because the MovieClip class is what is known as a *dynamic class*. In a dynamic class, if you refer to a property that doesn't exist in that class, the property will be created automatically. (If you try to refer to a property that doesn't exist in a nondynamic class, you will get an error message.)

The two most commonly used dynamic classes in ActionScript 3.0 are the MovieClip class and the Object class. Overall, you should assume that most other built-in classes are not dynamic.

If the concept of dynamic classes is not clear right now, don't worry; you may want to come back and re-read after you have a little more experience with ActionScript.

The full code so far should read:

```
for (var i:int = 0; i < 5; i++) {
 var rectangle = new Block();
 addChild(rectangle);
 rectangle.x = i * 100 + 25;
 rectangle.y = 100;
 rectangle.addEventListener(MouseEvent.CLICK, rectClick);
 rectangle.r = 0;
 rectangle.up = false;
}

function rectClick(e:MouseEvent):void {

}
```

Next, you will add code to make the rectangles rotate up when they are clicked.

Creating animation using ENTER_FRAME

You have recently created the `rectClick()` function, which will execute when any of the rectangles are clicked—a important preliminary step toward animating the rectangles when they are clicked. If you completed Lesson 3, "Creating Animation with ActionScript," you may remember that an easy way to animate one of an object's properties is to change that property repeatedly with an ENTER_FRAME listener.

Adding the ENTER_FRAME listener

In this section, you will add an `addEventListener()` method to the `rectClick()` function to start up the animation of each rectangle.

1   With the Actions panel still visible, locate the `rectClick()` function you added in frame 1 of the `actions` layer. It should read:

```
function rectClick(e:MouseEvent):void {

}
```

2   Add the following line within the body of the function:

```
function rectClick(e:MouseEvent):void {
  addEventListener(Event.ENTER_FRAME, rotateUp);
}
```

This will listen for and respond to the ENTER_FRAME event.

Using an event's target property

Now, you will add a new event handling function named `rotateUp()`. Before that, however, consider for a moment what we are trying to do. We have five instances of the `Block` class onstage; each one has been created in a single variable named `rectangle`. At this point, when the user clicks on any one of the rectangles, the `rectClick()` function is called, and starts an ENTER_FRAME listener, which animates the clicked rectangle.

But if the same ENTER_FRAME listener is going to be used for all five objects, and they are all referenced by the same name (`rectangle`), how is the ENTER_FRAME function going to know which one to animate?

Fortunately, there's an easy answer to this. When an event handling function is triggered, it automatically receives a property called `target`, which is a reference to the object that triggered it.

In this case, when the `rectClick()` function is triggered (by a rectangle being clicked), the target of the event references the particular rectangle. That reference will be stored in a variable, so it can be used by other functions. To that end, at the very top of the Actions panel, you will create a new variable to store references to the currently clicked rectangle.

1 In the Actions panel, place the insertion point at the very top of the code for frame 1 of the actions layer, and then press Enter.

2 In the new, empty first line, add the following code:

```
var clip:MovieClip;
```

Notice that the new variable, named clip, is of the data type MovieClip. It is given no initial value but instead will be given the current value of the most recently clicked rectangle whenever one of the rectangles is clicked.

3 In the Actions panel, locate the rectClick() function. On the line below the addListener() method, add the following line:

```
clip = e.target as MovieClip;
```

Now, any time a rectangle is clicked, the clip variable's value is changed to that of the newly clicked rectangle. The use of "as MovieClip" assures that the value stored in the clip is a MovieClip. This is called *casting*, and you will see it come again in later lessons.

The entire function should now read:

```
function rectClick(e:MouseEvent):void {
 addEventListener(Event.ENTER_FRAME, rotateUp);
 clip = e.target as MovieClip;
}
```

Creating the rotateUp() function

To recap, when a rectangle is clicked, it will start an ENTER_FRAME listener whose function name is rotateUp().

The intended purpose of the rotateUp() function is to animate the rotation of the clip up to −180 degrees. This function is also where you will set the up property of the selected rectangle to true so that Flash can keep track of whether this clip has already been clicked and opened. When the animation has finished, this function will call another function that will check if the currently clicked rectangle happens to have been the fifth and final rectangle to have been clicked open, which will indicate that the task is finished.

There are two conditions that must be met for the task to be complete:

• Has the rectangle been rotated all the way to −180 degrees?

• Have all five rectangles been clicked?

If you are thinking that you might use conditional statements to determine the answers to these questions, you are correct.

We'll use one conditional statement to check on the rotation of the currently clicked rectangle. Remember that the property r stores the rotation, and a reference to the currently clicked rectangle is stored in the clip variable.

1   In the Actions panel, on a new line below all the existing code for frame 1, add a new function named rotateUp:

```
function rotateUp(e:Event):void {

}
```

2   In between the curly braces of the new rotateUp() function, add code so that the function reads as follows:

```
function rotateUp(e:Event):void {
  if(clip.r > -180) {
    clip.rotationX=clip.r;
    clip.r -= 5;
    clip.up = true;
  }
}
```

Remember that this function repeats at the frame rate of the movie (which by default is 24 fps). Since the property r is initially set to 0, the first time this function runs, the rotationX property will be set to zero. Each time the function repeats, 5 degrees are subtracted from the rotationX property. The clip will rotate backward on its X axis, 5 degrees at a time, until it has reached a rotation of −180 degrees, at which point the condition (clip.r > -180) is no longer true, and the animation will stop.

Rotating in three dimensions

New to Flash CS4 is the ability to manipulate objects in 3D space. With ActionScript, you can now control the movement, rotation, and transformation of objects discretely in all three dimensions. The three dimensions, as described in ActionScript (and most other computer applications), are x (horizontal plane), y (vertical plane), and z (depth). So, for example, changing an object's rotationX property will rotate it on its horizontal plane, and changing its z property will make it appear closer or further away.

Adding an else statement

Once the rotation condition is no longer true and the animation has finished, the application should check to see whether all five clips have been clicked. And this is where our second conditional statement comes in: A function named testDone()

will soon be added to do this checking. One way to have something in a conditional statement happen when the condition is not true is to add an else statement at the end of the conditional statement, as in:

```
if(this == true) {
 doSomething();
} else {
 doSomethingElse();
}
```

When the rotationX of the clip is no longer more than −180 degrees, you'll call the testDone() function.

1 Add the following bold code to the existing rotateUp() function so that it now reads:

```
function rotateUp(e:Event):void {
 if(clip.r > -180) {
  clip.rotationX = clip.r;
  clip.r -= 5;
  clip.up = true;
 } else {
  testDone();
 }
}
```

When the animation is finished, there is no longer a reason for the ENTER_FRAME listener to continue running in the background, so it needs to be removed from the else statement.

▶ **Tip:** As you type your code, be sure that you have the correct number of left and right curly braces.

2 Within the else statement, above the call to the testDone() function, remove the ENTER_FRAME listener by adding this line:

```
removeEventListener(Event.ENTER_FRAME, rotateUp);
```

The full rotateUp() function should now read:

```
function rotateUp(e:Event):void {
 if(clip.r > -180) {
  clip.rotationX = clip.r;
  clip.r -= 5;
  clip.up = true;
 } else {
  removeEventListener(Event.ENTER_FRAME, rotateUp);
  testDone();
 }
}
```

Adding the testDone() function

Even if your code is all perfect, if you test the project at this point you would get an error, because the code contains a reference to the `testDone()` function—which does not yet exist. So, before you test it, add the shell for the final function in this lesson.

1   On the line below all the existing code, add the following code:

```
function testDone():void {

}
```

2   Test your movie, to see the state of your project as it is, before you add any more code.

3   Try clicking the various rectangle clips. Each one that is clicked should animate so that the clip rotates up.

When each clip is clicked, the ENTER_FRAME event handling function animates its `rotationX` property.

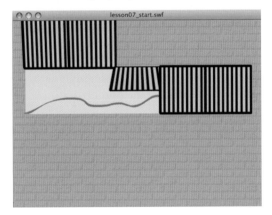

4   Close the lesson07_start.swf file to return to Flash.

Now, you will work on the `testDone()` function that checks if all the clips have been clicked. To do this, you will use two of the major tools in your existing ActionScript toolkit, the conditional statement and the `for` loop.

In the `testDone()` function, a `for` loop will be created to cycle through all of the onstage rectangle clips. Two conditional statements will be used: One will check if the clips' `up` properties have all been set to `true`; when they are all `true`, the second conditional statement will play the shape tween animation in the MovieClip that you examined way back at the beginning of the lesson.

However, there is still one piece missing. As mentioned earlier, all of the Block instances are referenced with the name `rectangle`, and the only way you have so far of identifying one of these clips is via the `target` property once the clip has been clicked. At this point, it would not be easy to cycle through the clips one at a time and check the value of their properties.

Wouldn't it be useful if, when the rectangle clips were created and given their initial properties, there were a way to add them to a list of all the existing rectangle clips, and then be able to cycle through this list and check the properties of the clips in the list?

Well, there is, and it will become an extremely important class for your ActionScript toolkit—the `Array`.

Introducing the array

An *array* is a Flash data type that allows a list of values to be stored in a single variable. Methods and properties of the `Array` class let you add to and remove elements from an array, sort the contents of an array alphabetically or numerically, and keep track of how many things are in a array at any given time. You can store lists of objects with multiple properties, and even store lists of lists.

There is an infinite number of uses for `Array` objects in a Flash project: a list of high scorers in a game, a list of contacts for an address book, a list of products that have been bought at an e-commerce site, and countless more. In this project, you will use an array to store a list of all the rectangles and their properties.

You create an array as you would any other variable. Here's the basic syntax:

```
var listOfThings:Array = new Array();
```

When you create a new array, you can populate it with a list of elements at the same time. However, in this project we want to create an empty array at the beginning of the code, and then populate it each time a new rectangle is created and given initial settings.

First create a new array called `rArray`.

1   With frame 1 of the `actions` layer selected, find the line of code at the top of the Actions panel that reads:

```
var clip:MovieClip;
```

2   Click to place the insertion point at the end of this line, and press Enter.

3   On the new line, type the following code to add a new `Array` instance:

```
var rArray:Array = new Array();
```

Soon you will add the rectangles to the new array as they are created. Remember that the `for` loop at the beginning of the code is where the rectangle clips are initially created. The code in the `for` loop should now read:

```
for(var i:int = 0; i < 5; i++) {
 var rectangle = new Block();
 addChild(rectangle);
 rectangle.x=i * 100 +2 5;
 rectangle.y = 100;
 rectangle.addEventListener(MouseEvent.CLICK, rectClick);
 rectangle.r = 0;
 rectangle.up = false;
}
```

Keeping track of arrays

A location in an array is referred to numerically by its *index*, and items in the array are referred to as *elements*. The first element in the array has the numeric index value of 0, the second element 1, the third element 2, and so on.

The following array has seven elements:

```
var colorArray:Array = new Array(red, yellow, blue, green,
 ➥tan, orange, black)
```

In ActionScript, when you wish to refer to a specific element in an array, you use the array's instance name, followed by square brackets that contain the element's index number. For example, to refer to element number 4 in an array called `colorArray`, you would write:

```
colorArray[4];
```

In this example, `colorArray[4]` would equal tan. Remember that elements in an array are counted starting at zero, not one.

Using the push() method

An object can be added to an array with a method of the `Array` class called `push()`. When data is pushed into an array, it is stored at the first open location in the array.

In our example, each time the `for` loop repeats and a rectangle is created with initial properties, the rectangle needs to be pushed into the `rArray`.

1   Add the following code above the closing curly brace of the `for` loop:

```
rArray.push(rectangle);
```

The full `for` loop should now read:

```
for(var i:int = 0; i < 5; i++) {
 var rectangle = new Block();
 addChild(rectangle);
 rectangle.x = i * 100 + 25;
```

(code continues on the next page)

(continued)

```
rectangle.y = 100;
rectangle.addEventListener(MouseEvent.CLICK, rectClick);
rectangle.r = 0;
rectangle.up = false;
rArray.push(rectangle);
}
```

When the `for` loop has completed, five rectangles will have been pushed into the `rArray`, in locations 0, 1, 2, 3, and 4. To find out how many elements are in an array, check the array's `length` property. Since there are currently five elements in the array, `rArray.length` would be 5. You will use this property in the `testDone()` function to cycle through all the rectangles and check their `up` property.

First, however, you need to add a new variable, `done`, to the beginning of the file, which will be used to indicate whether or not all five rectangles have been clicked.

2 Locate the code at the top of the Actions panel that reads:

```
var clip:MovieClip;
var rArray:Array = new Array();
```

3 Insert a new line below this code, and create a new variable named **done**:

```
var done:Boolean = false;
```

Notice that the data type for this variable is set to Boolean. A Boolean value can be only `true` or `false`. Variables with a data type of Boolean are used to store a value that can be one of only two possibilities, such as, in this case, whether or not all of the rectangles have been clicked. Since all the rectangles could not have been clicked when the application is first launched, the initial setting for the `done` variable is set to `false`.

Next, you will add code to the `testDone()` function to check if all the rectangles have been clicked, and set `done` to `true` when they have.

Checking the properties of elements in the rArray

Now that all information about the rectangle clips can be accessed in the `rArray`, you can add a `for` loop to the `testDone()` function to cycle through the elements of the array.

1 In the Actions panel, scroll down to the `testDone()` function, which should currently read:

```
function testDone():void {

}
```

2 Between the curly braces of the testDone() function, add a for loop so that the function now reads:

```
function testDone():void {
  for(var i:int = 0;  i <  rArray.length;  i++) {


  }
}
```

Notice that the second statement in between the parentheses is not comparing i to a specific integer but instead to whatever number of items is currently in the rArray. This means that if there are five elements in the rArray (which there are), then the for loop will execute five times. This is a very useful and common ActionScript technique for cycling through a list of items in an array.

The first time the loop runs, the first element in the rArray (which is the first rectangle that was created) is examined to see if its up property is true, and each subsequent time the loops runs, it checks the next element the same way.

3 Add code between the curly braces of the new for loop so that the full testDone() function now reads:

```
function testDone():void {
  for(var i:int = 0; i<rArray.length; i++) {
    if(rArray[i].up) {
      done = true;
    } else {
      done = false;
      break;
    }
  }
}
```

There are a couple of things to point out in this code. First, notice that the element of the rArray that is examined each time the code loops will be different. This is because instead of using an integer between the square brackets, the variable i is used. This means that the first time the code loops, it examines rArray[0].up, which is the up property the initial rectangle. The second time through the loop, i has a value of 1, and examines rArray[1] (the second rectangle created). The process continues until all the elements in the array (all the rectangles) have been examined.

Each time the conditional statement discovers that one of the rectangles has an up property of true, it will set done to true, but if one of the rectangles being examined has a condition of false, then done is also set to false, and then on the next line there is a break. The syntax break is used to stop the function altogether. This means that no matter where the code is in the for loop, if any of the rectangles has an up property of false, then the function will end with the done variable having a value of false. On the other hand, if all five rectangles have a value of true, then the function will not break, and done will have a final value of true.

Knowing all this, you can add one final conditional statement to the function that plays the *wave_mc* MovieClip (remember *wave_mc?*) if done is true.

4   Add code to the testDone() function so that the entire function now reads:

```
function testDone():void {
 for(var i:int = 0; i<rArray.length; i++) {
  if(rArray[i].up) {
   done = true;
  } else {
   done = false;
   break;
  }
 }
 if(done) {
  wave_mc.play();
 }
}
```

5   Test your movie. If you click all five rectangle clips one at a time, the underlying animation should play.

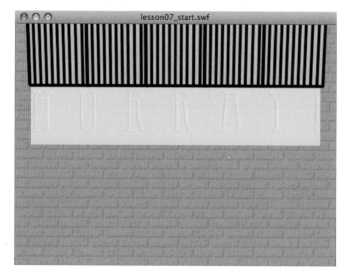

Here is the complete code for this lesson. You can also view it in the Lessons > Lesson07 > Complete > lesson07_complete.fla file.

```
var clip:MovieClip;
var rArray:Array = new Array();
var done:Boolean = false;

for (var i:int = 0; i < 5; i++) {
    var rectangle = new Block();
    addChild(rectangle);
    rectangle.x = i * 100 + 25;
    rectangle.y = 100;
    rectangle.addEventListener(MouseEvent.CLICK, rectClick);
    rectangle.r = 0;
    rectangle.up = false;
    rArray.push(rectangle);
}

function rectClick(e:MouseEvent):void {
    addEventListener(Event.ENTER_FRAME, rotateUp);
    clip = e.target as MovieClip;
}

function rotateUp(e:Event):void {
    if (clip.r > -180) {
        clip.rotationX = clip.r;
        clip.r -= 5;
        clip.up = true;
    } else {
        removeEventListener(Event.ENTER_FRAME, rotateUp);
        testDone();
    }
}

function testDone():void {
    for (var i:int = 0; i < rArray.length; i++) {
        if (rArray[i].up) {
            done = true;
        } else {
            done = false;
            break;
        }
    }
    if (done) {
        wave_mc.play();
    }
}
```

There is a lot of code here, so if you have any problems, go through your code carefully, using information provided by any error messages you receive. If you tested the movie throughout the lesson, fixed problems along the way, and got each section of the lesson working before going on, the animation will play.

You have made it this far, and have succeeded in getting this lesson to work (no matter how long it took). You absolutely have the patience and intestinal fortitude to become a great ActionScript programmer. Keep going!

In the next lesson, you will continue with the finished file from this lesson, and turn the project into an interactive quiz by creating an external ActionScript file.

Some suggestions to try on your own

Like this lesson, the next lesson will cover a lot of new material, and will require some stamina, so the first suggestion after this lesson is to take a break. Go for a walk in a beautiful place, watch a movie, do something that involves fun with other people who you like. Get away from the computer!

After that, you may want to try a few things for review before proceeding to the next lesson:

• Make a copy of your completed file and try some variations on the duplicate. Instead of creating five Block instances in the initial `for` loop, create more. Give them different properties. Play around with the values of the existing properties.

• Replace the *wave_mc* MovieClip with a new MovieClip of your own creation. Design it so that something different happens when all of the rectangles have been clicked.

• Try loading your finished file from this lesson into the UILoader component from Lesson 6, "Creating Preloaders in ActionScript 3.0."

Review questions

1   What needs to be done to a MovieClip symbol in the library before it can be controlled from ActionScript?

2   What is the basic syntax to use a for loop in ActionScript 3.0?

3   In an if conditional statement, what is the syntax to tell code to execute when the if conditions are not true?

4   What are the possible values for an object of the data type Boolean?

5   Name an ActionScript class that can be used to store a list of objects.

6   What is a method that could be used to add a new element to the next available location in an Array instance?

7   In ActionScript how could you identify the first element in an array named cars?

Review answers

1   To indicate that a symbol from the Library can be controlled with ActionScript, you need to set its linkage properties to Export for ActionScript.

2   The basic syntax to use a for loop is:

```
for(var i:int = 0; i< someNumber; i++) {
  doSomething();
}
```

3   To create code in an if statement that executes when the conditions are not true, you use an else statement. For example:

```
if(2+2 == x) {
   doSomething();

} else {
  doSomethingElse();
}
```

4   A Boolean object can evaluate to either true or false.

5   Array is a class that can be used to store a list of objects. An instance of an array can be created and stored in a variable like any other ActionScript data type. For example:

```
var employeeList:Array = new Array();
```

6   The push() method of the Array class could be used to add a new element in the next available location in the array. For example:

```
employeeList.push("John Smith");
```

7   Bearing in mind that the elements in an array are counted beginning with zero, the first element in an array named cars could be identified as cars[0].

8 CREATING A RADIO BUTTON QUIZ IN AN ACTIONSCRIPT FILE

Lesson overview

In this lesson, you will learn to do the following:

- Use private and public access modifiers in an ActionScript file.

- Create and work with radio buttons and radio button groups in ActionScript.

- Create new textFields with ActionScript.

- Set textField properties with ActionScript.

- Format text with ActionScript.

- Use a `switch` statement to check multiple conditions.

- Use the inequality operator (`!=`) to determine if a condition is false.

- Create a simple quiz and track users' responses.

- Communicate between an ActionScript file and code in the Flash timeline.

 This lesson will take approximately 3 hours.

In the previous lesson, you used ActionScript to animate open a series of five rectangular clips by clicking them one at a time. When all five doors were clicked open, the process was considered complete and a final animation played. In this lesson, you will start with the completed file from Lesson 7, and add new code so that each door will open when the user answers a quiz question correctly. The final animation will play when five questions are answered correctly.

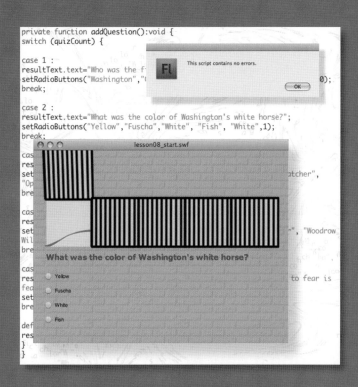

You will create a `RadioButtonsQuiz` class and use
it to add a quiz to the Lesson 7 project.

There is already quite a bit of code on frame 1 of the timeline from the previous lesson. So, rather than add a large amount of additional code to this file, you will create most of the code for this lesson in an external ActionScript file that will be integrated into the FLA file from Lesson 7.

While this lesson will not strictly adhere to object-oriented principles, it will introduce you to the concept of breaking up the code for larger projects into multiple files. This will provide you with a foundation for object-oriented programming (OOP) that will become very useful as your projects get more complex.

Examining the starting file

The starting file for this lesson can be found in the Lessons folder (Lessons > Lesson08 > Start > lesson08_start.fla). Open this file to begin the project. If you completed the Lesson 7 project, you will notice that this is the completed project from that lesson. If necessary, review Lesson 7 to understand the ActionScript in this file. You will make a few adjustments to this file towards the end of this lesson, but most of the additional functionality you will add to this project will be in an external ActionScript file that you will connect to this file.

Checking out the completed file

If you wish to view the completed file for this lesson, open Lessons > Lesson08 > Complete > lesson08_complete.fla. With the file open, choose Control > Test Movie, and try answering the questions that are presented to you. When five questions have been answered correctly, the animation from Lesson 7 will play.

Be sure to close this file before beginning work on your version of the lesson.

Creating a new ActionScript file

In Lesson 4, "Creating ActionScript in External Files," you learned the basics of creating an ActionScript class file. You will use many of these principles in this lesson to create much of the functionality for a simple quiz using radio buttons. If you need to review the basics of an ActionScript file see Lesson 4, "Creating ActionScript in External Files."

1　Choose File > New to create a new file.

2　In the New Document dialog box, select ActionScript File from the Type list, and click OK.

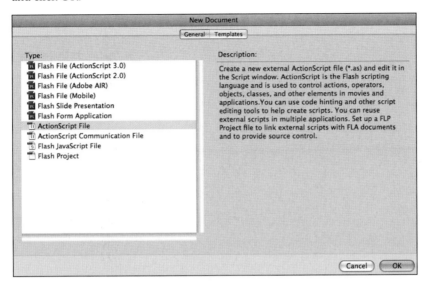

3　Save the file to the Lessons > Lesson08 > Start folder. Give the file the name **RadioButtonQuiz.as**. It is essential that the lesson08_start.fla file and the RadioButtonQuiz.as file be in the same folder.

Setting up the RadioButtonQuiz class

In Lesson 4, you learned the basics of setting up an ActionScript class file. You will use this same basic syntax to set up the RadioButtonQuiz class. Refer to Lesson 4 if you need to review this syntax.

Keeping in mind that all ActionScript in an .as file is contained within package tags, begin the RadioButtonQuiz.as by adding the following code:

```
package {

}
```

Since the RadioButtonQuiz.as file and the lesson08_start.fla file are in the same directory, you will not need to describe a path for the package.

Importing classes into the RadioButtonQuiz class

Remember that in an external ActionScript file, every class that will be referred to must be imported into the file.

Between the curly braces of the package tags, add the following code to import all the classes that will be used in this file. This may be the first time you have used some of these classes. These will be explained when they are used later in the lesson.

```
import flash.text.TextField;
import flash.text.TextFieldAutoSize;
import flash.text.TextFormat;
import flash.display.Sprite;
import flash.display.DisplayObjectContainer;
import flash.events.Event;
import fl.controls.RadioButton;
import fl.controls.RadioButtonGroup;
```

About importing classes in Flash

As you have seen, all classes that are referred to in an ActionScript file must be imported. When writing code in the Flash timeline, it is not always necessary to import the built-in classes of ActionScript; indeed, in earlier lessons you often used built-in classes on the Flash timeline without first importing them. However, many ActionScript programmers consider it a good practice to always import a class before using it; you may want to follow their lead and consider importing classes even in the Flash timeline.

Creating the RadioButtonQuiz class

Now you will create the class that this file will contain. Remember that ActionScript files typically contain a single class, and the class name and the filename need to match. Because the filename is RadioButtonQuiz.as, it is assumed that it will contain a class named RadioButtonQuiz.

On a line below all the `import` statements, create the `RadioButtonQuiz` class by adding the following code:

```
public class RadioButtonQuiz extends Sprite {

}
```

About Sprites

The class that you created in Lesson 4 extended the MovieClip class. If you recall from that lesson, extending a class means that the new class contains all the capabilities of the parent class as well as its own methods and properties.

The RadioButtonQuiz class you are creating extends the Sprite class. Sprites in Flash are very similar to MovieClips. They are both display objects with nearly identical capabilities. In fact the main difference between Sprites and MovieClips is that unlike MovieClips, a Sprite does not have a timeline. There are many situations when using ActionScript where you need MovieClip-like functionality but do not have a need for a timeline. In these cases, a Sprite is a more efficient object to use than a MovieClip.

The file should now read:

```
package {

    import flash.text.TextField;
    import flash.text.TextFieldAutoSize;
    import flash.text.TextFormat;
    import flash.display.Sprite;
    import flash.display.DisplayObjectContainer;
    import flash.events.Event;
    import fl.controls.RadioButton;
    import fl.controls.RadioButtonGroup;

    public class RadioButtonQuiz extends Sprite {

    }
}
```

Remember that all the code for the RadioButtonQuiz class will go between the left and right curly braces in the class.

Reviewing the format of the quiz

The RadioButtonQuiz class will create a single quiz with five questions. When this file launches, users will see an initial question in a text field. They answer the question by choosing what they believe is the correct answer from four possible answers displayed in radio buttons. If they choose the wrong answer, the text in the text field that contains the questions changes to give feedback that the answer was incorrect. Users can try as many times as they like until they get the correct answer. When the correct answer is selected, the text field automatically displays the next question, and the process repeats. When all five questions are answered correctly, a message will be sent to the FLA file to play the final animation.

To enable this functionality, you will create a single text field and four radio buttons using ActionScript, which will be used for all the questions in the quiz.

About radio buttons

Most people who have ever used a computer are familiar with using radio buttons—a common selection method in which, typically, only one item (or button) at a time can be selected within a discrete grouping. The metaphor is taken from older car radios, where you selected a station by pressing a button. When you selected one button, the previously selected button became deselected.

In Flash, radio buttons are available as components. To keep track of which radio buttons should work together, they are combined into a RadioButtonGroup. In ActionScript, there are a RadioButton class and a RadioButtonGroup class. You can create and control RadioButton and RadioButtonGroup instances much like the other class instances you have worked with. Here you see a typical group of radio buttons.

Adding variables to the RadioButtonQuiz class

The next thing you will add are some class variables that will be used to keep track of the elements that make up the quiz.

The convention for an ActionScript class file is that after all the `import` statements and Class declaration comes the class variables. Class variables in an ActionScript file are available to the entire file. The keyword private is used for variables that will be used only within the class file. The keyword public is used for variables that can be accessed by other files. The terms public and private are called *access modifiers.*

More about access modifiers

Access modifiers can be used on methods (the functions in a class file) and properties (the variables) in a class.

In addition to the public and private access modifiers, there are two additional access modifiers: protected (available to the class and to classes that extend it) and internal (available to all classes within the same package). If you don't give a method or property an access modifier, it will default to internal.

For more information on access modifiers, refer to Flash Help or to Colin Moock's book *Essential ActionScript 3.0* by O'Reilly Publishing.

1 Below the line that reads:

```
public class RadioButtonQuiz extends Sprite {
```

add variables that will be used to contain a text field, a RadioButtonGroup instance, a Sprite, and an array by adding the following code:

```
private var question:Sprite;
private var resultText:TextField;
private var rbg:RadioButtonGroup;
public var answers:Array;
```

Notice that the first three variables are set to private but the answers array is public. This is because information from the answers array will be passed to the lesson08_start.fla file, while all the other variables will be needed only within the scope of the RadioButtonQuiz.as file.

2 Below the code you just added, create three additional variables, and give them values that will be used to control the spacing of the textField and RadioButton instances:

```
private var currHeight:int = 250;
private var verticalSpacing:int = 30;
private var posX:int = 20;
```

All these variables will be used later in the file.

At this point, your file should read:

```
RadioButtonQuiz.as*  ×

 1   package {
 2
 3       import flash.text.TextField;
 4       import flash.text.TextFieldAutoSize;
 5       import flash.text.TextFormat;
 6       import flash.display.Sprite;
 7       import flash.display.DisplayObjectContainer;
 8       import flash.events.Event;
 9       import fl.controls.RadioButton;
10       import fl.controls.RadioButtonGroup;
11
12       public class RadioButtonQuiz extends Sprite {
13           private var question:Sprite;
14           private var resultText:TextField;
15           private var rbg:RadioButtonGroup;
16           public var answers:Array;
17           private var currHeight:int = 250;
18           private var verticalSpacing:int = 30;
19           private var posX:int = 20;
20       }
21   }
22
```

Line 22 of 22, Col 1

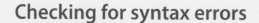

Checking for syntax errors

In addition to saving your file regularly as you work, it is a good idea to periodically check your code for syntax errors. The Check Syntax function (the blue check mark in the upper-left of the ActionScript file and the Actions panel) will check your code and give feedback on syntax errors without your having to test the movie.

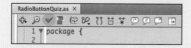

When you click Check Syntax, hopefully you will see this message.

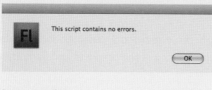

But seeing this:

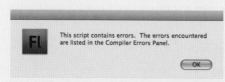

is also good, because it helps you track down potential problems as you go, rather than having to deal with many errors all at once further along in the project.

This type of error checking will identify errors in syntax, but some errors, such as mistakes in the spelling of files and property names, are not detected until runtime. Testing the movie will detect runtime errors.

Creating the quiz functionality

Now that the basic set up of the RadioButtonQuiz class is complete you are ready to add the functions that will make it work. The first function to add will be the constructor function. The constructor function in this class will call another function called quizInit() which will initialize the quiz settings.

Creating the constructor function

Lesson 4 introduced the concept of the constructor function. Remember that the constructor function is the one function in an ActionScript class with the same name as the class. The constructor function is called automatically any time an instance of the class is created. The constructor for this class needs to be named RadioButtonQuiz.

1 On a line below all the variable declarations, create the constructor function with the following code:

```
public function RadioButtonQuiz() {

}
```

The curly braces for the constructor function will contain the code that takes place when the class is instantiated. As an alternative to writing a lot of code inside the constructor function, it is fairly common to call one or more functions from the constructor. In this case, the constructor will call a function called quizInit().

2 Add a call to the constructor function so that the function now reads:

```
public function RadioButtonQuiz() {
  quizInit();
}
```

You'll create the quizInit() function that is called by the constructor next.

Creating the quizInit() function

The main purpose of this function is to create a text field that will display the quiz questions. It will also set a few of the text field's properties.

1 On a line below the closing brace of the constructor function, add the following code:

```
private function quizInit():void {

}
```

Notice that the access modifier for this function is set to private. That is because this function will only be called from within this file.

2 Add code to the quizInit() function so that it reads:

```
private function quizInit():void {
  resultText = new TextField();
  resultText.x = 25;
  resultText.y = 210;
  resultText.width = 450;
  resultText.wordWrap = true;
  resultText.text = "Select a Radio Button";
}
```

The code you just added creates a new instance of the TextField class in the variable named resultText, with an x position of 25 (pixels from the left) and y position of 210 (pixels from the top). When this class is used with the lesson08_start.fla file, these numbers will place the textField instance below the rectangular graphics onstage.

Next, the text field's width was set to 450 pixels.

In case the text displayed in the field does not fit on a single line, the text field's wordWrap property was set to true. Finally, the text property places the words "Select a Radio Button" in the field, to give the user some friendly initial instructions.

Creating a RadioButtonGroup

Now, you will add code to the quizInit() function to create the RadioButtonGroup that will contain all of the possible answers to the quiz questions.

1   Add a new line to the quizInit() function to create a RadioButtonGroup instance in the variable rbg. A single parameter is required: the name of the RadioButtonGroup. In this case, it is named answers:

```
rbg = new RadioButtonGroup("answers");
```

A RadioButtonGroup is not a physical object. It exists so that RadioButton objects can be associated with it. All RadioButton objects that are associated with the group work together, and only one RadioButton in a group at a time can be selected. When any button in a RadioButtonGroup is selected, that RadioButtonGroup fires a CHANGE event.

2   Below the line you just inserted, add a method that will listen for this CHANGE event:

```
rbg.addEventListener(Event.CHANGE, checkAnswer);
```

Remember that radio buttons you create in the rbg variable will soon contain all the possible answers to the questions in the quiz. When users select the answer they think is correct, the CHANGE event will call a function named checkAnswer().

The full code for the quizInit() function should now read:

```
private function quizInit():void {
 resultText = new TextField();
 resultText.x = 25;
 resultText.y = 210;
 resultText.width = 450;
 resultText.wordWrap = true;
 resultText.text = "Select a Radio Button";
 rbg = new RadioButtonGroup("answers");
   ➥rbg.addEventListener(Event.CHANGE, checkAnswer);
}
```

The last things that you will add to the `quizInit()` function are calls to two additional functions that you will soon create called `formatText()` and `addQuestion()`.

You will add the `formatText()` function in the next section; this function will be used to set the formatting for the `resultText` field.

The `addQuestion()` function will be created in the section that follows that and will contain quite a bit of code to create and keep track of the questions and answers for the quiz.

3   Above the closing brace of the `quizInit()` function, add the following two lines:

```
formatText();
addQuestion();
```

The final `quizInit()` function should now read:

```
                    RadioButtonQuiz.as  ×
25
26          private function quizInit():void {
27              resultText = new TextField();
28              resultText.x = 25;
29              resultText.y = 210;
30              resultText.width = 450;
31              resultText.wordWrap = true;
32              resultText.text = "Select a Radio Button";
33              rbg=new RadioButtonGroup("answers");
34              rbg.addEventListener(Event.CHANGE, checkAnswer);
35              formatText();
36              addQuestion();
37          }
```

Formatting text with ActionScript

When you wish to format text in the Flash interface, there is a wide range of options available in the Properties panel and from the Text menu. All of these options, and more, can also be set dynamically with ActionScript.

Many of the options in ActionScript for formatting text are part of the `TextFormat` class. These properties include many common options such as `font`, `size`, `color`, and `justification` (for the full list of formatting properties, see Flash Help). When you create a new `TextField` instance with ActionScript, it is given default formatting properties. For example, the default color for a textField is black, its default font size is 12 points, and its default font is Times on Macintosh and Times New Roman on Windows.

You create a new instance of the TextFormat class the same way you create any other class instance. Then properties for that TextFormat instance can be set. For example, to create an instance called arialBigBlue you could write:

```
var arialBigBlue:TextFormat = new TextFormat();
arialBigBlue.font = "Arial";
arialBigBlue.size = 60;
arialBigBlue.color = 0x0000FF;
```

You could then set the arialBigBlue instance as the TextFormat property for any TextField instances. For example, if you wanted to use arialBigBlue to format a text field with an instance name of user_txt, you could write:

```
user_txt.defaultTextFormat = arialBigBlue;
```

Any text in the user_txt field would now be displayed as blue, 60-point Arial.

Below the closing bracket of the quizInit() function add the formatText() function:

```
private function formatText():void {
    var format:TextFormat = new TextFormat();
    format.font = "Verdana";
    format.color = 0x3333AA;
    format.size = 16;
    format.bold = true;
    resultText.defaultTextFormat = format;
    addChild(resultText);
}
```

● **Note:** The font Verdana was chosen for this example because it is a common font on most Macintosh and Windows computers. Feel free to replace it in your code with any font installed on your computer.

This function creates a new TextFormat instance named format. The instance's font property is set to Verdana, its color to a medium blue, and its size to 16 points. It will display as bold text. Once the properties are all set, the format object becomes the defaultTextFormat property of the resultText field that was created earlier. The addChild() method is then used to display the formatted text onstage.

Your full code so far should now read:

```
package {

  import flash.text.TextField;
  import flash.text.TextFieldAutoSize;
  import flash.text.TextFormat;
  import flash.display.Sprite;
  import flash.display.DisplayObjectContainer;
  import flash.events.Event;
  import fl.controls.RadioButton;
  import fl.controls.RadioButtonGroup;

  public class RadioButtonQuiz extends Sprite {
    private var question:Sprite;
```

```
    private var resultText:TextField;
    private var rbg:RadioButtonGroup;
    public var answers:Array;
    private var currHeight:int = 250;
    private var verticalSpacing:int = 30;
    private var posX:int = 20;

    public function RadioButtonQuiz() {
      quizInit();
    }

    private function quizInit():void {
      resultText = new TextField();
      resultText.x = 25;
      resultText.y = 210;
      resultText.width = 450;
      resultText.wordWrap = true;
      resultText.text = "Select a Radio Button";
      rbg=new RadioButtonGroup("answers");
      rbg.addEventListener(Event.CHANGE, checkAnswer);
      formatText();
      addQuestion();
    }

    private function formatText():void {
      var format:TextFormat = new TextFormat();
      format.font = "Verdana";
      format.color = 0x3333AA;
      format.size = 16;
      format.bold = true;
      resultText.defaultTextFormat = format;
      addChild(resultText);
    }
  }
}
```

Creating the quiz

The heart of this RadioButtonsQuiz class file will be three functions that work together to manage the quiz. The addQuestion() function will store and set the question, the possible answers, and the correct answer for each entry of the quiz. This function will also call the setRadioButtons() function and pass it the question and answers each time the user proceeds to a new question. The createRadioButton() function will actually create and display the individual radio buttons.

At the start of each new question, the setRadioButtons() function creates a new Sprite to store the radio buttons for the quiz. It also creates a new array to store all the information for each question. Lastly, it calls the createRadioButton() method four times, to display all the possible answers to the current question. These radio buttons will be added to the Sprite that was created in the setRadioButtons() function.

These three functions will perform their tasks every time the user needs to be presented with a new quiz question. Therefore the script needs to keep track of which question the user is on, so you will add a new class variable named quizCount for this purpose.

1 Locate the list of variables that you created earlier in the lesson. This part of the code should currently read:

```
public class RadioButtonQuiz extends Sprite {
  private var question:Sprite;
  private var resultText:TextField;
  private var rbg:RadioButtonGroup;
  public var answers:Array;
  private var currHeight:int = 250;
  private var verticalSpacing:int = 30;
  private var posX:int = 20;
```

2 Below the existing variables, create a new variable called quizCount. The data type will be integer (int) and the initial value will be 1.

```
private var quizCount:int = 1;
```

The quiz will, of course, start at question 1, and each time the user correctly answers a question, the quizCount value will be incremented by one.

Now you will create the first of the three quiz-related functions.

Creating the addQuestion() function

As stated, the main purpose of this function is to set the questions and answers for the entire quiz. This will be the longest function of the class.

Below the closing brace of the textFormat() function, add the shell for the addQuestion() function with the following code:

```
private function addQuestion():void {

}
```

Adding a switch statement

The addQuestion() function will contain a large conditional statement that will examine the value of the quizCount variable. If quizCount is equal to 1, then this value will set the first quiz question. If quizCount equals 2, the second question will be set, and so on. Of course, this could be accomplished with a long `if` statement. However, for longer conditional statements that must check for a number of different possible conditions, many developers prefer an alternate way of writing the code: using a `switch` statement.

About switch statements

A `switch` statement performs the same function as an `if` statement but can be more convenient for situations where there are many conditions to check. The basic syntax for a `switch` statement is:

```
switch (condition to evaluate) {
  case possibleValue1 :
  doSomething1();
  break;

  case possibleValue2:
  doSomething2();
  break;

  //additional cases...
  default:
  }
```

For example, if you were checking to see if the weather was sunny, rainy, snowy, or something else, you could write an `if` statement such as:

```
if(weather == sunny) {
  goBeach();
}
else if(weather == raining) {
  goMovies();
}
  else if(weather == snowing) {
  goSkiing();
} else {
  goWeatherChannel();
}
```

The same result could be obtained with the following `switch` statement:

```
switch (weather) {
  case sunny:
  goBeach();
  break;

  case raining:
  goMovies();
  break
```

(continues on the next page)

(continued)

```
case snowing:
goSkiing();
break;

default:
goWeatherChannel();
}
```

Notice in the switch statement there is a break after each condition. If this were not present, then when one condition is found to be true, all the commands below it in the switch statement will be executed. With the break statement, only the command for the condition that is true is executed, and then the switch statement ends.

In your own projects you can use either if statements or switch statements to respond to multiple conditions.

In the addQuestion() function, you will use a switch statement to check the value of the quizCount variable and respond accordingly.

1   Place the cursor below the opening brace of the addQuestion() function, and press Enter.

2   Add the following code to create a switch statement that will be used to check the value of quizCount:

```
switch (quizCount) {

}
```

3   You will be checking for five possible values of quizCount—one for each of the questions in the quiz—so add five possible cases between the switch statement's curly braces:

```
switch (quizCount) {
 case 1:

 break;

 case 2:

 break;

 case 3:
```

```
    break;

 case 4:

 break;

 case 5:

 break;
 }
```

Now, for each separate condition (case 1, case 2, and so on), you will add the code that will execute for that condition. For each condition, you want to set the resultText field to display the corresponding question.

4 Add code to the `switch` statement to set the text in the resultText field for all five questions in the quiz:

```
switch (quizCount) {

case 1:
resultText.text = "Who was the first US President?";
break;

case 2:
resultText.text = "What was the color of Washington's white
 ➥horse?";
break;

case 3:
resultText.text = "Who was the US president during the Civil
 ➥War?";
break;

case 4:
resultText.text = "Who was the US president during WWI?";
break;

case 5:
resultText.text = 'Which US President said,"The only thing we
 ➥have to fear is fear itself"?';
break;
 }
```

Adding quotes inside a string

The switch statement in the sample code contains a string that is stored as part of case 5. The string contains a quote from FDR that is inside quotation marks. Normally this could cause some confusion in your code because as you know, ActionScript 3.0 delineates strings by placing them inside quotation marks. Fortunately, ActionScript strings can be enclosed in either a pair of single quotes or a pair of double quotes. If you start with a single quote, ActionScript will consider everything before the closing single quote to be part of the string, including any double quotes. This makes it simple to use quotation marks inside quotation marks.

For each step in the quiz, the possible answers, as well as the correct answer, will need to be stored. This will be done by passing this information as parameters to a function you will soon create named setRadioButtons().

5   Add a call to the (soon to be created) setRadioButtons() function for each condition in the switch statement. Every time the setRadioButtons() function is called, it will be passed six parameters. Update the switch statement to read:

```
switch (quizCount) {

case 1:
resultText.text = "Who was the first US President?";
setRadioButtons("Washington", "Coolidge", "Clinton", "Borat",
➥"Washington", 0);
break;

case 2:
resultText.text = "What was the color of Washington's white
➥horse?";
setRadioButtons("Yellow", "Fuscha", "White", "Fish", "White",
➥1);
break;

case 3:
resultText.text = "Who was the US president during the Civil
➥War?";
setRadioButtons("Grover Cleveland", "Abraham Lincoln",
➥"Margaret Thatcher", "Oprah Winfrey", "Abraham Lincoln", 2);
break;
```

```
case 4:
resultText.text = "Who was the US president during WWI?";
setRadioButtons("Herbert Hoover", "Kermit the Frog", "Herman
➥Munster", "Woodrow Wilson", "Woodrow Wilson", 3);
break;

case 5:
resultText.text = 'Which US President said, "The only thing we
➥have to fear is fear itself"?'
setRadioButtons("JFK", "FDR", "BBC", "MTV", "FDR", 4);
break;
}
```

Each call to the setRadioButton() function contains six parameters. The first four parameters represent the four possible answers for each question in the quiz. The fifth parameter stores the correct answer. For example, if the value of the quizCount variable is 5 (case 5), then the four possible answers to question 5 are the strings "JFK," "FDR," "BBC," and "MTV," and the correct choice is "FDR."

The final parameter will (soon) be used to control the animation of the rectangles in the lesson08_start.fla file. If you recall from Lesson 7, there are five rectangles that can be animated open. References to these rectangles were stored in an array called rArray. The final parameter of the setRadioButtons() function will be used later to pass a message to the rArray to indicate which rectangle should be animated open when a question is answered correctly. Remember that the elements in an array are counted beginning at zero, so this parameter will contain a number for an element between 0 and 4.

The final addition to the switch statement is a default condition at the end. The default condition will be reached only after all the questions have been completed; this will set the resultText field to display a message letting users know they have successfully completed the quiz.

6   In the switch statement, below the break statement for the final condition (case 5), add the following code:

```
default:
resultText.text = "You have successfully completed the quiz.";
```

The completed `addQuestion()` method should now read:

```
private function addQuestion():void {

    switch (quizCount) {
        case 1:
            resultText.text = "Who was the first US President?";
            setRadioButtons("Washington", "Coolidge", "Clinton", "Borat", "Washington",0);
            break;

        case 2:
            resultText.text = "What was the color of Washington's white horse?";
            setRadioButtons("Yellow", "Fuscha", "White", "Fish", "White", 1);
            break;

        case 3:
            resultText.text = "Who was the US president during the Civil War?";
            setRadioButtons("Grover Cleveland", "Abraham Lincoln", "Margaret Thatcher", "Oprah Winfrey", "Abraham Lincoln", 2);
            break;

        case 4:
            resultText.text = "Who was the US president during WW1?";
            setRadioButtons("Herbert Hoover", "Kermit the Frog", "Herman Munster", "Woodrow Wilson", "Woodrow Wilson", 3);
            break;

        case 5:
            resultText.text = 'Which US President said, "The only thing we have to fear is fear itself"?';
            setRadioButtons("JFK", "FDR", "BBC", "MTV", "FDR",4);
            break;

        default:
            resultText.text = "You have successfully completed the quiz.";
            }
}
```

Now that you have completed the `addQuestion()` function, you will add the `setRadioButtons()` function. This function will receive parameters passed from calls made in the `switch` statement you just created.

Adding the setRadioButtons() method

Each time the user begins a new question in the quiz, the `setRadioButtons()` function receives information from the `switch` statement in the `addQuestion()` function. The function creates a new Sprite in the `question` variable that will contain the radio buttons for the question.

It will then take the information in the passed parameters and store it in an array called `answers`.

Lastly, it will make four calls to the `createRadioButton()` function, passing one of the four possible answers to the question each time.

First, add the shell for the `setRadioButtons()` function:

1 Below the closing brace of the addQuestion() function, add the following code:

```
public function setRadioButtons(a1:String, a2:String,
➥a3:String, a4:String, a:String, q:int):void {

}
```

Creating functions with parameters

Throughout the lessons in this book, you have been working with functions that receive parameters. They have been mostly parameters for built-in events. In Lesson 4, you created an Ellipse class whose constructor function contained three parameters. With the setRadioButtons() method, you are creating a function that needs to receive six parameters in order to work.

Parameters are contained within the parentheses of a function. These parameters are really just variables that store values that can be passed to the function when it's called. Notice in the setRadioButtons() function that the parameters have data types just like other variables that you have worked with. Unlike other variables, however, they do not require the keyword var.

The a1, a2, a3, a4, and a parameters of the setRadioButtons() function all must receive a string of text. The q parameter receives an integer. If the parameters of a function don't contain an initial default value, then calls to the function must pass a value for the parameter, or an error message occurs. (See Lesson 4 for a review of creating functions with parameters.)

Each call to the setRadioButtons() function passes six parameters. For example, when the condition in the switch statement is 5, this call is made:

```
setRadioButtons("JFK","FDR","BBC", "MTV", "FDR",4);
```

Notice that the parameters include five strings and an integer. When the function receives these parameters, a1 will equal "JFK", a2 will equal "FDR", and so on.

By passing different parameters when a method is called, the same method can be used multiple times and perform differently each time.

Before working with the data in these parameters, you will add a new Sprite to the stage, which will be a container for the radio buttons that will soon be created.

2 Add the following code to the SetRadioButtons() function to add a new Sprite named question and place it onstage:

```
public function setRadioButtons(a1:String, a2:String,
➥a3:String, a4:String, a:String, q:int):void {
question = new Sprite();
addChild(question);
}
```

About variable scope

When discussing the *scope* of a variable, you are referring to where that variable can be referenced.

Remember that the variable `question` was created way back near the beginning of the file. For this reason, you do not have to use the keyword `var` when creating a new Sprite in the `question` variable. The variable already exists—you are just adding a new value to it.

By creating the variable outside the function, it becomes available to the entire file. If it were created within the function, it would not be recognized except within the function.

In a class file, variables created outside a method are considered *class* variables, and those created in a method are considered *method* variables. Choose where you create variables with care.

Calling the createRadioButton() method

Next you will add four calls to a method that will be created soon, which will be used to create the radio buttons and place them onstage. This method will be called `createRadioButton()` and will take three parameters.

Below the line that reads:

```
addChild(question);
```

insert the following code:

```
createRadioButton(a1, rbg, posX);
createRadioButton(a2, rbg, posX);
createRadioButton(a3, rbg, posX);
createRadioButton(a4, rbg, posX);
```

The first parameter of the `createRadioButton()` function receives one of the four possible answers to the current question. This means that the four lines you just inserted will create four new radio buttons, and each one will receive a different possible answer.

The second parameter, `rbg`, refers to the RadioButtonGroup that was created earlier in the file. This will be used by the `createRadioButton()` function to assign all four of the RadioButtons to the same RadioButtonGroup.

The third parameter, `posX`, also refers to a variable that was created earlier. This variable currently stores a numeric value of 20, which will be used to determine the horizontal position of the radio buttons.

Creating the answers array

Remember that all the parameters received by the setRadioButtons() function are available only within that function. Since the information in those parameters will need to be available later on in other methods, you will create a new array that will retain all of the parameter values. This way, those values can be used throughout the application. A variable named answers already exists with a data type of Array. This answers variable is where the new array and its values will be stored.

Below the line that reads:

```
createRadioButton(a4, rbg, posX);
```

add the following code to create the new array and store the setRadioButtons() parameters in it:

```
answers = new Array(a1, a2, a3, a4, a, q);
```

Keeping in mind what you learned in Lesson 7, you'll see that the possible answers to the current question are now stored as elements 0–3 of the new array, the answer to the current question is stored in element 4 (answers[4]), and the parameter named q is in answers[5]. This knowledge will be useful very soon.

At this point, the setRadioButtons() method should read:

```
public function setRadioButtons(a1:String, a2:String, a3:String,
  ➥a4:String, a:String, q:int):void {
  question = new Sprite();
  addChild(question);

  createRadioButton(a1, rbg, posX);
  createRadioButton(a2, rbg, posX);
  createRadioButton(a3, rbg, posX);
  createRadioButton(a4, rbg, posX);

  answers=new Array(a1,a2,a3,a4,a,q);
}
```

You will need to return to this function before you are finished, but first you will add the createRadioButton() method.

Adding the createRadioButton() method

After all this work to set up what have so far been theoretical radio buttons, you will finally create the radio buttons in this relatively simple function. You will also use this function to set a few properties for the radio buttons and add them to the stage.

1   Below the setRadioButtons() method, add the following code:

```
private function createRadioButton(rbLabel:String, rbg:
➥RadioButtonGroup, posX:int):void {

}
```

This function receives three parameters. rbLabel will receive the string that contains the question associated with that RadioButton instance, rbg will contain the RadioButtonGroup that this RadioButton will belong to, and posX will contain the integer that will be used to determine the radio button's x position. In the setRadioButtons() function, there were four calls made to this function, each of which passed values for these parameters.

2   Between the curly braces of the createRadioButton() function, create a new instance of the RadioButton class:

```
var rb:RadioButton = new RadioButton();
```

The label property of a radio button determines the text that will appear to the right of the button. You'll set this property to display the string in the rbLabel parameter.

3   Add this code below the previous line:

```
rb.label = rbLabel;
```

The group property of a RadioButton determines which RadioButtonGroup the RadioButton will belong to.

4   Set the group property to rbg by adding this code below the previous line:

```
rb.group = rbg;
```

The width property of a RadioButton, not surprisingly, sets the width of the RadioButton and its label.

5   Set the width property by adding this code below the previous line:

```
rb.width = 200;
```

The createRadioButton() function so far should read:

```
private function createRadioButton(
➥rbLabel:String, rbg:RadioButtonGroup, posX:int):void {
var rb:RadioButton = new RadioButton();
rb.label = rbLabel;
rb.group = rbg;
rb.width = 200;
}
```

The move property of a RadioButton takes two parameters that set the horizontal and vertical positions of the RadioButton.

6   Above the closing brace of the createRadioButton() function, set the move property of rb using the values of variables that were created earlier in the file:

```
rb.move(posX, currHeight);
```

The variable posX was set earlier to 20, so all the radio buttons will be placed 20 pixels from the left edge of the stage.

The original value of currHeight was set to 250. If the vertical positions were all set to currHeight as it is, each radio button would be at exactly the same location, and they would be very difficult to read. Instead, you'll add a little vertical space between the radio buttons by adding to the value of currHeight each time a button is created. Notice that earlier in the code you created a variable named verticalSpacing and gave it a value of 30. You will add this value to the current height after each new RadioButton is positioned. This way, each RadioButton in the group will be 30 pixels below the previous one.

7   Above the closing brace of the createRadioButton() function, add the following code:

```
currHeight += verticalSpacing;
```

The final step in this function will be to add the new RadioButton to the display list of the Sprite called question. All the RadioButtons for each question will be added to the same Sprite.

8   Above the closing brace of the createRadioButton() function, add the following code:

```
question.addChild(rb);
```

The final version of the createRadioButton() function should read:

```
private function createRadioButton(rbLabel:String, rbg:RadioButtonGroup, posX:int):void {
    var rb:RadioButton = new RadioButton();
    rb.label = rbLabel;
    rb.group = rbg;
    rb.width = 200;
    rb.move(posX, currHeight);
    currHeight += verticalSpacing;
    question.addChild(rb);
}
```

Checking to see if a condition is false

With what you now know about the createRadioButton() function, you can go back to the setRadioButtons() function and recognize a couple of potential problems.

The setRadioButtons() function should now read:

```
public function setRadioButtons(a1:String, a2:String, a3:String,
➥a4:String, a:String, q:int):void {
```

(code continues on the next page)

(continued)

```
question = new Sprite();
addChild(question);

createRadioButton(a1, rbg, posX);
createRadioButton(a2, rbg, posX);
createRadioButton(a3, rbg, posX);
createRadioButton(a4, rbg, posX);

answers = new Array(a1, a2, a3, a4, a, q);
}
```

This function will work brilliantly the first time it's called. However, the second time it's called (for the second question in the quiz), a second Sprite is created that adds radio buttons with the answers for question 2 below the existing radio buttons for question 1! Instead, each question should replace the previous one. You need a conditional statement to check to see if there is already an existing Sprite in the `question` variable.

A variable with a data type of Sprite that has nothing stored in it has a value of `null`. We therefore know that if the variable `question` is not `null`, then it must contain a Sprite.

To check to see if a condition is not true in ActionScript, you can use the operator `!=`, as in:

```
if(color != blue){
  paintMeBlue();
}
```

Add some code to the beginning of the `setRadioButtons()` function that will remove any previous question Sprites before adding a new one.

1 Above the line in the `setRadioButtons()` function that now reads:

```
question = new Sprite();
```

add the following code:

```
if(question != null) {
  removeChild(question);
}
```

This code will check to see if the question Sprite is not `null`. If it is not `null`, then it contains a Sprite that will then be removed so that the next question can replace it.

Within the conditional statement you just created, you need to add one more line. Remember that each time a new RadioButton is created, its horizontal position is incremented (by adding 30 to the `currHeight` property so that each question will have a series of radio buttons each 30 pixels below the previous one). When a new question is added, the `currHeight` value should be restored to the original setting so that the radio buttons for each question appear in the same spot.

About removeChild()

ActionScript keeps track of objects onstage in an internal display list. As you have seen, each time you use the `addChild()` method, a new object is added to the display list.

Just as objects are added to the display list and made viewable with the `addChild()` method, they are removed from the display list with the `removeChild()` method. This does not clear the object from memory; it only takes it off of the display list.

2   Below the line you just added that reads:

```
removeChild(question);
```

add this line:

```
currHeight = 250;
```

The final `setRadioButtons()` method should now read:

```
public function setRadioButtons(a1:String, a2:String, a3:String, a4:String, a:String,q:int):void {

    if (question != null) {
        removeChild(question);
        currHeight = 250;
    }
    question = new Sprite();
    addChild(question);

    createRadioButton(a1, rbg, posX);
    createRadioButton(a2, rbg, posX);
    createRadioButton(a3, rbg, posX);
    createRadioButton(a4, rbg, posX);

    answers=new Array(a1, a2, a3, a4, a, q);
}
```

Creating checkAnswer()—the final function

Pat yourself on the back: You have only one more function to write in the RadioButtonQuiz.as file and a few modifications to the lesson08_start.fla file to complete this lesson.

If you scroll up in the RadioButtonQuiz.as code to the function named `quizInit()`, you'll find the code that created the RadioButtonGroup named rbg:

```
rbg = new RadioButtonGroup("answers");
```

If you recall when that instance was created, an event listener was added to it that listened for a CHANGE event. This event takes place each time the user chooses an answer.

The line that added the listener is:

```
rbg.addEventListener(Event.CHANGE, checkAnswer);
```

The final function that needs to be written is the one to compare the user's choice to the correct answer and respond accordingly: the checkAnswer() function.

1   Below the closing brace of the createRadioButton() function, add the following code:

```
private function checkAnswer(e:Event):void {

}
```

This function checks to see if the RadioButton that the user selected matches the correct answer.

To identify the user's selection, the RadioButtonGroup that the CHANGE event came from needs to be identified, and then the RadioButton that the user chose needs to be stored locally.

2   To store the user's selection, add code to the checkAnswer() function so that it reads:

```
private function checkAnswer(e:Event):void {
  var rbg:RadioButtonGroup = e.target as RadioButtonGroup;
  var rb:RadioButton = rbg.selection;
}
```

The variable rb now represents the user's selection.

Remember that the correct answer that we wish to compare to the user's choice is stored in element 4 of the answers array (answers[4]).

3   To see if the label on the user selected RadioButton matches the correct answer, add the following code above the closing brace of the checkAnswer() function:

```
if(rb.label==answers[4] as String) {

}
```

If this condition is true, then the user's choice was correct. In this case, the user should proceed to the next question.

4   Add the bold code to the conditional statement so that it reads:

```
if(rb.label==answers[4] as String) {
  quizCount++;
  addQuestion();
}
```

Remember, the variable quizCount keeps track of the current question, so if the user answers question 1 correctly, then quizCount will increase to 2. If the user answers question 2 correctly, quizCount will become 3, and so on.

After quizCount is incremented, the addQuestion() method is called, and will use the new value of quizCount to set up the next question.

The other thing that should happen when the answer is correct is that the animations in the lesson08_start.fla file is triggered. Right now, these animations are being triggered in the Flash file using a function called rectClick(). This function was created in Lesson 7 to animate the rectangular doors when they were clicked.

Since, in this lesson, the animation should occur when an answer is correct, you will soon modify the rectClick() function and change its name to onCorrect(). This is because it is helpful to have the names of functions relate to their purpose.

Calling a function in the timeline from a class file

When an instance of an external class is created from the main Flash timeline, the external class is considered a child of that timeline. Conversely, the timeline is considered the parent of the external class. This will be the relationship between the RadioButtonQuiz.as file and the timeline of the lesson08_start.fla file.

1 To call a function named onCorrect() in the main timeline from your RadioButtonQuiz.as, add a new line to the conditional statement that currently reads:

```
if (rb.label == answers[4] as String) {
  quizCount++;
  addQuestion();
}
```

so that it now reads:

```
if (rb.label == answers[4] as String) {
  (parent as Object).onCorrect();
  quizCount++;
  addQuestion();
}
```

● **Note:** Calling a function in an ActionScript class file is not a common practice in OOP, since it is usually desirable to keep class files relatively self-contained. Ideally, class files should be as versatile as possible, so they can be reused in multiple projects.

The last thing to be added to this conditional statement, and to this entire file, will be an else statement that sets the resultText field to provide users with some feedback when they have chosen an incorrect answer.

2 Add an else statement to the new conditional statement so that it reads:

```
if (rb.label == answers[4] as String) {
  (parent as Object).onCorrect();
  quizCount++;
```

(code continues on the next page)

(continued)

```
    addQuestion();

  } else {
  resultText.text = rb.label + " is incorrect. Please try
    ➥again.";
  }
```

That's it for the class file. Here is the entire file:

```
package {
 import flash.text.TextField;
 import flash.text.TextFieldAutoSize;
 import flash.text.TextFormat;
 import flash.display.Sprite;
 import flash.display.DisplayObjectContainer;
 import flash.events.Event;
 import fl.controls.RadioButton;
 import fl.controls.RadioButtonGroup;

 public class RadioButtonQuiz extends Sprite {
  private var question:Sprite;
  private var resultText:TextField;
  private var rbg:RadioButtonGroup;
  private var currHeight:int = 250;
  private var verticalSpacing:int = 30;
  private var posX:int = 20;
  private var quizCount:int = 1;
  public var answers:Array;

  public function RadioButtonQuiz() {
   quizInit();
  }

  private function quizInit():void {
   resultText = new TextField();
   resultText.x = 25;
   resultText.y = 210;
   resultText.width = 450;
   resultText.wordWrap = true;
   resultText.text = "Select a Radio Button";
   rbg = new RadioButtonGroup("answers");
   rbg.addEventListener(Event.CHANGE, checkAnswer);
   formatText();
   addQuestion();
  }

  private function formatText():void {
   var format:TextFormat = new TextFormat();
```

```
      format.font = "Verdana";
      format.color = 0x3333AA;
      format.size = 16;
      format.bold = true;
      resultText.defaultTextFormat = format;
      addChild(resultText);
   }

private function addQuestion():void {
switch (quizCount) {

case 1:
resultText.text = "Who was the first US President?";
setRadioButtons("Washington", "Coolidge", "Clinton", "Borat",
 ➥"Washington", 0);
break;

case 2:
resultText.text = "What was the color of Washington's white
 ➥horse?";
setRadioButtons("Yellow", "Fuscha", "White", "Fish", "White", 1);
break;

case 3:
resultText.text = "Who was the US president during the Civil
 ➥War?";
setRadioButtons("Grover Cleveland", "Abraham Lincoln", "Margaret
 ➥Thatcher", "Oprah Winfrey", "Abraham Lincoln", 2);
break;

case 4:
resultText.text = "Who was the US president during WW1?";
setRadioButtons("Herbert Hoover", "Kermit the Frog", "Herman
 ➥Munster", "Woodrow Wilson", "Woodrow Wilson", 3);
break;

case 5:
resultText.text = 'Which US President said, "The only thing we
 ➥have to fear is fear itself"?'
setRadioButtons("JFK", "FDR", "BBC", "MTV", "FDR", 4);
break;

default:
resultText.text = "You have successfully completed the quiz.";
   }
}
```

(code continues on the next page)

(continued)

```
public function setRadioButtons(a1:String, a2:String, a3:String,
  ➥a4:String, a:String, q:int):void {

  if (question != null) {
    removeChild(question);
    currHeight = 250;
  }
  question = new Sprite();
  addChild(question);

  createRadioButton(a1, rbg, posX);
  createRadioButton(a2, rbg, posX);
  createRadioButton(a3, rbg, posX);
  createRadioButton(a4, rbg, posX);

  answers=new Array(a1, a2, a3, a4, a, q);
  }
private function createRadioButton(rbLabel:String,
  ➥rbg:RadioButtonGroup, posX:int):void {
  var rb:RadioButton = new RadioButton();
  rb.label = rbLabel;
  rb.group = rbg;
  rb.width = 200;
  rb.move(posX, currHeight);
  currHeight += verticalSpacing;
  question.addChild(rb);
  }

private function checkAnswer(e:Event):void {
  var rbg:RadioButtonGroup = e.target as RadioButtonGroup;
  var rb:RadioButton = rbg.selection;
  if (rb.label == answers[4] as String) {
    (parent as Object).onCorrect();
    quizCount++;
    addQuestion();
  } else {
    resultText.text = rb.label + " is incorrect. Please try
      ➥again.";
  }
  }
  }
}
```

Be sure to save this file before going back to the lesson08_start.fla file.

Integrating your new class into the Flash project

If you were ambitious enough to get this far in the lesson without a break, you might want to take at least a quick one before finishing this last bit of work.

Now that the quiz is completely done, you want to integrate it into the original Flash project by adding an instance to the file.

Adding an instance of the RadioButtonQuiz class

As you saw in Lesson 4, adding an instance of a custom class that you create is the same as adding an instance of an ActionScript built-in class. Here, you'll add an instance of the RadioButtonQuiz class in a variable named `quiz`.

If it is not already open, reopen the lesson08_start.fla (Lessons > Lesson08 > Start > lesson08_start.fla). If you like, close the RadioButtonQuiz.as file if it's in your way.

1   With frame 1 of the `actions` layer selected and the Actions panel visible, place the cursor on the line below the code that reads:

```
var clip:MovieClip;
var rArray:Array = new Array();
var done:Boolean = false;
```

2   Add the following two new lines of code:

```
var quiz:RadioButtonQuiz = new RadioButtonQuiz();
addChild(quiz);
```

This creates the `quiz` instance of the class you just created and adds it to the stage.

3   Scroll down and locate the line that reads:

```
rectangle.addEventListener(MouseEvent.CLICK, rectClick);
```

4   Select the entire line of code, and press the Delete key to remove it.

The line you just removed was used in Lesson 7 to open the rectangle instances when clicked. You will replace this functionality with the functionality that already exists in the `RadioButtonQuiz` class.

5   Locate the function named `rectClick()`.

6   Change the function's name to **onCorrect**().

7   Remove the parameters between the parentheses of the `onCorrect()` function. It should now read:

```
function onCorrect():void {
 addEventListener(Event.ENTER_FRAME, rotateUp);
 clip = e.target as MovieClip;
}
```

8   Select and delete the line that reads:

```
clip = e.target as MovieClip;
```

9   Place the cursor above the line that reads:

```
addEventListener(Event.ENTER_FRAME, rotateUp);
```

and insert the following code:

```
clip = rArray[quiz.answers[5]] as MovieClip;
```

Recall that element number 5 in the answers array contains the number of
the rectangle that corresponds with the current question. Remember also that
quiz is the instance name of the RadioButtonsQuiz class instance. So to get
element 5 from the answers array of that class, you refer to quiz.answers[5].
That entire phrase will evaluate to the number of the rectangle that needs to
be opened. Remember the rectangle references are stored in an array called
rArray. So rArray[quiz.answers[5]] will return the correct rectangle each
time. The bit of final syntax, as MovieClip, casts the result so that it can be
treated as a MovieClip and instructed to animate its rotationX property.

10 Find the rotateUp() function below the onCorrect() function. Locate and
    cut (Edit > Cut) the line that reads:

```
clip.up = true;
```

11 Back in the onCorrect() function, place the cursor at the end of the line that
    reads:

```
addEventListener(Event.ENTER_FRAME, rotateUp);
```

and press Enter.

12 Paste (Edit > Paste) the line that you cut into this new line, so that the entire
    onCorrect() function now reads:

```
function onCorrect():void {
 clip = rArray[quiz.answers[5]] as MovieClip;
 addEventListener(Event.ENTER_FRAME, rotateUp);
 clip.up = true;
}
```

All the remaining code in the lesson08_start.fla can remain as it is; however, in
order for the completed project to work, the RadioButton component needs to be
made available to the project so that the ActionScript that you wrote can access it.

Adding the RadioButton to the library

The final steps of the project are perhaps the easiest. You will be adding the RadioButton component to the library so that it is available to the ActionScript code you have written.

1　Open both the Library panel and the Components panel so that they are both visible.

2　Drag an instance of the RadioButton component into the library so that it is available to this file.

3　Test the movie.

4　The text for the questions should be formatted with the format object (large, blue, Verdana). Select a correct answer from the radio buttons. The first rectangle should open. Answer the remaining questions, and the other rectangles will open. Try an occasional incorrect answer; the text field should give appropriate feedback. When all five questions are answered, the final animation should display "Hurray!" Celebrate your triumph.

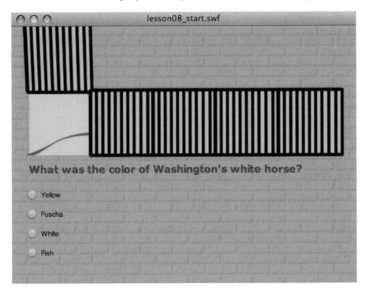

This lesson covered quite an ambitious amount of code, so don't be surprised if errors occur when you test your project. The usual troubleshooting techniques will help you track down any issues that come up. If you need to compare your file to a finished working version, the Lessons > Lesson08 > Complete folder contains a finished working version of both the FLA file and the RadioButtonQuiz.as file.

Some suggestions to try on your own

To become more comfortable with the many new techniques introduced in this lesson, try a few of the following:

- Consult Flash Help and become familiar with additional properties of the TextFormat class.

- Modify the format instance in the RadioButtonQuiz class. Look up the various properties of the TextFormat class in the help system and explore different formatting possibilities.

- Create a few new TextFormat instances in the RadioButtonQuiz class. Use a list component or button instances to change the formatting of the text field using different TextFormat instances. (The list of components is covered in Lesson 5, "Using ActionScript and Components to Load Content.")

- Modify the switch statement in the addQuestion() function to change the questions and possible answers in the quiz.

- Reposition the radio buttons by modifying the currHeight, verticalSpacing, and posX values.

- Change the content (and maybe even the format) of the feedback users get when they choose an incorrect answer.

- Add a text field onstage that reports to users the number of correct and incorrect choices that they have made.

Review questions

1 Name the four access modifiers available in an ActionScript 3.0 class.

2 How are RadioButton instances associated with a RadioButtonGroup using ActionScript?

3 What is an alternate to an `if` conditional statement that is useful to check a large number of possible conditions?

4 What method can be used to remove an object from the display list?

Review answers

1 ActionScript 3.0 uses the access modifiers public, private, protected, and internal.

2 A RadioButton is associated with a RadioButtonGroup in ActionScript by setting the `group` property of the RadioButton. For example:

```
radioButton1.group = rbg;
```

3 A `switch` statement is a type of conditional statement that is commonly used when many conditions need to be checked.

4 The `removeChild()` method removes a specific item from the display list so that it is no longer seen by the user.

9 CONTROLLING SOUND WITH ACTIONSCRIPT

Lesson overview

In this lesson, you will learn to do the following:

- Create instances of the Sound, SoundChannel, and SoundTransform classes.

- Control the loading and playback of external MP3 files.

- Use the SoundTransform class to control volume and panning of sounds.

- Use the Slider component to control the properties of the SoundTransform class.

- Use an array to store a playlist of MP3 files.

- Use methods of the TextField class to add to and remove characters from text strings.

- Use the ID3 tags of an MP3 file to access information about the file.

This lesson will take approximately 2.5 hours.

Sound is one of the most effective ways to evoke strong responses from your audience. By making the audio in your Flash projects interactive using ActionScript, sounds can respond to your users and significantly enhance their experience. Whether employing simple sound effects that occur as the user interacts with an interface, or a full interactive soundscape in a game, ActionScript 3.0 makes it possible to immerse your users in a responsive aural environment.

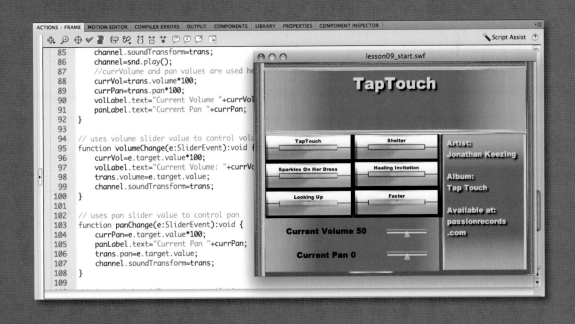

A simple Flash music player controlled by
ActionScript.

In this lesson, you will create one of the most primary uses of ActionScript-controlled sound: a simple music player. You will add basic sound control to your ActionScript repertoire and gain comfort with a number of sound-related ActionScript techniques.

There are a number of ActionScript classes that work with sound. This lesson will focus on three: the Sound, SoundChannel, and SoundTransform classes. These three classes work together to give you control over individual sound files. A fourth class, not covered in this lesson, is the SoundMixer class, which is used to control multiple channels of sound simultaneously.

Examining the completed file

To get an idea what you will be doing in this lesson, take a look at the completed version, Lessons > Lesson09 > Complete > lesson09_complete.fla. The file uses six MP3 music files that are in the Lesson09 > MP3 folder. Open lesson09_complete.fla and test it (Control > Test Movie) to see the results of this lesson. When clicked, each of the six jukebox titles plays a different song by loading it at runtime from the MP3 folder. When a song is loaded, information is displayed about that song.

You will add additional controls to this music player project in Lesson 10, "Working with an XML Playlist."

Examining the starting file

The starting file for this lesson—lesson09_start.fla—can be found in the Lessons > Lesson 09 > Start folder. Open this file to begin the lesson.

1 With the Flash timeline visible, notice that there are three layers with content. The background layer is a full-screen static graphic. The song buttons layer contains six MovieClip instances that will be used to select and play six different songs. There is also a layer with text fields that you will control with ActionScript later in the lesson.

2 If it is not already visible, open the Properties panel, and, one at a time, select the six MovieClips onstage that look like the background graphics of classic jukebox elements. Notice that they have instance names of *song1* through

song6. These clips will be used to let the user select the song they wish to play. You will add ActionScript to give these "song" clips functionality.

3   Double-click any of the "song" clips onstage to go into that symbol's timeline. You will see that inside each clip is a dynamic text field with the instance name of title. These text fields will display the titles of the songs in the music player.

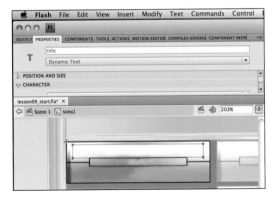

4   Click the tab in the upper-left of the stage labeled Scene 1 to return to the main timeline.

5   On the main timeline, the text fields layer has four dynamic text fields: one at the top of the stage, one in the lower-right, and two in the lower-left. With the Properties panel still visible, select these fields one at a time. Notice that the top field has an instance name of songTitle, the right field has an instance name of info, and the two in the lower-left are named volLabel and panLabel. You will control the contents of all these fields with ActionScript.

Adding sliders to the project

The only graphical content items for this project not already provided are the sliders that you will use to give the user control over the volume and panning of the songs. These sliders will be instances of a User Interface component that ships with Flash CS4 called Slider.

1 With frame 1 of the `sliders` layer selected, open the Components panel (Window > Components) and, from the directory of User Interface components, locate the Slider component.

2 Drag two instances of the Slider component to the stage, one to the right of the panLabel text field, and one to the right of the volLabel field.

3 With the Properties panel visible, select the Slider instance to the right of the volLabel text field. Give this slider the instance name **volSlide**.

4 Select the slider to the right of the panLabel text field. Give this slider the instance name **panSlide**.

All the remaining additions to this project will be done with ActionScript. In this lesson, the ActionScript to control the project will all be added in frame 1 of the timeline's `actions` layer. So, let's get the workspace ready.

Next you set the starting settings for the two Slider instances in the Component Inspector.

5 With the volSlider selected, make the Component Inspector panel visible (Window > Component Inspector).

6 Set the initial settings for the volSlide instance to match those in the image below. This will give the volume slider a range from 0 to 1 and an initial setting of .5 (50%) volume.

7 Next select the panSlide instance and give it these settings in the Component Inspector.

These settings will give the slider a range that represents the range between the left and right speaker and sets the initial value to represent the center of the stereo field.

8 With frame 1 of the `actions` layer selected, open the Actions panel if it is not already visible.

The first code in the file will import the `SliderEvent` class.

You will use several ActionScript classes in this project, but only one of them needs to be imported into the file. This is a class called `SliderEvent` that is used when the user adjusts the volume and panning using the sliders. Later in the lesson the sliders will be programmed to control the volume and panning of sound.

9 With frame 1 of the `actions` layer selected, add the following code on the first line in the Actions panel:

```
import fl.events.SliderEvent;
```

With the sliders set up, the graphics for the file are all set and you are ready to begin coding the sound controls. The first step will be to create variables to store references to the three classes that you will use to work with sound: Sound, SoundChannel, and SoundTransform.

The Sound, SoundChannel, and SoundTransform classes

As stated earlier, ActionScript 3.0 contains a number of classes that control sound. These classes often work together on the same sound file to load the sound into the project and determine how and when the sound plays. In this project, you will use an instance of each of three classes to control your sounds. Here's a brief overview of how these three classes work together: The Sound class is used mainly to load sounds into a Flash project and play them. There are also features in this class to read text data that is stored in MP3 files. New features have been added to the Sound class in Flash CS4 for generating sounds from scratch in Flash.

When a sound is played in a Flash project, it is automatically assigned to a SoundChannel object. The SoundChannel class is used to stop playback of individual sounds as well as to monitor the volume and panning of sound. The SoundChannel class works with the SoundTransform class, which controls the volume and panning of sounds. You can also create instances of the SoundChannel class and assign specific sounds to a specific SoundChannel. A Flash project can have many separate sounds, all playing in their own SoundChannel simultaneously. Each SoundChannel instance can be controlled individually.

About import statements

For classes whose package description begins with "flash," it is optional to import that class before using it in the Flash timeline. Other classes should be imported.

If you are not sure which classes need to be imported into a Flash project and which are optional, or what the path is for a class, you can find out in Flash Help by looking in the ActionScript 3.0 Language and Components Reference, where you will see a menu of all the classes in Flash. This is a great resource for researching an ActionScript class and learning about its methods, properties, and events.

When you select a class from the menu, at the top of the reference page for that class you will see a reference to that class's package. In the illustration below, you can see the reference for the SliderEvent class. Notice that its package is listed as fl.events.

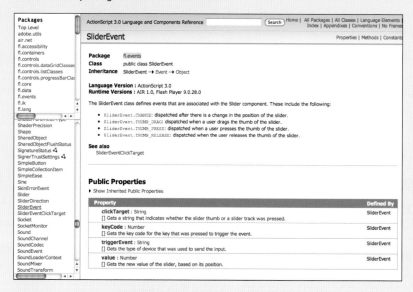

In an import statement for this class, you would use the package path followed by a dot and the class name:

```
import fl.events.SliderEvent;
```

Most of the built-in classes in ActionScript 3.0 have a path description that begins with the word "flash," as in:

```
import flash.media.Sound
```

An option to importing a class that you may want to consider for your own custom classes is to set class paths associated with your Flash project. You can use the Publish settings (File > Publish Settings) to set class paths for a single Flash file, or you can globally set class paths for all your Flash projects using the Flash Preferences (Edit > Preferences on Windows, File > Preferences on Mac). For more information on setting class paths, see Flash Help.

Remember, when you are writing code in external ActionScript files, you must import every class you reference.

Creating Sound, SoundChannel, and SoundTransform instances

In this lesson, you will create an instance of the Sound class that loads and plays songs that the user selects. You will associate the Sound class instance with an instance of the SoundChannel class, and then associate the SoundChannel instance with a SoundTransform instance so that the user will be able to adjust the volume and panning in the songs.

Start by creating three variables to store the instances of these three classes.

In the Actions panel below the line that reads:

```
import fl.events.SliderEvent;
```

add the following code:

```
var snd:Sound;
var channel:SoundChannel;
var trans:SoundTransform;
```

The variable named snd has a data type of Sound, the variable named channel has a data type of SoundChannel, and the trans variable has a data type of SoundTransform. These variables have no initial values but will soon contain instances of their respective classes.

Adding comments to your files

While you are writing code, it may seem perfectly clear to you what you are trying to create, but often when you come back to a file later (sometimes much later!), it is less obvious what your thought process was at the time.

Adding comments in your ActionScript to explain key points of the code can be extremely helpful to you when you may have to recall the development process. Clear comments can also be very useful when a team is working together on a project or when sharing your code with others.

You designate a single-line comment in ActionScript with two forward slashes, as in:

```
// this code doesn't do anything but provides useful information
```

For multiline comments, you surround the comment with the tags /* and */, as in:

```
/* this line and the
lines below this
are all
commented out
until the asterisk-end
characters */
```

(continues on the next page)

(continued)

It's a good idea to get in the habit of adding generous comments to your ActionScript files. As you progress through the lessons, add whatever comments you think might be helpful to you when you go back to review them later or to apply the techniques you learn in the lesson to your own projects.

For example, when you're reviewing this lesson in the future, you may be grateful that you added a comment before the code you added to create class instances, as in:

```
//these variables will store instances of sound-related classes
var snd:Sound;
var channel:SoundChannel;
var trans:SoundTransform;
```

If you look at the code in the lesson09_complete.fla file, you will see a number of comments that help clarify the ActionScript.

Adding more variables

In this project, you'll also use variables to keep track of the currently selected song as well as the current volume and pan settings. So, while you are declaring variables for the project, add three more.

1   In the Actions panel, below the code you just added, skip a line and use the following code to create three more variables:

```
var currSong:String;
var currVol:Number = .5;
var currPan:Number = 0;
```

The variable currSong will hold a string that contains the name of the currently selected song. The currVol and currPan variables will store numeric values for the current volume and pan settings respectively. They are given initial values of .5 and 0 respectively. The range of values for volume and pan will be covered later in the lesson.

Next, you will add one more variable with a data type of Array to hold the playlist.

Creating the songList array

If you completed Lesson 7, "Using Arrays and Loops in ActionScript 3.0," and Lesson 8, "Creating a Radio Button Quiz in an ActionScript File," you are familiar with the technique of storing a list of data in a single variable as an array. In this lesson, you will use an array to store the list of songs that the user can choose from. In a later lesson, you will change this array to a list that can be updated and modified easily, but for now, you will just add six songs directly to the array.

With frame 1 of the `actions` layer still selected, add the following line below the existing code in the Actions panel:

```
var songList:Array = new Array("TapTouch.mp3", "Sparkles On Her
➥Dress.mp3", "Looking Up.mp3", "Shelter.mp3", "Healing
➥Invitation.mp3", "Faster.mp3");
```

You'll find these songs in the Lessons > Lesson09 > MP3s folder. After completing the lesson, you may want to change this list to use some of your own MP3 files, but unless you are already familiar with ID3 tags and know that your files have tags in the ID3 version 2.4 format, it's best to work with the files provided for now. ID3 tags will be discussed later in more detail.

Setting the song titles using a for loop

The six MovieClips on stage that look like classic jukebox selections have instance names of *song1* through *song6*. You will use these as buttons with which the user can choose the various songs in the `songList` array. When the project runs, these song clips will display the titles of the songs. As you have seen, each song clip has a dynamic text field, named title, inside of it. To control these text fields using ActionScript in the main timeline, you could refer to them by the path (using *song1* as an example):

```
this.song1.title
```

The keyword `this` in ActionScript refers to the location that the ActionScript is referenced from, which in this case is the main timeline.

Because the song clips have instance names that vary only by the number at the end, and there are the same number of song clips as items in the `songList` array, it will be easy to set up a `for` loop that assigns the names of the songs in the `songList` array to the title text fields in the clips.

1 Below the existing code in frame 1 of the `actions` layer, add the following `for` loop:

```
for(var i = 0; i < songList.length; i++) {
 this["song" + (i + 1)].title.text = songList[i] as String;

}
```

A number of useful techniques are being implemented here. In the first line of the `for` loop, notice that the number of times the code repeats is based on the length of the `songList` array. (For a review of `for` loops and arrays, see Lesson 7.)

```
for(var i = 0; i < songList.length; i++) {
```

The second line of code introduces the technique of evaluating the path of a MovieClip using square brackets. Each time the `for` loop repeats, the text in between the brackets is combined to produce one of the clip names. The `i` variable in the `for` loop begins at 0 and increment up to 5, and 1 is added to the current value of `i` in each iteration, so the loop evaluates from 1 to 6, which numbers correspond with the song MovieClip instance names. So the first time the `for` loop runs the code

```
this["song" + (i + 1)]
```

it will evaluate to `this.song1`, the second time, `this.song2`, and so on. This can be a very useful way to loop through a group of objects with similar names.

The remaining part of the line:

```
songList[i] as String
```

evaluates to a different element of the array each time the loop repeats, the result will set all six song clip titles to the six songs stored in the array.

2 Test the movie. The filenames of the songs appear in the text fields of the song clips.

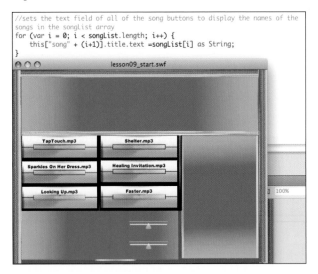

Modifying text fields with the replace() method

When you tested the movie, you probably noticed that the text fields display the full names of the song files, including the suffix .mp3. Since it's not really desirable to display the suffix in the interface, you can use a method of the `TextField` class to remove it. The `replace()` method takes two parameters between the parentheses. The first parameter is the text to be removed; the second is what you wish to add in place of the removed text. If you have used the find-and-replace feature in any software application, you are familiar with the concept of `replace()`.

In this example, you will replace the suffix .mp3 with no text, which will be described by empty quotation marks ("").

To write the names of the songs without the suffixes, you will modify the for loop you just created. You'll add a new variable named str to store the original filenames of the songs, and then you'll modify that variable with the replace() method. This new string will then be what is placed in the title fields of the song clips.

1 Rewrite the code in the for loop that you added:

```
for(var i = 0; i < songList.length; i++) {
  this["song" + (i + 1)].title.text = songList[i] as String;


}
```

So that it instead reads:

```
for(var i = 0; i < songList.length; i++) {
  var str:String = songList[i] as String;
  str = str.replace(".mp3" , "");
  var clip = this["song" + (i + 1)].title;
  clip.text = str;
}
```

2 Test the movie. Notice that now the names of the songs display without the file suffix.

3 Close the lesson09_start.swf file to leave the testing environment.

Making the sliders invisible until needed

Since the two sliders that you added to the stage won't be needed until the user selects a song to play, it makes sense to set their visible properties to `false` to hide them. Later in the lesson, you will add code to make them both visible and functional when a song is chosen.

1   With frame 1 of the `actions` layer of the timeline still selected, insert a new line in the Actions panel below your existing code, and add the following two lines:

```
panSlide.visible = false;
volSlide.visible = false;
```

2   Test the movie once more. The sliders should no longer be visible.

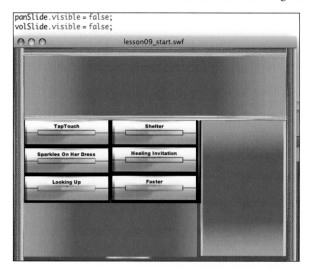

3   Close the lesson09_start.swf file to leave the testing environment.

Next, you will add the event listeners that will let users click to select a song.

Programming the buttons to select songs

The six song clips onstage will be used to call a function that will determine which song will be played. Start by creating six `addEventListener()` calls for these clips.

Adding event listeners to the song buttons

The six clips with the instance names *song1* through *song6* will all call the same function. This function will use a long conditional (`switch`) statement to determine which song to play.

First, add six addEventListener() methods to listen for when the clips have been clicked.

On a new line below the existing code, add the following six listeners:

```
song1.addEventListener(MouseEvent.CLICK, chooseSong);
song2.addEventListener(MouseEvent.CLICK, chooseSong);
song3.addEventListener(MouseEvent.CLICK, chooseSong);
song4.addEventListener(MouseEvent.CLICK, chooseSong);
song5.addEventListener(MouseEvent.CLICK, chooseSong);
song6.addEventListener(MouseEvent.CLICK, chooseSong);
```

Creating the chooseSong() function

Next, you will create the shell for the chooseSong() function that all of these events will call. On a new line below the existing code, add this function:

```
function chooseSong(e:MouseEvent):void {

}
```

This function will do much of the work for the entire movie player project and will contain quite a bit of code. It will store the name of the sound that the user selects, create a new Sound instance, and create and set the properties for related SoundChannel and SoundTransform instances to control the sound. It will also make the sliders visible (since they will of course be needed once a song has been selected) and set the initial volume and pan settings for the sliders.

Creating a switch statement for the song selection

The first thing to be done in this function is to store the name of the song that the user selects. The selected song will be stored in the variable that you created earlier named currSong. A long switch statement will be used to check which song was selected and set the currSong variable to contain a string that describes the path to that song. For example, when the first song in the songList Array is selected (songList[0]), then the currSong variable will be set to:

```
"../MP3s/" + songList[0] as String;
```

The string "../MP3s/" refers to the folder where songs are stored. The two dots and initial forward slash (../) tell that the MP3s folder is found in the parent folder of the current Flash file. (If you need to review switch statements, see Lesson 8.)

Add the full switch statement to the chooseSong() function so that the entire function reads:

```
function chooseSong(e:MouseEvent):void {

  switch (e.currentTarget.name) {
   case "song1":
```

(code continues on the next page)

(continued)

```
      currSong = "../MP3s/" + songList[0] as String;
      break;

    case "song2":
      currSong = "../MP3s/" + songList[1] as String;
      break;

    case "song3":
      currSong = "../MP3s/" + songList[2] as String;
      break;

    case "song4":
      currSong = "../MP3s/" + songList[3] as String;
      break;

    case "song5":
      currSong = "../MP3s/" + songList[4] as String;
      break;

    case "song6":
      currSong = "../MP3s/" + songList[5] as String;
      break;
  }
}
```

Now the currSong variable will store any song the user selects. You will now create and work with three instances. The variable you created called snd will be an instance of the Sound class, the variable called channel will be a SoundChannel instance that will contain the snd instance, and the trans instance will refer to the SoundTransform object you will create to manipulate the volume and pan of snd.

You will create all these instances and set their initial properties in the chooseSong() function.

Creating a Sound class instance and checking for existing instances

Since the chooseSong() function may be called at any time while a user is interacting with this project, you want to make sure that multiple songs don't overlap: that is, if a snd instance is already playing, it needs to stop before a new one begins. You will use an if statement to check if the snd variable contains a value. If snd does have a value, then that sound should be stopped, and only after that will a new snd instance be created.

Below the closing curly brace of the `switch` statement and above the closing brace of the `chooseSong()` function, add the following code:

```
if (snd != null) {
  channel.stop();
}
snd = new Sound();
```

Keeping in mind that all audio in the `snd` instance will play through the `channel` instance (which you be working with very soon), the code you just wrote states that if a sound already exists in the `snd` object (`snd != null`), then the sound playing in `channel` will be stopped (`channel.stop()`). After this, a new instance of the Sound class will be created in the `snd` object (`snd = new Sound()`).

The result of this code is that each time the user clicks one of the song clips, a new Sound object is created; if a song is playing, it will stop.

Loading a sound into a Sound instance

To load a sound into an instance of the Sound class, you use the `load()` method.

Keeping in mind the song that the user wishes to play has already been stored in the variable `currSong`, add the following code below the code you just added and above the closing brace of the `chooseSong()` function:

```
snd.load(new URLRequest(currSong));
```

Creating the SoundChannel and SoundTransform instances

As mentioned, in order to control the stopping, panning, and volume of a Sound instance, it needs be associated with a SoundChannel and SoundTransform instance. You will create those now.

1   Below the line the reads:

```
snd.load(new URLRequest(currSong));
```

add a new SoundChannel instance in the variable called `channel`:

```
channel = new SoundChannel;
```

Next, you need an instance of the `SoundTransform` class in the variable called `trans`. The constructor for the `SoundTransform` class takes two required parameters: one for volume and one for pan.

2   On the next line, type the following code:

```
trans = new SoundTransform(currVol, currPan);
```

● **Note:** In projects where you are loading sounds from external locations, it is a good idea to track the loading progress of a sound and check for errors in the loading. For information on how to do this, look up `load()` in Flash Help. Because the files for this lesson are local, and in order to concentrate on the features in the Sound classes, this lesson does not track loading progress.

This SoundTransform takes its volume property from the variable you created earlier named currVol; recall that this variable had an initial value of .5. The pan value comes from the value of the variable currPan, whose initial value is 0.

To play the sound that has been loaded into the snd instance inside of channel, use the play() method of the Sound class.

Values for volume and pan: listeners, beware!

The SoundTransform class has properties that take numeric values (or expressions that evaluate to numbers) to indicate the volume and pan settings.

Volume in ActionScript is measured between 0 (silent) and 1 (full volume of the original audio). A common mistake is to assume that volume is measured between 0 and 100. This can have dire consequences, because numbers over 1 overdrive the sound level. A volume setting of 2 will play the sound twice as loud as the original file, a setting of 5 will be 500% of the original volume, and therefore a volume setting of 100 is, you got it, 100 times louder than the original sound! This is obviously an unfortunate level for eardrums and sound cards, so it is important to remember the actual volume range.

Pan is measured between –1 and 1. A setting of –1 will play the sound exclusively in the left speaker. A pan setting of 1 will play in the right speaker only. A pan setting of 0 will play a sound exactly in the center of the stereo field.

3 On the next line, type the following code:

```
channel = snd.play();
```

Next, you need to associate the sound playing in the channel object with the new SoundTransform instance.

4 Add the following code on the next line:

```
channel.soundTransform = trans;
```

This will apply the volume and pan settings in the trans instance to the channel object and therefore the playing sound.

At this point, the entire chooseSong() function should read as follows:

```
function chooseSong(e:MouseEvent):void {
    switch (e.currentTarget.name) {
        case "song1":
            currSong = "../MP3s/"+songList[0] as String;
            break;

        case "song2":
            currSong = "../MP3s/"+songList[1] as String;
            break;

        case "song3":
            currSong = "../MP3s/"+songList[2] as String;
            break;

        case "song4":
            currSong = "../MP3s/"+songList[3] as String;
            break;

        case "song5":
            currSong = "../MP3s/"+songList[4] as String;
            break;

        case "song6":
            currSong = "../MP3s/"+songList[5] as String;
            break;
    }
    if (snd != null) {
        channel.stop();
    }
    snd = new Sound();
    snd.load(new URLRequest(currSong));

    channel = new SoundChannel   ;
    trans = new SoundTransform(currVol,currPan);
    channel = snd.play();
    channel.soundTransform = trans;
}
```

5   Test the movie. You should be able to click any of the song clips and hear the related song play back. Choose multiple songs, and notice that only one song at a time will play.

6   Close the lesson09_start.swf file to leave the testing environment.

There are still a few more things to add to the chooseSong() function, starting with the volume and pan sliders and their text fields.

Controlling the visibility of the volume and pan controls

Earlier, you set the volume and pan sliders to be invisible. Once the user selects a song to play, the sliders will of course be needed again to control the volume and pan. So in the body of the chooseSong() function, make the sliders visible.

1   Above the closing brace of the chooseSong() function and below the line that reads:

```
channel.soundTransform = trans;
```

insert the following two lines to make the sliders visible:

```
panSlide.visible = true;
volSlide.visible = true;
```

Next, you will use the values of the `currVol` and `currPan` variables to display the volume and pan levels in the text fields next to the sliders.

2 Below the code you just added, insert these four new lines:

```
volLabel.text = "Current Volume " + int(currVol * 100);
panLabel.text = "Current Pan " + int(currPan * 100);
```

Most users are intuitively more comfortable with volume and pan sliders that range up to 100 rather than up to 1, which is why the `trans.volume` and `trans.pan` values were multiplied by 100. These values will only be used for display in text fields.

Notice also that the values of `currVol` and `currPan` are both cast as integers. This is because unlike instances of the data type `Number`, integers (`int`) cannot contain fractions. This will prevent numbers with decimal places from being displayed in the volume and pan text fields.

3 Test the movie once more. Notice that when a song is selected, the pan and volume sliders become visible and their initial settings are displayed in the text fields.

Notice that moving the sliders around has no effect at this point on the volume or panning of the music or the text in the text fields. You will add code soon to change this.

4 Close the lesson09_start.swf file to leave the testing environment.

Before you add the listeners to respond to movement of the volume and pan sliders, there is one more line of code to add to the `chooseSong()` function. This will be used to listen for data that is stored within MP3 files.

Adding a listener for the ID3 tags of an MP3 file

The MP3 file format allows for the insertion of text-based data into the file. These "ID3" tags in an MP3 file are typically used to store information about the file such as the name of the song, the artist, album, date of release, and so on.

ActionScript is capable of reading and displaying this ID3 data from a loaded MP3 file. There is even a built-in event in the Sound class that responds to the successful loading of ID3 tags from an MP3 file. You will use this ID3 event to call a function to display information about the currently playing song in your interface.

Below the last line of code that you inserted and above the closing brace of the chooseSong() function, add the following line:

```
snd.addEventListener(Event.ID3, id3Handler);
```

When a load() method loads an MP3 file that has ID3 tags, the successful loading of those tags triggers the ID3 event. In this case, when the event occurs, a function named id3Handler() is called. Next, you will create that function.

Creating the id3Handler() function

The ID3 format contains dozens of possible tags also affords you the ability to create your own custom tags.

In this lesson, you will use only three of the most common tags (you can look up other ID3 tags in Flash Help)—the ones that contain the name of the song in the MP3 file, the artist, and the album that the song is from. The data you retrieve from these tags will be used to populate the songTitle and info text fields onstage.

First add the shell for the id3Handler() function.

1 With frame 1 of the actions layer still selected, add a new line below all the existing code in that frame, and insert the following function structure:

```
function id3Handler(event:Event):void {

}
```

Remember that this function will be called every time new data from a loaded MP3 file is available. This data will be automatically stored in the id3 property of the Sound class instance that loaded the MP3 file—in this case, the snd instance.

The first thing you will add to the new function is a local variable to contain all the loaded ID3 data.

(*continues on page 209*)

Using iTunes to check and set ID3 tags

Most MP3 files contain some ID3 tags, but not all of them are in the correct format to work with Flash and ActionScript. ActionScript 3.0 works best with ID3 tags in the version 2.4 format. You can view and create these tags, as well as save them to the correct version, with a number of audio applications. One of the most popular of these is Apple's iTunes (available free for Macintosh and Windows).

To view and set the ID3 tags of an MP3 file, open it in iTunes. If you see name, artist, and other information for the file in the iTunes library, the source of that data is the ID3 tags. To set the ID3 tags to the correct version, select the song in the iTunes library and choose Advanced > Convert ID3 Tags.

In the dialog box that opens, make sure that the ID3 tag version box is selected, and choose v2.4. Then click OK.

Finally, to make sure that you are viewing the updated version of the file with the correct tags, right-click the song in the iTunes Library and select Show In Finder (on the Mac) or Show in Windows Explorer (in Windows).

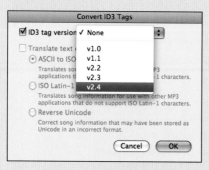 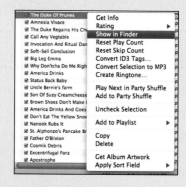

You can now be confident that ActionScript can read and use these tags.

2   In the `id3Handler()` function, add the following new line so that the function now reads:

```
function id3Handler(event:Event):void {
  var id3:ID3Info = snd.id3;
}
```

If an MP3 file has ID3 tags at all, it is almost certain that those tags include a songName property. However, it's a good idea to be certain of this before trying to use this information in the project, so you'll add a conditional statement to check if there is a songName property. If there is, it will display the name in the songTitle text field onstage.

3   Add the code to the `id3Handler()` function so that it reads:

```
function id3Handler(event:Event):void {
  var id3:ID3Info = snd.id3;
  if (id3.songName != null) {
    songTitle.text = id3.songName;
  }
}
```

4   Test the movie. Select a song. In addition to the song playing, the title should now appear at the top of the screen. Try other songs; the title will update automatically.

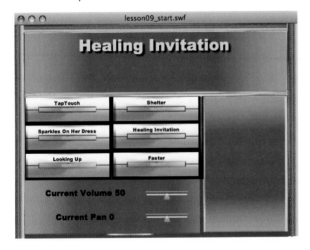

5   Close the lesson09_start.swf file to leave the testing environment.

Adding the Artist and Album information

If songName information is available in the ID3 tags, then you can assume that artist and album information will also be available. In your own projects, you may want to use additional conditional statements to check on the existence of data in each tag separately.

1 Add code to the id3Handler() function to set the info text field to display information using the artist and album properties. The final function should read:

```
function id3Handler(event:Event):void {
 var id3:ID3Info = snd.id3;
 if (id3.songName != null) {
  songTitle.text = id3.songName + "\n";
  info.text = "Artist: \n" + id3.artist + "\n \n";
  info.appendText("Album: \n" + id3.album);
  info.appendText("\n\n" + "Available at: \n" +
   ➥"passionrecords \n.com");
 }
}
```

This new code has a couple of things that you may not have encountered before. The first new line uses the tag \n to force new lines in a string of text in the text field.

The second and third new lines add text to the existing info text field with the appendText() method.

2 Test the movie. Now when a song is selected, in addition to the title appearing at the top, artist and album information from the ID3 tags as well as the string for the label's website appear in the info field on the right side.

3 Close the lesson09_start.swf file to leave the testing environment.

Adding a text format object

In Lesson 8, you learned to format text with the TextFormat class. You will now create a TextFormat instance and apply it to the info field. Since most of this code is familiar from Lesson 7, add it all at once.

1   With frame 1 of the `actions` layer still selected in the timeline, insert a new line in the Actions panel below all the existing code.

2   Create a new `TextFormat` instance, and set its properties with the following code:

```
var format:TextFormat = new TextFormat();
format.font = "Arial Black"; //If your computer does not have
//this font installed on it, use the installed font of
//your choice.
format.color = 0xFFFF00;
format.size = 14;
format.url = "http://www.passionrecords.com/";
```

If you completed Lesson 7, all of this code is familiar to you, with the exception of the `url` property of the `TextFormat` class. Setting the `url` property of a `TextFormat` instance is a very easy way to add a hyperlink to ActionScript formatted text. In this case, any text that has the `format` instance as its `TextFormat` property will go to www.passionrecords.com when clicked.

3   Apply the new format object to be the `defaultTextFormat` property of the info field by adding this line below all the existing code:

```
info.defaultTextFormat = format;
```

4   Test the movie. Choose a song and notice the formatting of the text on the right. Click that text. If you are connected to the Internet, your default browser should load and display www.passionrecords.com.

5   Close the lesson09_start.swf file to leave the testing environment.

Adding the slider controls

The last thing that you will add to this project is code to make the sliders control volume and panning of the currently playing song.

Like the List component that you used in Lesson 5, "Using ActionScript and Components to Load Content," the Slider component has a built-in CHANGE event that occurs whenever the user drags a slider's handle.

● **Note:** Many developers like to organize their files by placing all the addEventListener() calls in the same section of the file. If you would prefer to place the two lines that you just added with the rest of the addEventListener() methods for this file, feel free to cut and paste them below the addEventListener() methods for the six buttons that you created earlier. They will work exactly the same way in either location.

Below all the existing code for frame 1, create an addEventListener() method that listens for the CHANGE event for each onstage Slider instance:

```
volSlide.addEventListener(SliderEvent.CHANGE, volumeChange);
panSlide.addEventListener(SliderEvent.CHANGE, panChange);
```

Adding the volumeChange() and panChange() functions

When the user changes the volume (using the volume slider), a function named volumeChange() is called. Add the shell for that function below all the existing code for frame 1.

1   On a new line below all the existing code for frame 1, add the following code:

```
function volumeChange(e:SliderEvent):void {

}
```

The syntax e.target.value will describe the value that the slider gets moved to. This value will update the volLabel text field as well as set the volume of the Sound object.

2   Add two new lines to the volumeChange() function to update the volLabel's text property of volLabel to show the new volume setting. The function should now read:

```
function volumeChange(e:SliderEvent):void {
  currVol = e.target.value;
  volLabel.text = "Current Volume: " + int(currVol * 100);
}
```

To actually set the volume, you will use the slider's value to be the volume property of the SoundTransform instance named trans. Each time you update the properties of a SoundTransform instance, it needs to be reapplied to the SoundChannel instance to hear the change. The last line of this function will do that.

3   Add two more lines to the volumeChange() function to apply the slider's current value to be the volume of the playing song. The completed function should read:

```
function volumeChange(e:SliderEvent):void {
 currVol = e.target.value;
 volLabel.text = "Current Volume: " + int(currVol * 100);
 trans.volume = currVol;
 channel.soundTransform = trans;
}
```

Before you test the completed lesson file, add one final function, panChange().
This is very similar to the volumeChange() function, but uses the pan property
of the SoundTransform class.

4   Insert the panChange() function below all the existing code:

```
function panChange(e:SliderEvent):void {
 currPan = e.target.value;
 panLabel.text = "Current Pan " + int(currPan * 100);
 trans.pan = e.target.value;
 channel.soundTransform = trans;
}
```

5   Test the completed movie. Select a song and try sliding the volume and pan
controls. The volume slider should vary from silent to full volume, and, if you
have stereo speakers, you should hear the panning control send the sound from
the left speaker to the right.

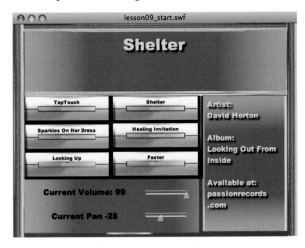

Congratulations—you now have the ability to create projects with full interactive
control over sound! This is a solid foundation on which you can build endless and
powerful variations.

Some suggestions to try on your own

There are a number of other ways to control sounds with ActionScript. You will see some of them in the coming lessons, but it would also be a good idea to consult the ActionScript 3.0 language reference found in Flash Help, especially reading through all the methods, properties, and events of the three sound-related classes used in this lesson. Play with some of the example code in the reference. In addition, here are a few suggestions for going deeper into using sound with ActionScript:

- Use the techniques covered in this lesson and add ID3 tags to your own MP3 files. Try replacing the sound files in the songList array of the lesson09_start.fla file with your MP3 files.

- Add information about some of the other ID3 tags in your MP3 files to the text fields onstage. Add additional text fields. For information on the names of other default tag names, see Flash Help.

- Create a new TextFormat object and set its properties to your taste. Set it to format the songTitle field at the top of the stage.

- Research the Microphone and SoundMixer classes in Flash Help. These two ActionScript 3.0 classes offer many other audio capabilities.

- Research the computeSpectrum() method of the SoundMixer class in Flash Help. This method can be used to create graphics from audio data.

- Research the Sound class's new sampleData event, which can be used to create new sounds entirely with ActionScript.

Review questions

1 What are three ActionScript classes you can use to load, play, and control an external audio file?

2 What are two properties of a sound file that can be controlled with the SoundTransform class?

3 What is a method of the TextField class that be used to replace text in a text field? What is a method to add to an existing text field?

4 What event of the Sound class can respond to the loading of text data from an MP3 file?

Review answers

1 The Sound class, the SoundChannel class, and the SoundTransform class all work together in ActionScript to load, play, and control sound files with ActionScript.

2 The SoundTransform class can control the volume and panning of sound with ActionScript.

3 The replace() method of the TextField class can find and replace text in a field. The appendText() method can concatenate text to a text field.

4 The ID3 event of the Sound class occurs when the ID3 text data of an MP3 file has successfully loaded.

10 WORKING WITH AN XML PLAYLIST

Lesson overview

In this lesson, you will learn to do the following:

- Understand the basic structure of an XML file.

- Understand how you can use XML in a Flash project.

- Create an XML object in Flash with ActionScript.

- Use the URLLoader class to load an external XML file.

- Respond to the COMPLETE and ERROR events of the URLLoader class.

- Access data in an XML file from Flash using the XML features of ActionScript 3.0.

- Use XML data to control a music player application.

 This lesson will take approximately 2 hours.

This lesson will show how to use the data in external XML files in a Flash project by taking advantage of the enhanced XML capabilities in ActionScript 3.0.

A music player powered by ActionScript and XML.

XML is a very easy-to-use markup language that has become a standard for organizing data. It is a tag-based language that is very similar to HTML; however, unlike HTML, XML does not have predefined tags and is therefore completely flexible—you can define your own tags to describe the data you are storing in an XML file.

In this lesson, you will work with an XML file that includes a playlist and song information that will drive the music player application that was created in Lesson 9, "Controlling Sound with ActionScript."

Understanding the basic structure of an XML file

XML files are really just text files with the suffix ".xml," so they can be created and edited with any application that supports text files.

ActionScript 3.0 has very strong support for XML. ActionScript 3.0 is based on the ECMAScript programming standard defined by the ECMA International standards committee. Part of this standard includes native support for XML. (To learn more about XML and ECMAScript, visit www.ecma-international.org/publications/standards/Ecma-357.htm.)

ActionScript 3.0 is capable of reading and writing XML. Common uses of XML in Flash projects include:

- Working with RSS feeds

- Creating podcasts

- Creating blogging applications

- Communicating with server software

- Creating captioned applications and subtitles

- Working with video and audio playlists

● **Note:** While it is possible to open an XML file directly in Flash, it is not recommended. Flash's default color-coding is based on ActionScript and can be misleading for XML.

To understand the basics of how an XML document is set up, open the XML file that you will use for this lesson: songlist.xml, from the Lessons > Lesson10 > Start folder. The figures in this lesson will show this file opened in Dreamweaver, but you can use any application that supports plain text files. If you do not own Dreamweaver but wish to use it to work with XML files, a free 30-day download is available at

https://www.adobe.com/cfusion/tdrc/index.cfm?promoid=BONQP&product=dreamweaver.

It is helpful to remember that the code in an XML file is not intended to *do* anything—XML files are used only to store and organize data. If you have worked with data in spreadsheets before, then much of XML's structure should be familiar to you.

The songlist.xml file has a simple structure but contains the basic format common to all XML files. The following figure shows songlist.xml open in Dreamweaver.

The first line of an XML file contains a declaration tag that tells parsers which version of XML and what type of encoding the file uses.

```
<?xml version="1.0" encoding="utf-8"?>
```

Since by default ActionScript ignores this line, you don't have to be too concerned with it for now.

The two lines below the first `<songList>` tag in the songlist.xml file are comments. These serve the same purpose as ActionScript comments (discussed in Lesson 9), which is to leave notes for yourself and others. Comments in an XML file are contained between the characters `<!--` and `-->`, as in:

```
<!-- This is an XML comment -->
<!-- similar to an HTML comment -->
```

ActionScript ignores XML comments by default, so you can too.

After those initial lines comes the body of the songlist.xml document, which is made up of tagged data. Every XML document used with ActionScript must have a single root pair of tags. In this case, that tag-pair is named songlist. As may look familiar to you, an opening tag in XML is contained within greater than and less than characters (for example, `<songlist>`) and a closing tag adds a forward slash

> ● **Note:** If you need to access XML comments using ActionScript, you can use the `ignoreComments()` method of the XML class. For more information, see the ActionScript 3.0 Language Reference.

after the less than character (`</songlist>`). All opening tags in XML must have a corresponding closing tag. Another word for a tag in XML is an *element*.

All the additional elements of the XML document are contained between the opening and closing root tags. In your own XML documents you can make up any names you want for the tags, which is the main reason the language is so versatile and useful.

XML is set up in a hierarchy of parent and child tags.

In the songlist.xml file, the `<songlist>` tag is the parent of all twelve sets of `<song>` tags (elements).

Each song element has five child elements. These elements are named file, name, artist, album, and itunes.

```
<song>
    <file>../MP3s/TapTouch.mp3</file>
    <name>Tap Touch</name>
    <artist>Jonathan Keezing</artist>
    <album>Taptouch</album>
    <itunes> http://phobos.apple.com/WebObjects/MZStore.woa/wa/viewAlbum?i=208135545&id=208135393&s=143441  </itunes>
</song>
```

Visualizing the various tags or elements in a table format may help you to understand the format of the songlist.xml file. Each song element could be considered the equivalent of a record, or entry, or a "row," in a spreadsheet or table. The child elements provide various values or information for each song element.

`<song>`	`<file>`	`<name>`	`<artist>`	`<album>`	`<itunes>`
`<song>`	../MP3s/TapTouch.mp3	Tap Touch	Jonathan Keezing	Taptouch	http://phobos.apple.com...
`<song>`	../MP3s/Healing Invitation.mp3	Healing Invitation	Chris Florio	Quartets and Quintets	http://phobos.apple.com...
`<song>`	>../MP3s/Faster.mp3	Faster	Chris Florio	Quartets and Quintets	http://phobos.apple.com...
`<song>`	>../MP3s/Shelter.mp3	Shelter	David Horton	Looking out from inside	http://phobos.apple.com...
`<song>`	>../MP3s/Sparkles On Her Dress.mp3	Sparkles on her Dress	Chris Florio	Butterfly/Gymsock	http://phobos.apple.com...
`<song>`	etc.				

An XML file can have as many levels of nested children as needed. This simple example just contains a series of song elements, each with its child elements. You can add as many song elements as you like by repeating the structure.

For now, close the songlist.xml file. Later, you'll load the data in this file into a Flash project using ActionScript.

Examining the starting file

This lesson will begin with a slightly modified version of the completed file from Lesson 9. You'll delete the array that was used to determine the songs available in the music player and instead use the data from the songlist.xml file. By getting this data from the XML file, you make it easy for anyone to add to or modify the song list without ever having to recreate or even open the existing Flash file.

1   Open the lesson10_start.fla file from the Lessons > Lesson10 > Start folder.

2   Open the Actions panel if it is not visible, and examine the code on frame 1 of the `actions` layer. If you completed Lesson 9, you will recognize the code from that lesson. With the exception of a few added comments for clarity, this is the same as the ActionScript in the completed version of Lesson 9.

3   Examine the stage. Notice that two new buttons have been added to the project. With the Properties panel visible, select the button in the lower-left that has the text "more songs." Notice that this button has the instance name more_btn. Since in the interface there are only six song choices visible at a time, you will add ActionScript to the file to allow the user to click this button to view additional songs.

4   Select the button in the upper-right of the stage that has Apple's iTunes logo. Notice in the Properties panel that this button has an instance name of link_btn. You will add ActionScript to the file so that when this button is clicked it will launch iTunes and navigate to the iTunes location of the song that is currently selected in the Flash project. The iTunes locations of these songs are stored as URLs in the songlist.xml document.

Now you can begin adding this new functionality to the file.

Replacing the songList array with an XML instance

As mentioned earlier, this project replaces the `songList` array from Lesson 9 with the contents of the songlist.xml file. You'll begin by deleting the array from the existing code.

1 With frame 1 of the `actions` layer selected, locate the `songList` array in the Actions panel.

2 Select the entire array (as well as related comments), and press Delete.

```
 8    //create variables to store values for the current song and it's volume and pan settings.
 9    var currSong:String;
10    var currVol:int;
11    var currPan:int;
12
13 ▼  // Array of all the songs in the current playlist.
14    var songList:Array=new Array("TapTouch.mp3","Sparkles On Her Dress.mp3","Looking Up.mp3",
   ▲  "Shelter.mp3","Healing Invitation.mp3","Faster.mp3");
15
```

Next, you will insert two new variables into the file. These will be used later on in the lesson to keep track of current songs.

3 In the Actions panel, on frame 1, locate the code that declares these variables:

```
var currSong:String;
var currVol:int;
var currPan:int;
```

4 Below this code, insert the following lines:

```
var songCount:int = 0;
var songNum:int;
```

Now you will create a new XML object that will be used to contain the data from the songlist.xml file and a URLLoader object to load the XML into Flash.

Creating new XML and URLLoader instances

The XML class is used to store XML data that has been created in a Flash project or loaded from an external XML file. The XML class also has methods and properties for working with XML data.

The class that is used for loading data into Flash is called the URLLoader class. If you completed Lesson 5, "Using ActionScript and Components to Load Content," you used the URLLoader class to load text into Flash from external files. In this lesson, you will use an instance of this class to load the songlist.xml file.

Add code to this project to create a new instance of the XML class and a new instance of the URLLoader class.

1   Locate the following variables declarations:

```
var currSong:String;
var currVol:int;
var currPan:int;
var songCount:int = 0;
var songNum:int;
```

2   Place the cursor below these lines, and press Enter to add a new line.

3   Add the following two lines of code:

```
var songList_XML:XML;
var xmlLoader:URLLoader = new URLLoader();
```

The songList_XML variable will contain the data from the songlist.xml file. That data has not loaded yet, so this variable has no initial value.

You have also created the xmlLoader variable and given it a new instance of the URLLoader class.

Loading an external playlist using the URLLoader class

The URLLoader uses the load() method to bring data from an external source into a Flash project. When URLLoader data is requested, events of the URLLoader class provide feedback that let you respond when data has loaded or in the case of an error.

This load() method requires one parameter: the URL of the data you wish to load. Often, as you saw in Lesson 2, "Working with Events and Functions," that parameter takes the form of a new URLRequest object. You will use the load() method to load the data from the songlist.xml file.

On a new line, below the line that reads:

```
var xmlLoader:URLLoader = new URLLoader();
```

insert the following code:

```
xmlLoader.load(new URLRequest("songlist.xml"));
```

● **Note:** When testing Flash projects that are on your local machine in a browser, you will occasionally get security errors. This depends on your Flash Player settings. These settings, as well as information on how to use them, can be accessed by right-clicking any Flash file that is playing in your browser and choosing Settings from the menu. Using Control > Test Movie should not present any security issues with the lesson files.

● **Note:** The line that you just added assumes you have a file named songlist.xml in the same folder as your Flash file (which you do). If the file that you wish to load is on a remote server, you would type the entire URL to that file as the URLRequest parameter.

Responding to COMPLETE and IO_ERROR events

The URLLoader has built-in events that give feedback on the loading of data. In this project, you will use two of them. The COMPLETE event fires once when the data that you have instructed it to load has successfully completed loading. You should always use the COMPLETE event to check that data is available before writing code that requires the use of that data! If for some reason the data fails to load, then the IO_Error event takes place. It is a good idea to listen for this event, to help you take into account situations where your users are unable to load data that might be an important part of your projects.

An additional URLLoader event—not used in this lesson but worth knowing about—is the PROGRESS event, which can be used to monitor the progress of larger files that may take a while to load.

You will add event listeners to this project for the COMPLETE and IO_ERROR events.

1   In the Actions panel, below the last line of code that you entered, add the following two addEventListener() methods:

```
xmlLoader.addEventListener(Event.COMPLETE, xmlLoaded);
xmlLoader.addEventListener(IOErrorEvent.IO_ERROR,
➥errorHandler);
```

If the songlist.xml file fails to load, then the listener you just added calls a function named errorHandler(). Now you will insert that function.

2   On a line below the code you just added in the previous section, insert the following code:

```
function errorHandler(event:IOErrorEvent):void {
 songTitle.text = "XML loading error: " + event;
}
```

Now, if an error occurs, an error message is placed in the songTitle text field in the upper part of the stage. In your own projects, you may want to use error events to take the user to alternate content that does not require the material that failed to load.

If the file loads successfully, the xmlLoaded() function will be called instead. This function performs much of the setup for the music player.

Start by adding the shell for this function.

3   Below the errorHandler() function, add the following code:

```
function xmlLoaded(event:Event):void {

}
```

Now that you know the songlist.xml data has loaded successfully, you can place that data in the XML instance you created previously.

4 Between the curly braces of the xmlLoaded() function, add the following line:

```
songList_XML = new XML(xmlLoader.data);
```

Now all the elements from the songlist.xml file can be accessed from within the songList_XML instance. And now that you can be confident that the XML data is loaded and stored, you will copy some of the existing ActionScript from the previous lesson into the xmlLoaded() function, sure in the knowledge that code requiring the XML elements will not execute until the XML data is available.

Moving the event listeners into the xmlLoaded() function

Right now this file has six addEventListener() methods—one for each of the song clips onstage. They are currently set to start listening as soon as the file launches. It will be safer to put them in the xmlLoaded() function so that the clip listeners won't be active until the song list data is available.

1 Below the code that you just added, locate the following lines:

```
song1.addEventListener(MouseEvent.CLICK, chooseSong);
song2.addEventListener(MouseEvent.CLICK, chooseSong);
song3.addEventListener(MouseEvent.CLICK, chooseSong);
song4.addEventListener(MouseEvent.CLICK, chooseSong);
song5.addEventListener(MouseEvent.CLICK, chooseSong);
song6.addEventListener(MouseEvent.CLICK, chooseSong);
```

2 Select all this code, and cut it (Edit > Cut) to the clipboard.

3 Place the cursor above the closing brace of the xmlLoaded() function, and paste the code. The xmlLoaded() function should now read:

```
function xmlLoaded(event:Event):void {
songList_XML = new XML(xmlLoader.data);

song1.addEventListener(MouseEvent.CLICK, chooseSong);
song2.addEventListener(MouseEvent.CLICK, chooseSong);
song3.addEventListener(MouseEvent.CLICK, chooseSong);
song4.addEventListener(MouseEvent.CLICK, chooseSong);
song5.addEventListener(MouseEvent.CLICK, chooseSong);
song6.addEventListener(MouseEvent.CLICK, chooseSong);

}
```

Creating the setSongs() function

The other thing that should not occur until the XML data has loaded is the labeling of the onstage song clips. This is now taking place inside a `for` loop below the code you just added. The loop currently reads:

```
for(var i = 0; i < songList.length; i++) {
  var str:String = songList[i] as String;
  str = str.replace(".mp3", "");
  var clip = this["song" + (i + 1)].title;
  clip.text = str;
}
```

You will modify this code so that it gets its information from the XML data, and move it into a new function called `setSongs()`. You will then call this function when the XML data is loaded.

1 Below the closing brace of the `xmlLoaded()` function, add the shell for the `setSongs()` function:

```
function setSongs():void {

}
```

2 Locate the `for` loop below the `setSongs()` function. It currently reads:

```
for(var i = 0; i < songList.length; i++) {
  var str:String = songList[i] as String;
  str = str.replace(".mp3", "");
  var clip = this["song" + (i + 1)].title;
  clip.text = str;
}
```

3 Select the entire `for` loop, and cut it (Edit > Cut) to the clipboard.

4 Paste the code between the curly braces of the `setSongs()` function. The `setSongs()` function should now read:

```
function setSongs():void {
for(var i = 0; i < songList.length; i++) {
  var str:String = songList[i] as String;
  str = str.replace(".mp3", "");
  var clip = this["song" + (i + 1)].title;
  clip.text = str;
}
}
```

Be sure you have the correct number of curly braces in this function, remembering that both the `for` loop and the function itself require closing braces.

Now, taking one line at a time, modify this `for` loop to work with the XML array.

The first line of the `for` loop now reads:

```
for(var i = 0; i < songList.length; i++) {
```

This was appropriate when you were working with an array whose `length` property represented the only six songs that were available for play in the Lesson 9 project. However, now this project uses an external XML file that can be modified to store an indefinite number of songs. The `length` of the songlist no longer necessarily corresponds with the six song choices.

The purpose of this `for` loop is to set the song clip's text fields to the currently available songs. Since there only six clips, you will set the `for` loop to simply repeat six times.

5 Change the first line of the `for` loop to read:

```
for(var i = 0; i < 6; i++) {
```

Accessing song title and artist from the XML data

The second line of the `for` loop you are working with currently reads:

```
var str:String = songList[i] as String;
```

The `str` variable stored the names of the songs from the `songList` array that you removed. The XML file contains significantly more information than the array, and you be working with some of it soon. The first modification of this line is a simple name change that makes this variable's purpose clearer.

1 Change the variable name `str` to `titleText`. The line should now read:

```
var titleText:String = songList[i] as String;
```

2 Change the value of the `titleText` variable to take the song-title information from the XML `name` property.

```
var titleText:String = songList_XML.song[i].name;
```

Since artist information is available from the XML data in the same manner, it makes sense to create an additional variable to store that information.

3 Select and copy (Edit > Copy) the line that currently reads:

```
var titleText:String = songList_XML.song[i].name;
```

4 On the line directly below the line you just copied, paste a new copy of the line.

5 Change the new copy of the line to read:

```
var artistText:String = songList_XML.song[i].artist;
```

About XMLLists and accessing data from XML elements

The code that you just inserted:

```
var titleText:String = songList_XML.song[i].name;
```

takes advantage of a number of very useful features in ActionScript 3.0 for working with XML data.

Recall that the original songlist.xml file contained a series of song elements, each including a set of elements.

In ActionScript, you can access elements in XML data using the same dot notation that you would use for other ActionScript paths.

The XML instance in which the XML data was stored takes the place of the root element of the XML file. The child elements of the XML file can be accessed with dots. For example, to access the song elements of the XML data you are working with, you would write:

```
songList_XML.song
```

Requesting `songList_XML.song` would access all 12 separate song elements in this file. When there are repeating elements in XML data, ActionScript 3.0 automatically stores them in what is called an XMLList. An XMLList works very similarly to an array. (For a review of arrays in ActionScript, see Lessons 7 through 9.)

For example, if you wish to access the first song element in the songList_XML data, you could write:

```
songList_XML.song[0]
```

If you want to get the value stored in the name tag of the third song element, you could write:

```
songList_XML.song[2].name
```

This makes working with XML data very similar to the ways that you have already worked with other data. If you reexamine the for loop as it stands now:

```
for(var i = 0; i < 6; i++) {
var titleText:String = songList_XML.song.[i].name;
}
```

it is apparent that the loop will one at time store the names of the first six song elements in the XML data.

The entire `for` loop should now read:

```
for(var i = 0; i < 6; i++) {
 var titleText:String = songList_XML.song[i].name;
 var artistText:String = songList_XML.song[i].artist;
 str = str.replace(".mp3", "");
 var clip = this["song" + (i + 1)].title;
 clip.text = str;
}
```

Setting the song clips' title and artist fields

The last three lines of code in the `for` loop were used to set the text fields in the Lesson 9 project. These need to be modified for the XML version of the project.

The first of these three lines now reads:

```
str = str.replace(".mp3", "");
```

This code was used in the previous lesson to remove the file suffix (.mp3) from the array elements. This is no longer needed, since the filename and song title are separate elements in the XML data.

1 Select and delete the line that reads:

```
str = str.replace(".mp3", "");
```

The next line reads:

```
var clip = this["song" + (i + 1)].title;
```

This is used to store the path to the text field named title in the individual song clips. If you recall from Lesson 9, each time the `for` loop repeats, it evaluates this line to return `song1.title`, `song2.title`, `song3.title`, and so on. There is still a need to set the titles, but since you will also set the artists in this example, the only change you will make to this line is to change the name of the variable.

2 In the line that reads:

```
var clip = this["song" + (i + 1)].title;
```

change the name of the variable from `clip` to `clipTitle` so the line now reads:

```
var clipTitle = this["song" + (i + 1)].title;
```

The onstage clips named *song1* through *song6* have text fields inside of them with an instance name of title. The `clipTitle` variable will be used to set their text properties. These clips also have a second text field named artist, so create a second variable to store the path to those text fields. Since this path is nearly identical to the one you just created, you can copy and paste the previous line.

3 Select and copy the line you just modified, which currently reads:

```
var clipTitle = this["song" + (i + 1)].title;
```

4 On a new line below the line you copied, paste a new version of this line.

5 Modify the new line so that it reads:

```
var clipArtist = this["song" + (i + 1)].artist;
```

The for loop should now read:

```
for(var i = 0; i < 6; i++) {
 var titleText:String = songList_XML.song[i].name;
 var artistText:String = songList_XML.song[i].artist;
 var clipTitle = this["song" + (i + 1)].title;
 var clipArtist = this["song" + (i + 1)].artist;
 clip.text = str;
}
```

The final line within the brackets of the for loop sets the song clips' title text fields to the names of the songs gathered from the XML data. Since the variable that stores references to the song clips was changed from clip to clipTitle and the variable that stores the song names was changed from str to titleText, update the code to reflect these changes.

6 Change the code that currently reads:

```
clip.text = str;
```

so that it reads:

```
clipTitle.text = titleText;
```

This sets the titles of the individual song clips when the for loop runs. One final line in the for loop will do the same for the artist text in the song clips.

7 Below the line that reads:

```
clipTitle.text = titleText;
```

insert the following code:

```
clipArtist.text = artistText;
```

You will make a slight modification to this code later, but for now this completes the for loop as well as the setSongs() function. The entire function should now read:

```
function setSongs():void {
for(var i = 0; i < 6; i++) {
    var titleText:String = songList_XML.song[i].name;
    var artistText:String = songList_XML.song[i].artist;
    var clipTitle = this["song" + (i + 1)].title;
    var clipArtist = this["song" + (i + 1)].artist;
    clipTitle.text = titleText;
    clipArtist.text = artistText;
 }
}
```

Adding a call to the setSongs() function

The setSongs() function you just created needs to take place when the file is first launched, but not until after the XML data (which is used to set the songs) is available. You already have a function named xmlLoaded() that is called on the completion of the XML data being loaded; that would be a good place in which to call the setSongs() function.

1   In the Actions for frame 1, scroll up to locate the xmlLoaded() function.

2   Above the closing brace of this function, insert this line to call the setSongs() function:

```
setSongs();
```

The xmlLoaded() function should now read:

```
function xmlLoaded(event:Event):void {
 songList_XML = new XML(xmlLoader.data);

 song1.addEventListener(MouseEvent.CLICK, chooseSong);
 song2.addEventListener(MouseEvent.CLICK, chooseSong);
 song3.addEventListener(MouseEvent.CLICK, chooseSong);
 song4.addEventListener(MouseEvent.CLICK, chooseSong);
 song5.addEventListener(MouseEvent.CLICK, chooseSong);
 song6.addEventListener(MouseEvent.CLICK, chooseSong);

 setSongs();
}
```

There are quite a few more things to add to this project, but you only need one more in order to test the project—updating the switch statement that determines which song will be played when a song clip is clicked.

Updating the chooseSong() function

If you recall from Lesson 9, when any of the song clips (*song1* through *song6*) is clicked, the chooseSong() function is called. For this lesson's version of the project, most of this functionality will remain the same. The one thing that you will need to modify, to take into account the XML source of the song data, is the switch statement that determines the currently playing song.

1   Locate the switch statement in the chooseSong() function. The first few lines of this statement should read:

```
switch (e.currentTarget.name) {

 currSong = "../MP3s/" + songList[0] as String;
 break;
```

To keep track of the songs in the list, you'll give a different value (depending on which song clip is clicked) to the variable that you created earlier called songNum.

2 Below the line that reads:

```
case "song1":
```

add the following new line:

```
songNum = 0;
```

Very soon it will be clearer how this value will be used.

Notice that the currSong variable is still taking its value from the songList array that you deleted earlier. Update this value so that it now gets the current song from the XML data.

3 Change the line that reads:

```
currSong = "../MP3s/" + songList[0] as String;
```

so that it now reads:

```
currSong = songList_XML.song[songNum + songCount].file;
```

Notice that this is similar to the way that you retrieved the title and artist information for the song clips, only now you are retrieving the file element from the XML data. Since the value of songCount is initially 0, it will have no effect when added to songNum at this point. However, you will make use of this variable soon.

The first condition in the switch statement should now read:

```
case "song1":
songNum = 0;
currSong = songList_XML.song[songNum + songCount].file;
break;
```

4 Update the rest of the switch statement in a similar manner. The full switch statement should read:

```
switch (e.currentTarget.name) {
 case "song1":
   songNum = 0;
   currSong = songList_XML.song[songNum + songCount].file;
   break;

 case "song2":
   songNum = 1;
   currSong = songList_XML.song[songNum + songCount].file;
   break;
```

```
    case "song3":
     songNum = 2;
     currSong = songList_XML.song[songNum + songCount].file;
     break;

    case "song4":
     songNum = 3;
     currSong = songList_XML.song[songNum + songCount].file;
     break;

    case "song5":
     songNum = 4;
     currSong = songList_XML.song[songNum + songCount].file;
     break;

    case "song6":
     songNum = 5;
     currSong =s ongList_XML.song[songNum + songCount].file;
     break;
    }
```

You should now be able to test the file without getting error messages.

5 Test the movie to see the results so far.

The file should now work approximately the way that it did at the end of Lesson 9. The buttons should load and play the associated songs when clicked, and the volume and pan sliders should still work, with the ID3 tags displaying the same information as before. As a matter of fact, the only difference in this file for the user so far is that the artist's name appears on the song clips and there are two onscreen buttons that don't do anything yet ("more songs" and "Buy on iTunes").

That was a lot of effort to get a file that does about the same as when you started. But you should congratulate yourself—you are now able to integrate XML data into a Flash project! You will soon add some new functionality to this project that uses some of the other data in the XML file.

Next, you will create the code to make the two additional buttons onstage functional.

Creating hyperlinks using XML data

The XML data that you loaded into the Lesson 10 file contains a link element with a URL for the location of each song on iTunes. The link_btn in the upper-right corner of the Flash stage will use ActionScript's `navigateToURL()` method with the link element's URL data to create a hyperlink for each song. In order for these links to work, the user must have iTunes installed on their machine.

1   In the Actions for frame 1 of the lesson10start.fla file, locate the `addEventListener()` methods in the `xmlLoaded()` function.

2   On a line below the existing `addEventListener()` methods for the six song clips, insert a new `addEventListener()` for the link_btn with the following code:

```
link_btn.addEventListener(MouseEvent.CLICK, iTunesLink);
```

When the link_btn is clicked, it will call a function called `iTunesLink()`, which you will now create.

3   Scroll to the end of the code for frame 1 and, below all the existing code, add the shell for the `iTunesLink()` function:

```
function iTunesLink(e:MouseEvent):void {

}
```

You access the iTunes element of the XML data similarly to the way you accessed the name, artist, and file elements.

4   Within the braces of the `iTunesLink()` function, add this line:

```
var link:String = songList_XML.song[songNum + songCount].
➥itunes;
```

Which itunes element from the XML data will be used is determined by adding the number stored in the `songNum` variable to the number in the `songCount` variable. Recall that the `switch` statement sets the `songNum` variable based on which song clip the user selected. Up until this point `songCount` equals 0, so the link element will match the song clip that was selected (you will work more with `songCount` soon).

Once the appropriate link from the XML data has been stored in the `link` variable, you can use that variable in a `navigateToURL()` method to create the actual hyperlink.

5 On a line above the closing brace of the `iTunesLink()` function, add the following code:

```
navigateToURL(new URLRequest(link), "_blank");
```

This code will open the URL stored in the `link` variable, and the link itself will launch iTunes and go to the appropriate location. The full function should read:

```
function iTunesLink(e:MouseEvent):void {
 var link:String = songList_XML.song[songNum + songCount].
   ➥itunes;
 navigateToURL(new URLRequest(link), "_blank");
}
```

6 Test the movie. Select a song, and then click the iTunes link. If iTunes is installed on your machine, it should open and automatically navigate to the page for the song you selected.

In the final step of this lesson, you'll add code for the button in the lower left of the stage that contains the text "more songs". This code will make it possible for the Flash project to display and play as many songs as you wish to include in the XML file.

Navigating through the song list

The more_btn will be used to display additional songs from the songlist.xml file in the onstage song clips. When there are no more songs in the songList data to display, then the list will repeat, so that the user can click this button repeatedly to cycle through the song list.

First add a new listener for this button.

1   In the Actions for frame 1 of the lesson10_start.fla file, locate the addEventListener() methods within the xmlLoaded() function.

    Below the existing addEventListener() methods, add the following line:

    ```
    more_btn.addEventListener(MouseEvent.CLICK, moreSongs);
    ```

    This calls a function named moreSongs() when the button is clicked—the final function for this lesson, which you'll add now.

2   Below all the existing code for this project, add the shell for the moreSongs() function:

    ```
    function moreSongs(e:MouseEvent):void {


    }
    ```

    To understand what moreSongs() needs to do requires a little review of the functionality already in this file. When the user clicks one of the six buttons onstage, a switch statement is called. The switch statement determines which song will be played, using the number associated with the selected song clip. That number is stored in a variable called songNum. If you recall, it also adds the value of the songCount variable to that number. By default, songCount is zero, so it has no effect on which song is selected.

    The reason for the more songs button is to allow the user to select from more than six songs. It does this by incrementing the songCount value. Each time the user clicks more songs (more_btn), the songCount value increases by one. When this button is pressed (one time), then the songCount goes from 0 to 1, and the six buttons—instead of selecting songs 0 through 5—will select songs 1 through 6. If the songCount variable equals 5, then songs 5 through 10 will be selected. A conditional statement will be added to the moreSongs() function to make sure that the songCount never exceeds the total number of songs in the XML data minus six (the number of buttons onstage for selecting songs).

3   Add code to the moreSongs() function so that it reads:

    ```
    function moreSongs(e:MouseEvent):void {

      if(songCount < songList_XML.song.name.length() - 6) {
        songCount++;
    ```

```
  } else {
    songCount = 0;
  }
}
```

4 Test the movie. Click one of the song buttons. Now click the more songs button. Again, click the same song button you originally clicked. This time, a different song should play. Press the more songs button once more, and then press the same song button again; a totally different song plays. However, the labels on the buttons are not yet changing! This is a problem with an easy solution.

Updating the song buttons

The setSongs() method is where the song labels are being assigned, so that is where we will go to fix our label problem.

1 In the code for frame 1 of the actions layer, locate the setSongs() function and find these lines:

```
var titleText:String = songList_XML.song[i].name;
var artistText:String = songList_XML.song[i].artist;
```

Because these two lines are within a for loop set to repeat six times, these lines are always going to set the labels of the song clips from the first six songs in the XML data, because the value of the variable i will always loop from 0 to 5.

However, if you add the value of the songCount variable to i, then when the more songs button is clicked, the song and artist labels will increment to match the songs in the XML data.

2 Alter the two lines in Step 1 so that they read:

```
var titleText:String = songList_XML.song[i + songCount].name;
var artistText:String = songList_XML.song[i + songCount].
➥artist;
```

To update the song-clip labels each time the more_btn is clicked, you call the setSongs() function within the moreSongs() function.

3 Scroll all the way back down to the moreSongs() function and, above the closing brace, add the following line to call the setSongs() function:

```
setSongs();
```

The full moreSongs() function should now read:

```
function moreSongs(e:MouseEvent):void {
  if(songCount < songList_XML.song.name.length() - 6) {
    songCount++;
  } else {
    songCount = 0;
  }
  setSongs();
}
```

4   Test the movie once more. Now when you click the more songs button, all the labels will update. If you click enough times and go through all the songs in the XML data, it returns to the original songs, allowing for a continuous loop through the *song list*.

No matter how many songs are added to the songlist.xml file, the ActionScript will continue to work and navigate through all the songs. This means that by using XML, once a project is built, all you need to do in order to add and remove content from the project is to change the XML file.

The same principle that was applied here for a music player can be used for any type of content or data. You will apply this in the next lesson using video content.

Some suggestions to try on your own

Here are a few things you can do on your own in order to get more comfortable with some of the techniques introduced in this lesson.

- Try adding additional song elements to the songlist.xml file, making sure each element has the same child elements as the existing songs do.

- Add additional children to all the song elements in the songlist.xml file. For example, you could add elements for genre, time, rating, and so on.

- Try placing your own version of this file on a server and loading the files from that server. Use your favorite ftp software to modify the songlist.xml file on the server.

- Create multiple XML files with different playlists, create buttons that let the user choose which XML files determine the playlist that is used. For example, create playlists for different artists or musical styles.

- Add an event listener for the PROGRESS event of the URLLoader instance in this lesson. Try tracing a message to the output window as the loading progresses.

- Use the navigateToURL() and URLRequest() methods to create links to other online content associated with artists in your XML playlists.

- Create your own XML files based on the structure of the songlist.xml file. Try loading and using that data in a Flash project.

Review questions

1 What is another term for an XML tag?

2 What is the main class for working with XML in ActionScript 3.0?

3 What class can be used to load data in ActionScript 3.0?

4 Name and describe three events of the URLLoader class.

5 In XML data that has multiple versions of the same element, how can ActionScript access a specific element?

Review answers

1 Another term for an XML tag is an element.

2 The main class in ActionScript 3.0 for working with XML is the XML class (not exactly a trick question).

3 The load() method of the URLLoader class can be used to load data into a Flash project.

4 The COMPLETE event of the URLLoader class is triggered by the successful loading of requested data. The IO_ERROR event is triggered if the requested data fails to load. As data is loading, the PROGRESS event is repeatedly triggered while data is loading.

5 ActionScript uses dot notation and Array notation (square brackets) to locate the individual elements of an XML list. For example, to locate the title child element of the third song element in XML data, you could refer to it in ActionScript as:

```
song[2].title
```

11 USING ACTIONSCRIPT AND COMPONENTS TO CONTROL VIDEO

Lesson overview

In this lesson, you will learn to do the following:

- Use the FLVPlayback component to work with Flash video files.

- Set the properties of the FLVPlayback component in the Component Inspector.

- Set the properties of the FLVPlayback component with ActionScript.

- Use the FLVCaptioning component.

- Work with a Timed-Text XML file for video captions.

- Use the ColorPicker component to set the background color of a video skin.

- Use the Slider component to adjust the transparency of a video skin.

- Create ActionScript that responds when a video file is finished playing.

- Create ActionScript that works with an XML video playlist.

- Work with the Allow Full Screen template to view full-screen video in a browser.

This lesson will take approximately 2.5 hours.

In the last few years, Flash video has exploded in popularity to become the dominant video format for the web. It is extremely easy to get started working with Flash video. Adobe Flash CS4 Professional

A video player with customizable controls connected
to an XML playlist.

ships with all the tools needed to create Flash video files and integrate them into Flash projects. You can place video in a Flash file and give the user video-player controls without using any ActionScript. However, integrating ActionScript with Flash video will offer vast creative possibilities. This lesson will introduce quite a few ActionScript techniques for working with the video components that ship with Flash CS4. Keep in mind that entire books have been written about ActionScript and Flash video. We hope the techniques in this lesson will inspire you to pursue the subject more deeply.

Examining the Lesson11 folder contents

This lesson will be created largely from external media and data files and from Flash CS4 components. You will use ActionScript to connect all these pieces together to create a simple video player application.

If you open the Lessons > Lesson11 folder, you will see that in addition to the Start and Complete folders, there is a folder called video. This folder contains seven F4V files. F4V is Adobe's version of the industry standard H.264 video format.

The Lessons > Lesson11 > Start folder contains two XML files and an FLA file. The captions.xml file will be used with a component in Flash to create synchronized subtitles for a video clip. The vidlist.xml file will work similarly to the way you used the songlist.xml file in Lesson 10, "Working with an XML Playlist," and will supply filenames and information about a list of video clips to be played in your project.

The actual Flash file for this lesson contains no precreated material. Open the Lessons > Lesson11 > Start > lesson11_start.fla file. You will create most of the Flash content for this project using Flash components. All the components and text that you will add to this file will be placed in the empty layer named content, and all the code will go in the actions layer.

F4V and FLV video files

F4V is one of two native Flash video file formats, the other being FLV. While F4V files tend to give better image quality than FLV files of the same size, F4V files also require that your users have a more recent version of Flash Player (9.0.115 or later) and a faster processor. Also, F4V files do not support alpha channels. If you have video experience and are used to working with H.264 files with other suffixes (.mp4, .mov), you can use some but not all of them with Flash. For more information on the F4V format, visit www.adobe.com/devnet/flv.

The FLV format does support full alpha channel transparency (with On2VP6 compression), and FLV video files will work as far back as Flash Player 7. FLV files also tend to perform better than F4V on older machines. Flash CS4 Professional and the Adobe Media Encoder that ships with Flash can create both FLV and F4V files, making it easy to use whichever format is more appropriate for your projects.

Adding the FLVPlayback component

One of the most powerful components to ship with Flash CS4 is the FLVPlayback component. While it is possible to play and manipulate external video files in Flash without this component, the FLVPlayback component contains all the functionality most users need for working with Flash video, and in fact is often the best way to work with video. You can use an FLVPlayback instance to play and manipulate any external FLV or F4V file. The FLVPlayback class in ActionScript is associated with the FLVPlayback component and has an extensive number of methods, properties, and events for working with video. It is worth a serious study if you are interested in interactive video. We will look at some of the ActionScript tools for working with the FLVPlayback component soon, but first let's look at how much can be done without any code.

1   With the stage visible and the first frame of the content layer selected, open the Components panel (Window > Components).

2   From the Video folder of the Components panel, locate the FLVPlayback component.

Note: Your default playback controls may vary.

3 Drag an instance of the FLVPlayback component to the lower-right of the stage.

4 In the Properties panel, give the onstage FLVPlayback component the instance name **vidPlayer**.

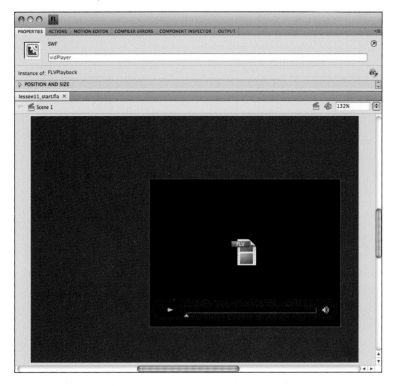

Setting FLVPlayback properties in Flash

As mentioned earlier, much of the video functionality required by the average project can be accomplished easily without code, using Flash's intuitive Component Inspector to set common properties. In the case of the FLVPlayback component, the Component Inspector offers the ability to choose the initial video file that will play in the component as well as set the type of controls with which the user can manipulate the video, and even what the controls will look like. Even on projects where you plan to manipulate these settings with ActionScript, it's very convenient to be able set the initial values in the interface. This is what you will do now.

1 With the vidPlayer component selected onstage, open the Component Inspector if it is not already visible (Window > Component Inspector).

As you can see in the figure, there are many properties that can be set for the video and its playback. You will leave most of these settings at their defaults, but a few you will set now. Keep in mind that all these settings can also be controlled with ActionScript. The most important setting for the FLVPlayback component is the one that determines which video file will play in the component. This is the `source` property.

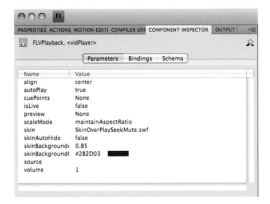

2 In the Component Inspector, select the field to the right of the `source` property.

When this field is selected, a magnifying glass icon appears.

3 Click the magnifying glass icon, browse to the Lessons > Lesson11 > video folder, and select the Solution5.f4v file. After choosing this video file and clicking OK, the path to the video file that you selected will appear to the right of the `source` property.

4 Test the movie. The video that you selected will play inside the FLVPlayback component.

The set of controls that the user is given for an instance of the FLVPlayback component are known as the component's *skin*. Unless you consciously set the `skin` property of this component, the controls that appear for the video will be whatever skin was last selected and may not be what you want for your project. So those are what you will set next.

Setting the FLVPlayback controls

Flash CS4 ships with a large number of prebuilt sets of video controls that can be associated with instances of the FLVPlayback component. These *skins* are set with the `skin` property of the FLVPlayback component, either in the Component Inspector or with ActionScript. For now, you will set the initial skin in the Component Inspector.

1 With the `vidPlayer` instance still selected and the Component Inspector still visible, locate the `skin` property, and select the field to the right of the property.

Again, a magnifying glass icon will appear.

2 Select the magnifying glass icon to open the Select Skin dialog box.

3 In the drop-down list that appears in the Select Skin dialog box, navigate to and select the SkinUnderAll.swf skin, and then click OK.

About FLVPlayback skin files

The skins that appear in the Skin Select dialog box are actually SWF files created to work with the FLVPlayback component. All these SWF files, as well as the original FLA files from which they were made, are installed on your hard drive when you install Flash CS4 Professional. There are many variations of the possible controls; the filenames describe the controls each contains. For example, the skin named SkinOverPlayMuteCaptionFull.swf contains controls that appear directly "over" the video file. This skin will give the user control over playing the video and muting the audio as well as toggling on and off captions and viewing in full-screen mode. The skin you selected in this exercise, SkinUnderAll.swf, appears "under" the video and contains "all" the possible controls for the FLVPlayback component.

You will soon see that it's simple to modify the color and transparency of these prebuilt skins. If the overall design of these skins doesn't match the intended look of your project, you can also very easily create your own custom-designed skins that offer the same functionality as the built-in skins. For more information, see Flash Help or visit the video section of the Flash developer site at www.adobe.com/devnet/video/.

Setting skin color and transparency

Next you will set the color and transparency of the skin for your video—first in the Component Inspector, but then using ActionScript, to give users the ability to change these properties while the project is running.

1. With the `vidPlayer` component still selected, locate the `skinBackground` color property in the Component Inspector, and double-click the color chip to the right of the property name.

2. Select the color that you want your video controls to be.

3. Select the `skinBackgroundAlpha` property, and enter a value between 0 and 1 to set the transparency of the color that you selected. A good initial setting would be between .7 and 1. Remember that a setting of 0 would mean that the background color you selected would not be visible.

4. Test the movie again. The video will play once more, but this time with the skin that you selected and with your color and transparency choices.

   Try some of the video controls. You should be able play and pause the video, scrub it, and adjust the volume of the audio. Notice that at this point the two controls on the far right, which are for toggling on and off captions and full-screen mode, don't do anything. You will add that functionality later in the lesson.

5. Close the lesson11_start.swf file to leave the testing environment.

Adding ActionScript control of FLVPlayback properties

Using ActionScript to set any of the properties of an FLVPlayback instance is as simple as setting the properties of a MovieClip or any other ActionScript class. For example, to set the `rotation` property of a MovieClip instance named *clip1* to 90 degrees, you would write:

```
clip1.rotation = 90;
```

Similarly, if you wanted to set the `source` property of an FLVPlayback instance named `vid1` to play a movie named *vid1.f4v*, you could write:

```
vid1.source = "vd1.flv";
```

Keeping this in mind, if you know the available properties for the `FLVPlayback` class (many of which you have already seen in the Component Inspector), then you can easily look up their possible values in Flash Help and control them with ActionScript.

Remember, when you want to set a property only once and leave it that way, you can do this in the Component Inspector, but when you want to make a property dynamic and interactive, then use ActionScript. As an example, you will use two UI components—the Slider and the ColorPicker—to let the user change the settings for the color and transparency of the FLVPlayback skin.

Adding a slider to control transparency

If you completed Lessons 9 and 10, then you are already familiar with the Slider Component and its use. It will be easy at this point to use the same technique for the `skinBackgroundAlpha` property of your video player.

1 Open the Components panel if it is not already visible.

2 From the User Interface components folder, select the Slider component.

3 With the `contents` layer of the timeline selected, drag an instance of the Slider component to the upper-left area of the stage.

4 In the Properties panel, give the new Slider component the instance name of **alphaSlide**.

5 With the `alphaSlide` instance selected, make the Component Inspector visible (Window > Component Inspector).

6 Set the `minimum` property of the `alphaSlide` to 0 and the `maximum` to 1. Remember this is the same as the range of the `skinBackgroundAlpha` property.

7 Set the other settings for the `alphaSlide` instance as they appear in the following image.

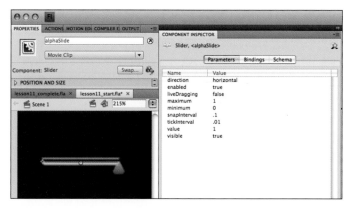

Now you'll create a text element to give the user a clue about the intended purpose of this slider.

8 Select the Text tool from the Tools panel and drag out a text field above the slider.

9 Type **Video Player Transparency** or a similar phrase in the text field.

10 Since this text will be for display only, set the text type to Static from the dropdown list in the Properties panel. Set the font style and color of the text any way that you wish.

Next, you'll add the ActionScript to make the slider work.

Adding the initial slider ActionScript

If you recall from Lesson 9, "Controlling Sound with ActionScript," before you can work with the Slider component in ActionScript, the `SliderEvent` class needs to be imported.

1 With frame 1 of the `actions` layer selected, and the Actions panel open, insert the following code on the first line of the Actions panel:

```
import fl.events.SliderEvent;
```

Since you will be using a number of other classes soon that also require being imported, this is a good time to add those additional `import` statements.

2 Below the line you just typed, add the following code:

```
import fl.controls.ColorPicker;
import fl.events.ColorPickerEvent;
import fl.video.FLVPlayback;
import fl.video.VideoEvent;
```

Now you will be ready to work with the FLVPlayback classes and the ColorPicker component, but first let's finish the code for the `alphaSlide` component.

If you recall from Lesson 9, the CHANGE event is what responds when the user moves a Slider instance. Add this event to your code.

3 On the line below the existing code, add the following line:

```
alphaSlide.addEventListener(SliderEvent.CHANGE, alphaChange);
```

The code for the `alphaChange()` function should be familiar to you from similar code you have used in previous lessons.

4 Add the `alphaChange()` function below the line you just added by typing:

```
function alphaChange(e:SliderEvent):void {
 vidPlayer.skinBackgroundAlpha = e.target.value;
}
```

As with the Slider components you worked with in previous lessons, the value that the user drags the slider to (`e.target.value`) is what is used to set a specific property, in this case the `skinBackgroundAlpha` property of the flvPlayer component.

5   Test your movie. While the video is playing, scrub the slider. Each time you release it, the color of the skin background should fade in or out accordingly.

6   Close the lesson11_start.swf file to leave the testing environment.

Next you will use an additional component to let the user choose a color for the video controls.

Working with color

You may use color pickers regularly in many applications without really thinking about it. In fact, if you do any design work in Flash, you probably use a color picker to choose fill, stroke, or text colors. With the ColorPicker component in Flash, you can easily add this functionality to your own projects. For this lesson, you will add a standard color picker with the basic settings, but in other projects you can use ActionScript to modify the ColorPicker component in many ways, including offering your users custom palettes with as many colors as you wish.

Adding the ColorPicker component

Like the Slider and other components, ColorPicker fires off the CHANGE event when the user makes a change to a component instance—in this case, when the user selects a new color.

1 With the `contents` layer of the timeline selected, and the Components panel visible, locate the ColorPicker component in the User Interface folder.

2 Drag an instance of the ColorPicker to the stage above the `alphaSlide` component.

3 In the Properties panel, give the new ColorPicker component the instance name of **colorChoose**.

4 Place descriptive text by the `colorChoose` instance by copying and pasting the text that you placed by the slider and changing the wording to read **Video Player Color** or the equivalent. Position the text near the `colorChoose` instance.

5 Test the movie. The color picker responds when you click it because this is the component's built-in behavior, but the color you choose will not be applied to anything. You will set that next with ActionScript.

6 Close the lesson11_start.swf file to leave the testing environment.

Setting the skinBackgroundColor

As mentioned earlier, the CHANGE event is what is listened for to determine when the user has selected a color. You've already set up the CHANGE event; now you'll insert the listener.

1 In the Actions panel, add the following code below the existing code for frame 1 of the `actions` layer:

```
colorChoose.addEventListener(ColorPickerEvent.CHANGE,
➥changeHandler);
```

2 Now add the `changeHandler()` function below that with this code:

```
function changeHandler(e:ColorPickerEvent):void {
var cp:ColorPicker = e.currentTarget as ColorPicker;
vidPlayer.skinBackgroundColor = Number("0x" + cp.hexValue);
}
```

Much of this should be starting to look familiar.

It is important to note that in both lines within the function's braces, the data type of the value that is set is specifically indicated.

About casting to a data type

There are many situations where ActionScript will not recognize data as being in the format in which would like to use it. For example, ActionScript might be treating data as a string of literal characters when you want it to be treated as a Number. Or maybe you want to take a list of MovieClips from an array, but ActionScript doesn't recognize the objects listed in the array as MovieClips. Telling ActionScript that specific data should be recognized as belonging to a certain data type is called *casting*. In earlier lessons, you have already written code that has cast data, but it's worth taking a closer look at the two main ways of casting in ActionScript. The function you just wrote uses both techniques.

In the line of the `changeHandler()` function that says:

```
var cp:ColorPicker = e.currentTarget as ColorPicker;
```

e.currentTarget is the item that triggers the function, and it is explicitly identified or cast as the data type ColorPicker. In this line, the ActionScript keyword as is used to indicate that the preceding term should be cast as a specific type of data—in this case, "as" a ColorPicker.

Similarly, in the second line:

```
vidPlayer.skinBackgroundColor = Number("0x" + cp.hexValue);
```

the skinBackGround color is selected by combining in parentheses the literal characters "0x" (remember 0x identifies a hexadecimal color in ActionScript) with the hexadecimal value that the user chooses from the color picker. This combined phrase is cast as a Number. This is an example of the other way that data can be cast to a data type.

Most of the time these two casting techniques can be used interchangeably. There are a few situations such as when casting arrays that the first technique (using the as keyword) should be used. If you are not certain which to use, then use the as type of casting.

Your code so far should read:

```
import fl.events.SliderEvent;
import fl.controls.ColorPicker;
import fl.events.ColorPickerEvent;
import fl.video.FLVPlayback;
import fl.video.VideoEvent;

alphaSlide.addEventListener(SliderEvent.CHANGE, alphaChange);

function alphaChange(e:SliderEvent):void {
    vidPlayer.skinBackgroundAlpha = e.target.value;
}

colorChoose.addEventListener(ColorPickerEvent.CHANGE, changeHandler);

function changeHandler(e:ColorPickerEvent):void {
    var cp:ColorPicker = e.currentTarget as ColorPicker;
    vidPlayer.skinBackgroundColor = Number("0x" + cp.hexValue);
}
```

3   Test your movie. Now when you select a new color with the color picker, it will assign that color to the background of the video controls. While the movie is running, you should be able to freely modify the background color with the ColorPicker and transparency with the Slider.

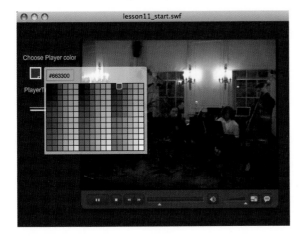

4 Close the lesson11_start.swf file to leave the testing environment.

Next, you will add some captions to the video file. These will take advantage of the built-in FLVCaptioning component that ships with Flash CS4. The captions can be toggled on and off with the captions button included on the far right of the skin that you assigned your FLVPlayback instance.

Adding the FLVCaptioning component

In Lesson 10, you learned how to use an XML file as a playlist. You wrote ActionScript to load and use the playlist information in a Flash project. Later in this lesson, you will get some additional practice with this technique using an XML file as a video playlist.

Another use of an XML file is to store captions or subtitles for a video file. You can create an XML file that contains the specific times in a video clip at which captions should appear as well as the text that should be displayed at that point in the video. You can even store information about how that text can be formatted. Of course, you could then write ActionScript to load and use the information from that XML file, as you already have seen in Lesson 10. However, there is an even easier way to do this.

If you create the XML file with your captions using a specific protocol called the Timed Text format, then the FLVCaptioning component in Flash will take care of all the ActionScript for you! The component will load the XML file and connect all the information in the XML file with the video that is played in an FLVPlayback instance.

For this lesson, an XML file in the Timed Text format has been provided. You will add captions to your video using this file with an instance of the FLVCaptioning component. First, let's look at the Timed Text code in the captions.xml file.

Examining the captions.xml file

In the Lessons > Lesson11 > Start folder, locate the captions.xml file, and open it in Dreamweaver or the text editor of your choice.

If you completed Lesson 10 or are familiar with XML, then the basic format of the file should be familiar.

The top-level <tt> tag in this file indicates that this file is in the Timed Text format.

Within the body of code, there is a series of tags to indicate where the captions should appear while a video file plays. The <begin> tags indicate the place where a caption begins. These times are indicated in hours:minutes:seconds:milliseconds format (for example, 00:03:40:50). The <dur> tags indicate how long the text will appear on stage; this can be measured in seconds (s) or milliseconds (ms). The file also contains a variety of `<tts>` formatting tags to format the caption text. Most of these tags are fairly intuitive (textAlign, color, fontStyle, and so on), especially if you have worked with HTML code.

```xml
<?xml version="1.0" encoding="UTF-8"?>
  <tt xml:lang="en" xmlns="http://www.w3.org/2006/04/ttaf1"  xmlns:tts="http://www.w3.org/2006/04/ttaf1#styling">

      <body>
          <div xml:lang="en">
              <p begin="00:00:00.50" dur="7000ms" tts:textAlign="center" tts:color="#cccc99" tts:backgroundColor="#333300">Seven Possible Solutions</p>
              <p begin="00:00:11.50" tts:textAlign="center" tts:color="#cccc99">Live at the Goethe Institute, Boston, Mass<br/>June 10, 2008</p>
              <p begin="00:00:22.40" dur="10s">Hiro Honshuku - <span tts:fontWeight="bold" tts:color="#ccc333" tts:fontStyle="italic">Flute and Electronics</span> </p>
              <p begin="00:00:33.50" dur="10s" tts:textAlign="left">Mimi Rabson <span tts:fontWeight="bold" tts:color="#ccc333" tts:fontStyle="italic">Violin</span> </p>
              <p begin="00:00:44.50" tts:textAlign="center">Peter Cokkinias <span tts:fontWeight = "bold" tts:color="#ccc333" tts:fontStyle="italic">Saxophone and Bass
Clarinet</span></p>
              <p begin="00:00:54.50" tts:textAlign="center">  Thomas Sanger Elnaes <span tts:fontWeight = "bold" tts:color="#ccc333" tts:fontStyle="italic">Piano</span>
</p>

              <p begin="62s" tts:textAlign="right">Chris Florio   <span tts:fontWeight="bold" tts:color="#ccc333" tts:fontStyle="italic">Guitar Composition</span></p>
              <p begin="74s" dur="10s" tts:textAlign="right">Mike Rivard  <span tts:fontWeight="bold" tts:color="#ccc333" tts:fontStyle="italic"> Contrabass</span></p>
          </div>
      </body>
  </tt>
```

You can use this file as a template for your own Timed Text files. For more information on the Timed Text format, see http://help.adobe.com/en_US/AS3LCR/Flash_10.0/TimedTextTags.html.

When you have finished examining the captions.xml file, close that file and return to the lesson11_start.fla file in Flash, where you will integrate the captions.xml file into your project.

Adding the FLVCaptioning component

The FLVCaptioning component adds no graphical content to your project. Instead, it contains the functionality to connect the captions in a Timed Text file to an instance of the FLVPlayback component. When you drag an instance of the FLVCaptioning component to the stage, a rectangular placeholder appears, but this is not visible to your users.

1 Back in the lesson11_start.fla file, with the `contents` layer selected and the Components panel open, locate the FLVCaptioning component in the Video folder.

2 Drag an instance of this component to anywhere on the stage.

3 With the new FLVCaptioning instance selected onstage, open the Component Inspector.

4 In the Component Inspector, set the flvPlaybackName property to vidPlayer. This connects your captions with the FLVPlayback instance onstage.

5 Set the source property to captions.xml. This is the XML Timed Text file that you previously examined. The component will automatically load this file and associate the tags in the file with the video that plays in the vidPlayer component.

6 Notice that the captionTargetName is set to auto. When this is the case, the FLVCaptioning component will create a new text field automatically, and display the captions of the video. If you wish to create a text field specifically for your captions, you could indicate its instance name here, in the captionTargetName property. For now, leave it set to auto.

7 Close the Component Inspector and test the movie. The captions with their formatting should appear at the times indicated in the captions.xml file. While a caption is visible, try toggling the button on the far-right of the FLVPlayback skin.

Now that you have working captions, this button will let your users toggle them on and off. This is great for giving your users the option of subtitles. You could even use a technique similar to the one covered in Lesson 2, "Working with Events and Functions," to give your user the option of subtitles in multiple languages by using a conditional statement that chooses between multiple captions files.

8 Close the lesson11_start.swf file to leave the testing environment.

The next feature that you will add to this project will change it from an application that plays a single video file to one that automatically plays a series of video files using an XML file as a playlist.

Playing multiple video files from an XML playlist

The process of adding a video playlist to this project will review a number of techniques from previous lessons. It will also introduce techniques for playing multiple video files in the same FLVPlayback component, and listening and responding when a video file that was playing has reached its end.

You will load in a list of video files from a simple XML playlist. Then, you'll create an event listener that will play the next video file from the playlist when the current video is complete.

Examining the vidlist.xml file

The first step in this section will be to take a look at the code in the vidlist.xml file that will be used as a video playlist.

1   In Dreamweaver or the text editor of your choice, open the vidlist.xml file found in the Lessons > Lesson11 > Start folder.

If you completed Lesson 10, then the code in this file should be very familiar to you. It is very similar to the songlist.xml file that you used for that lesson but is even simpler. There is only one main element within the root vidlist tags called vid. Each vid element contains two child elements. The file elements contain the names of video files. The name element contains text that you will use in a text field in Flash.

```xml
<?xml version="1.0" encoding="utf-8"?>
<vidlist>
<!-- All vids © copyrght Passion Records -->
    <!-- www.passionrecords.com -->
    <vid>
        <file>../video/solution5.f4v</file>
        <name>Nan Jing in Performance</name>
    </vid>

    <vid>
        <file>../video/solution2.f4v</file>
        <name>7 Possible Solutions (mvmt.2)</name>
    </vid>

    <vid>
        <file>../video/solution4.f4v</file>
        <name>Hope (excerpt)</name>
    </vid>

    <vid>
        <file>../video/perahara1.f4v</file>
        <name>Kandy Perhara</name>
    </vid>

    <vid>
        <file>../video/perahara2.f4v</file>
        <name>Filmed in Kandy Sri Lanka</name>
    </vid>
```

2   Close the vidlist.xml file and return to the lesson11_start.fla file in Flash.

You will now add the ActionScript to use of the vidlist.xml file.

As mentioned, the technique you will use to load and use the vidlist.xml file is very similar to the way you used the songlist.xml file in the previous lesson.

Adding a title text field

The first step in preparing to load and use the XML playlist will be to add a new dynamic text field to the Flash stage. This will be used to display the text obtained from the name elements in the vidlist.xml file.

1 With frame 1 of the `contents` layer selected, choose the Text tool from the Tools panel, and drag out a new text field above the FLVPlayback instance onstage.

2 In the Properties panel, set the type of text in this field to be Dynamic Text.

3 Give the new text field the instance name of **title_txt**.

4 Choose any font or formatting that you wish for this field. You could do this in the Properties panel or you could get ambitious and create a TextFormat object in ActionScript (see Lesson 8, "Creating a Radio Button Quiz in an ActionScript File").

5 Type some text in the field. This will be the text that appears onscreen while the first video is playing. You will replace this text with ActionScript when other video files play.

Loading the vidlist.xml file with ActionScript

Now for some ActionScript, first you will add a few variables.

1 With frame 1 of the `actions` layer selected in the timeline and the Actions panel open and visible, locate the code that contains all the initial `import` statements:

```
import fl.events.SliderEvent;
import fl.controls.ColorPicker;
import fl.events.ColorPickerEvent;
import fl.video.FLVPlayback;
import fl.video.VideoEvent;
```

2 On a new line below this code, create a new variable named **vidList_XML** that will be used to store an XML object:

```
var vidList_XML:XML;
```

3   The next variable that you will create will be used to store the name associated with each vid element in the vidlist.xml file. Insert the following code below the line you just added:

```
var vidTitle:String;
```

It will be necessary to keep track of which video from the playlist should be played next. To do that, you will need to create a variable called count.

4   Add the following on the line below the code you just entered:

```
var count:int = 0;
```

Notice that the initial value of count is 0. This will be used soon to determine the first video that will play from the vidlist.xml data.

To load the data from the XML file you will use an instance of the URLLoader class.

5   Insert a variable on the next line to contain this instance:

```
var xmlLoader:URLLoader = new URLLoader();
```

Now you will use the load() method of the URLLoader instance to load the vidlist.xml file.

6   On the line below the code you just added, insert the following line:

```
xmlLoader.load(new URLRequest("vidlist.xml"));
```

In the previous lesson, you learned that it is important to confirm that data has been loaded before using that data. You will listen for the COMPLETE event of the URLLoader class to make sure the data in the vidlist.xml file has completely loaded before working with it.

7   On the line below the load() method that you just added, create an addEventListener() for the COMPLETE event:

```
xmlLoader.addEventListener(Event.COMPLETE, xmlLoaded);
```

Creating the xmlLoaded() function

The xmlLoaded() function, which will be called when the vidlist.xml data is available, will be used to work with the XML data.

1   Below the code listener you last added, insert the shell for the xmlLoaded() function:

```
function xmlLoaded(event:Event):void {

}
```

The first thing this function should do is store the XML data that was loaded in the XML object you created a few steps back.

2   Between the curly braces of the `xmlLoaded()` function, insert this line:

```
vidList_XML = new XML(xmlLoader.data);
```

The next thing you will add within this function is an event listener that responds whenever video in the vidPlayer instance finishes playing. The event that will do this is the COMPLETE event of the `FLVPlayback` class.

Distinguishing between COMPLETE events

You have already worked with COMPLETE events a number of times in this and earlier lessons. You have worked with the COMPLETE event of the `URLLoader` class, the `Loader` class, and the `UILoader` class. In all of these cases, the COMPLETE event is listening for the successful completion of the loading of external content.

Even though the name is the same, when you are listening for the COMPLETE event of the FLVPlayback component, you are not listening for when a video file is completely loaded. Instead, you are listening for when a video file has reached the end of its playback and is complete. Because video files are streaming files they can be downloading and playing at the same time, and therefore don't need to be completely loaded before they can begin playing. It is therefore much more common to need to listen for when video is finished *playing* than when it is finished *loading*. This is what you will do now.

3   On the next line of the `xmlLoaded()` function, add a listener for the vidPlayer's COMPLETE event with this code:

```
vidPlayer.addEventListener(VideoEvent.COMPLETE, changeVid);
```

The complete function should now read:

```
function xmlLoaded(event:Event):void {

  vidList_XML = new XML(xmlLoader.data);
  vidPlayer.addEventListener(VideoEvent.COMPLETE, changeVid);
}
```

Next you will add the `changeVid()` function that will be triggered each time a video file completes playing.

Creating the changeVid() function

Remember that the `changeVid()` function occurs every time the vidPlayer instance fires the COMPLETE event. The purpose of `changeVid()` is to identify the next video from the loaded playlist and set it to be the source file of the vidPlayer. The final step of the `changeVid()` function will be to increment the count variable so that it can be used to play a different video each time the `changeVid()` function is called.

1 On a line below the closing brace of the xmlLoaded() function, insert the shell of the changeVid() function:

```
function changeVid(e:VideoEvent):void {

}
```

The first thing this function will do is store the string for the next video in the list. This will be assembled in a new variable using the value of count to determine from which element of the vidlist.xml data to get the file information.

2 Between the curly braces of the changeVid() function, add the following line:

```
var nextVid:String = "../video/" + vidList_XML.vid[count].
➡file;
```

Next you will use the value of this new variable to be the source of the vidPlayer instance.

3 Add this line below the code you just typed:

```
vidPlayer.source = nextVid;
```

Now you will use the name element from the current vid element (vid[count]) as the text in the onscreen title_txt field.

4 Below the last line you entered, add the following lines of code:

```
vidTitle=vidList_XML.vid[count].name;
title_txt.text = vidTitle;
```

Just because you can, set the background color of the vidPlayer to change every time a new video plays.

5 On the next line of code, add the following:

```
vidPlayer.skinBackgroundColor = Math.random() * 0xFFFFFF;
```

Finally, to make sure that a new video is played the next time this function is called, increment the value of the count variable by one.

6 Add this line above the closing brace of the changeVid() function:

```
count++;
```

The completed changeVid() function should read:

```
function changeVid(e:VideoEvent):void {
 var nextVid:String = "../video/" + vidList_XML.vid[count].
  ➡file;
 vidPlayer.source = nextVid;
 vidTitle = vidList_XML.vid[count].name;
 title_txt.text = vidTitle;
 vidPlayer.skinBackgroundColor = Math.random() * 0xFFFFFF;
 count++;
}
```

The code for the entire file should now read:

```
import fl.events.SliderEvent;
import fl.controls.ColorPicker;
import fl.events.ColorPickerEvent;
import fl.video.FLVPlayback;
import fl.video.VideoEvent;

var vidList_XML:XML;
var vidTitle:String;
var count:int = 0;
var xmlLoader:URLLoader = new URLLoader();
xmlLoader.load(new URLRequest("vidlist.xml"));
xmlLoader.addEventListener(Event.COMPLETE, xmlLoaded);

function xmlLoaded(event:Event):void {
 vidList_XML = new XML(xmlLoader.data);
 vidPlayer.addEventListener(VideoEvent.COMPLETE, changeVid);
}

function changeVid(e:VideoEvent):void {
 var nextVid:String = "../video/" + vidList_XML.vid[count].
  ➥file;
 vidPlayer.source = nextVid;
 vidTitle = vidList_XML.vid[count].name;
 title_txt.text = vidTitle;
 vidPlayer.skinBackgroundColor = Math.random() * 0xFFFFFF;
 count++;
}

alphaSlide.addEventListener(SliderEvent.CHANGE, alphaChange);

function alphaChange(e:SliderEvent):void {
 vidPlayer.skinBackgroundAlpha = e.target.value;
}

colorChoose.addEventListener(ColorPickerEvent.CHANGE,
 ➥changeHandler);

function changeHandler(e:ColorPickerEvent):void {
 var cp:ColorPicker = e.currentTarget as ColorPicker;
 vidPlayer.skinBackgroundColor = Number("0x" + cp.hexValue);
}
```

7 Test the movie. When the first video is finished playing (you can scrub toward the end if you get impatient), the next video in the vidlist data should automatically start. Notice that the title_txt field changes each time a new video file loads. If you let the movie continue, it will play through all of the video files contained in the vidlist.xml file. Also notice that each time a new video file is loaded, the background color of the skin changes.

There is one last thing to attend to in the test file. If you click the second button from the right, which is designed to toggle in and out of full-screen mode, you'll see that nothing happens.

Fortunately, it is very simple to address this small problem. Unfortunately, full-screen mode does not work in the testing environment, so close the lesson11_start.swf file. After adjusting the publish settings, you'll preview the full-screen feature in the browser.

Using the full-screen publish settings

The easiest way to make full-screen video work in Flash is to use the FLVPlayback skins that toggle full screen and to let Flash write code into your HTML file to allow the page to make use of full-screen mode. Since you have already used an FLVPlayback component with a full-screen toggle, the final step of the lesson is to set the publish settings to use the Allow Full Screen template.

1   With the lesson11_start.fla file still open in Flash, choose File > Publish Settings. In the Formats tab of the Publish Settings dialog box, make sure both the Flash and HTML options are selected.

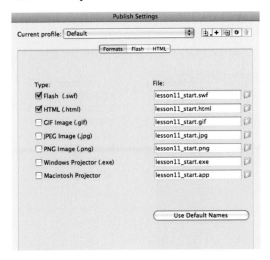

2   Click the HTML tab.

3   From the Templates drop-down list, choose Flash Only - Allow Full Screen, and then click OK.

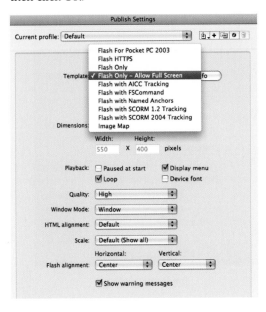

4 Test this project in your default browser by choosing File > Publish Preview > Default - (HTML).

● **Note:** As always, if you had any trouble with your code, try troubleshooting by using the error messages that you receive as guides. If you still have problems, compare the code to the lesson11_complete.fla file in the Lessons > Lesson11 > Complete folder.

5 Your project should play in the browser the same way it did when you viewed it in the Flash testing environment. Now, however, when you toggle the full-screen button, the video file that is playing should take over the full screen. Press the Escape key in order to return to the normal view of the project.

Some suggestions to try on your own

Having made it all the way through the lesson, you now have a great collection of tools to work with for integrating Flash video into your projects. By experimenting with the other features in the classes and components that you used in this lesson, you will discover many other easy-to-use possibilities for working with video in Flash.

Digging a little deeper and exploring other video-related ActionScript classes including the `NetConnection`, `Video`, `Camera`, and particularly `NetStream` will open up even more options.

Finally, to go even further with Flash video, investigate Adobe's Flash Media Server technology and its possibilities. You will find that there are many good reasons why Flash video has become such a popular format.

You may also want to make a few modifications to the project file for this lesson to solidify your understanding of the covered materials.

- Try experimenting with the captions.xml file. Change the timing, the text, and/or the formatting of the captions. (It is a good idea to save a backup copy of the original file before you do this.)

- Try adding to or replacing the video files supplied in the video folder with your own FLV or F4V files. You can make video files in these formats from many standard video formats, including QuickTime movies and AVI files. For help doing this, see Flash Help.

- Create additional vid elements in the vidlist.xml file to add your videos to the playlist.

- Add additional child tags to the vid elements in the vidlist.xml playlist. Use your new elements in the Flash project to display additional information in text fields or in other creative ways.

- Explore the other properties of the `FLVPlayback` class. Try changing some of these settings in the Component Inspector or with ActionScript.

Review questions

1 Name a Flash component that is used to play and control Flash video files.

2 What are the two Flash video file formats?

3 What is the format for creating files that work with the FLVCaptioning component?

4 What event is used by the FLVPlayback class to respond when a video file has reached the end of the file?

Review answers

1 The FLVPlayback component is used to play and control Flash video files.

2 Flash supports the .flv video format and the .f4v video format.

3 The FLVCaptioning component reads XML files in the Timed-Text format.

4 The COMPLETE event of the FLVPlayback class fires any time a video playing in an FLVPlayback instance reaches its end.

DELVING DEEPER INTO GRAPHICS AND ANIMATION WITH ACTIONSCRIPT

Lesson overview

In this lesson, you will learn to do the following:

- Use the new inverse kinematics (IK) tools in Flash CS4.

- Use the new IK classes in Flash CS4 to create advanced animation with ActionScript.

- Check if users have a video camera or webcam available to their computers.

- Access and display video from a webcam or connected camera using ActionScript.

- Create bitmap graphics with ActionScript.

- Take screen captures of Flash objects and save them as bitmap data.

- Examine the Adobe Pixel Bender Toolkit.

- Work with filters in ActionScript.

- Use an external class file to load filters created in the Pixel Bender Toolkit.

- Apply Pixel Bender filters to a snapshot from a live camera.

- Use a slider to perform live modifications to the properties of a filter.

 This lesson will take approximately 3.5 hours.

In this lesson, you will take advantage of some terrific and fun tools available in ActionScript 3.0 for creating and manipulating graphics and animations. A number of these features are available for the

Inverse kinematics and Pixel Bender filters are some of
new Flash CS4 features used in this lesson.

first time in Flash CS4 and will require your user have Flash Player 10 or later. Depending on when you are reading this book, Flash Player 10 may not have completely permeated the market, so if you use some of the features in this lesson in your own projects, be sure to take the user's player version into account (see "Getting Started").

Inverse kinematics in Flash CS4

One of the most exciting new features in Flash CS4 is a full set of tools to work with *inverse kinematics* (IK), which is the process of calculating the movement of a series of objects that are connected with bones at joints. For example, in an animation of a human walk cycle, rather than separately animating a character's feet, lower legs, upper legs, and hips, the IK tools in Flash would let you link the individual parts together with bones so that when one part is animated the entire chain moves. By setting the range of motion for each joint, you can then easily create realistic movements. Flash CS4 offers tools for setting up an IK animation in the timeline. It also offers full ActionScript control over IK using a number of new classes.

However, you should be aware that you can't create IK systems with ActionScript. As of Flash CS4, these systems are created only in the Flash interface itself. Once they are created, they can then be manipulated either in the interface or with ActionScript. As always, the interface is often best for linear animation, and ActionScript makes more sense for interactive animation, such as in a game.

This lesson will work with IK using ActionScript, but before you begin that project, open a file that contains an IK example that can be controlled in the timeline so that you can see how IK is created in Flash.

Viewing the IKSample file

An *IK system* is a group of graphics that are connected to move together in a system of joints. IK systems can be created in Flash from shapes or from symbols. However, if you intend to work with IK using ActionScript, it's best if the individual pieces of the system are MovieClip instances.

Open the Lessons > Lesson12 > IKSample.fla file. If you have not worked with IK in Flash CS4 before, you may notice a number of things that are new. On the timeline, you'll see that there is only one layer with a single frame. The layer is called `Armature` and has a new icon on it. A armature layer is automatically generated by Flash as soon for each IK system that is created.

You create an IK system in Flash by connecting graphics together using the Bone tool in the Tools panel. This system, referred to as an armature in Flash, can be thought of as a chain of graphics connected together at joints. These joints control the movement of all the objects in the system when any one of the objects is moved. To create a connection between two graphics, you simply select the Bone tool from the Tools panel and drag from the desired joint location of one object to the desired location of a joint of another. In this sample file, this has been done for you, but you may want to experiment with creating your own files and experiment with creating IK animations.

About IK Bones

Bones allow symbol instances and shapes to move in relation to each other. You can add bones to multiple symbol instances or to the interior of a single shape. You can use the Properties panel or ActionScript to constrain the movement of the separate parts of an IK system. Bones cannot be created with ActionScript; they must be created in the Flash interface. They can then be controlled in the timeline or with ActionScript. For more details on how to create bones in Flash see "Using Inverse Kinematics" in Flash CS4 Help.

The armature in the sample file is composed of four MovieClips that make up a robotic arm—three rectangular clips and a fourth clip with a hand pointer. If you select any one of these graphics, you will see the "*bones*" (represented in purple) that have been created to connect them. When a specific bone is selected, it turns green. Click anywhere on the armature and move the mouse around; the entire system moves and the individual pieces bend at the joints. Try selecting different parts of the armature and moving them around.

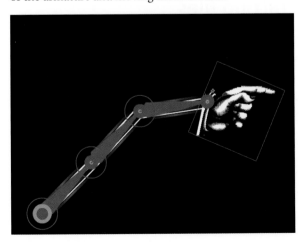

Notice that even when it's not selected, the joint furthest from the hand remains green. This indicates that it is the root joint. In any armature, there is only one root—the origin point for the armature. When you work with IK and ActionScript, the root joint will be a useful point of reference.

Creating animation in the timeline with IK in Flash is very similar to other Flash animation techniques. If you are already used to working with "regular" Flash animation, you should have no trouble getting up and running using the IK features in the timeline. (For details, see "Using Inverse Kinematics" in Flash CS4 Help.) However, in this lesson, you will focus on using ActionScript to create IK animation.

Switching between authortime and runtime IK

IK animation created in the timeline is considered *authortime* IK. IK animation created with ActionScript is considered *runtime*. Once an armature layer is created, you can indicate whether it will be used for authortime or runtime animation by setting the properties for that layer. Remember that either way, the IK system must be created in the timeline.

1 In the IKSample.fla file, select frame 1 of the Armature layer.

2 With the Properties panel visible, select the Type drop-down list from the Options section. You will see that the two options are Authortime and Runtime.

Remember that if you intend to create an IK system that will be controlled with ActionScript, it must be set to runtime. This will be done for you in the Lesson 12 project file, which you will begin next. Feel free to experiment with IK in the time-line as much as you like before moving on.

Examining the starting files

This lesson includes quite a few new techniques, starting with ActionScript control of IK. Before beginning, take a look at the contents of the Lessons > Lesson12 > Start folder.

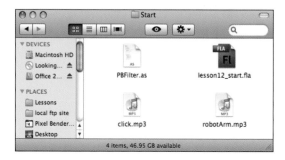

Notice that in addition to the lesson12_start.fla file there are two MP3 audio files. You will use ActionScript to control these sound-effects files in your project. In addition, there is an external ActionScript class file for this lesson. You will work with this file later in the lesson.

Now open the Lessons > Lesson12 > Start > lesson12_start.fla file in Flash CS4 and take a look at the assets that are provided with the file.

There are four layers in the timeline of this file. The `actions` layer is currently empty. All the code that you will add to this project will go here.

The `interactive content` layer contains two buttons, a text field, and a Slider component. Select them one at a time. If you select the area on the lower-left that includes the text that reads Take a Snapshot, you will see that it is a button instance. Make the Properties panel visible while this button is selected, and you will see that the button has an instance name of snapshot_btn.

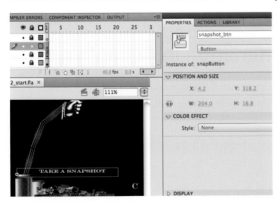

The text that says CHOOSE A FILTER is a dynamic text field that has been given the instance name valueText. The slider below that text is an instance of the Slider component that has the instance name of fSlider, and the red button to the left of the slider has the instance name of filter_btn. You will write ActionScript in this lesson to interact with all four of these elements.

The Armature_1 layer contains a copy of the same armature that you viewed in the IKsample.fla file. With the Properties panel visible, select frame 1 of this layer in the timeline. Notice that the Type field for the armature is set to Runtime. That is because you will create animation for this armature with ActionScript. This layer has been locked to maintain the initial position of the graphics. You won't have to unlock the layer for this lesson, but if you wish to unlock it in order to experiment with this graphic, it would be a good idea to make a backup copy first, since the initial position of the graphics is essential to the functionality you're adding in this lesson.

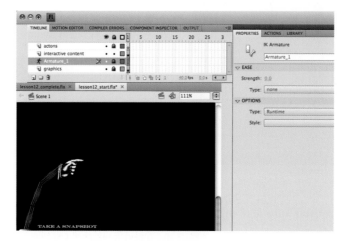

The bottom layer (graphics) in the timeline contains static design elements that will not be made interactive.

The first ActionScript you will work with in this lesson will introduce the new IK classes in Flash CS4.

Working with IK animation in ActionScript

There are a number of new classes in Flash CS4 to work with inverse kinematics. The first code you will add to this project imports all these classes so they will be available to the project.

With frame 1 of the actions layer selected and the Actions panel visible, add this line of code:

```
import fl.ik.*;
```

Using the IKArmature and IKManager classes

The `IKManager` class is used to keep track of all the IK armatures in a single Flash document. The `IKArmature` class is used to describe a single `IKArmature` instance in the document. Unlike with most other ActionScript classes that you've worked with so far, you don't have to create new instances of the `IKManager` or `IKArmature` classes. As already mentioned, IK systems can be created only in the Flash interface, and when you create IK on the Flash timeline, an `IKManager` is generated in the background automatically. An `IKArmature` instance is automatically created for each armature in the timeline as well.

If you wish to let the user drag around IK armatures the same way you yourself did with the IKSample file, you'd set the `trackAllArmatures` property of the IKManager to `true`. But for this project, ActionScript, rather than the user, should move the armature, so set this property to `false`.

1 Below all the `import` statements in the Actions panel, add this line of code:

```
IKManager.trackAllArmatures(false);
```

The IKManager for a file automatically keeps a list of all the `IKArmature` instances in the file. You can make a reference to any armature in a Flash file using the `IKManager.getArmatureAt()` method. You will use this method to make an ActionScript reference to the onstage armature so that you can manipulate it in code.

▶ **Tip:** If you have a project containing multiple armatures, you can reference them by their number using `getArmatureAt()` or give them names and refer to them with the `getArmatureByName()` method.

2 Below the previous line of code you added, type the following code:

```
var arm0:IKArmature = IKManager.getArmatureAt(0);
```

The new variable `arm0` stores a reference to the armature onstage. Since there is only one armature on the stage, it's an accurate assumption that it is in position 0 in the IKManager list.

You can keep track of the individual joints in an IK armature using the `IKJoint` class. Once you have stored a reference to an `IKJoint`, you can animate it using the `IKMover` class. When a single joint in an IK system is moved using ActionScript, the whole system will automatically respond accordingly, just as you saw on the timeline of the IKsample file. In this project, the goal is to move the joint that is furthest from the root to animate the whole system.

As mentioned, each IK armature in Flash has only one root joint. You can reference this root using the `rootjoint` property of an IKArmature.

3 On the line below the existing code, create a reference to the root joint of the onstage armature.

```
var rt0:IKJoint = arm0.rootJoint;
```

Once a reference has been stored to the root of the armature, all the other joints can be referenced as children of the root. For example, the first joint attached to the root could be referenced as:

```
rt0.getChildAt(0);
```

4 In order to reference the third joint away from the root, which is the one you will animate, add the following code below the line you added in Step 3:

```
var jt0:IKJoint = rt0.getChildAt(0).getChildAt(0).
➥getChildAt(0);
```

Now you will apply animation to the joint stored in `jt0`. Remember that animation applied to one joint of an IK armature will move the entire armature chain similarly to the way you saw it move in the IKSample file. You will use the `IKMover` class to do the animation.

Using the IKMover class

The IKMover class is used to animate joints in an IKArmature. Once a new instance of the `IKMover` class is created, you can use the `moveTo()` method of this class to move any joint to any location. You'll create an instance of this class now.

Add this code below all the code you have added so far:

```
var mover0:IKMover = new IKMover(jt0, jt0.position);
```

The first required parameter of a new IKMover instance is the name of the joint that will be moved—in this case, jt0. The second parameter is the starting point of the movement. In this case, that point will be derived from the current position of jt0. Once that's established, the moveTo() method can be used to move the jt0 joint to a new location.

You will initiate this movement when the snapshot_btn instance is clicked.

Adding an event listener to the snapshot_btn

A function that occurs when the user clicks the Take A Snapshot button onstage will trigger an ENTER_FRAME function that will start the armature animating. You've already had quite a bit of experience with the basics of this technique, so much of it will be familiar to you.

1 Below the existing code, insert an addEventListener() method for the snapshot_btn:

```
snapshot_btn.addEventListener(MouseEvent.CLICK, onSnapshot);
```

2 Now add the shell for the onSnapshot() function below the previous line:

```
function onSnapshot(e:MouseEvent):void {

}
```

As mentioned, this function will initiate an ENTER_FRAME function.

3 Within the braces of the onSnapshot() function, add this code:

```
stage.addEventListener(Event.ENTER_FRAME, moveDown);
```

The moveDown() function will animate the armature. While that is occurring, it would not be desirable for the user to take another snapshot, so while this function occurs the snapshot button should be hidden.

4 Below the last line you typed and above the closing brace of the onSnapshot() function, add this line:

```
snapshot_btn.visible = false;
```

The full onSnapshot() function should now read:

```
function onSnapshot(e:MouseEvent):void {
    stage.addEventListener(Event.ENTER_FRAME, moveDown);
    snapshot_btn.visible = false;
}
```

Adding the moveDown() function

When the user clicks the snapshot button, the armature should animate down to the camera graphic on the stage, take a picture, and animate back up. You will add the code to "take the picture" later in the lesson. Now, you will add the up and down animation. Because a number of things will be occurring in your code when the animation has finished moving down, you will separate the down movement and the up movement into separate ENTER_FRAME functions. A moveDown() function is triggered when the user clicks the snapshot_btn instance, and a moveUp() function is triggered when the downward movement is complete.

Start by adding the shell for the moveDown() function.

1 Below the existing code, add the following:

```
function moveDown(e:Event) {

}
```

The moveDown() function, which will occur on every frame, should move the armature a little closer to its target on each frame. The armature will have reached its target when it gets to a y position of 305, so you will use a conditional statement to check if the target has been achieved. When it has, you will turn off the moveDown() listener and initiate the moveUp() function.

2 Add a conditional statement to the moveDown() function so that it now reads:

```
function moveDown(e:Event) {

  if(jt0.position.y < 305) {

  } else {


  }
}
```

Now you will add to this function the actual movement of the armature, using the moveTo() method of the IKMover class. The moveTo() method takes a single parameter. This is the point that the joint, stored in the IKMover instance, should be moved to. In this case, the amount that will be moved in each frame will be relative to the current position of jt0. So, first create a variable that stores a point that is five pixels to the right and five pixels below the jt0 joint's current location. That point will be used as the parameter for the moveTo() method.

3 Below the line that reads:

```
if(jt0.position.y < 305) {
```

add the following two lines:

```
var pt0:Point = new Point(jt0.position.x + 5,jt0.position.y + 5);
mover0.moveTo(pt0);
```

As mentioned, when the target position has been reached, this function should be disabled and a new ENTER_FRAME function initiated that will move the armature back to its original location.

4   Below the line that reads:

```
} else {
```

add the following lines:

```
stage.removeEventListener(Event.ENTER_FRAME, moveDown);
stage.addEventListener(Event.ENTER_FRAME, moveUp);
```

The entire moveDown() function so far should read:

```
function moveDown(e:Event) {

    if(jt0.position.y < 305) {
        var pt0:Point = new Point(jt0.position.x + 5, jt0.position.y + 5);
        mover0.moveTo(pt0);
    } else {
        stage.removeEventListener(Event.ENTER_FRAME, moveDown);
        stage.addEventListener(Event.ENTER_FRAME, moveUp);
    }
}
```

If you tested the movie at this point you would get an error, because the moveUp() function has been referred to but does not yet exist. So before you test what you have so far, add the shell for the moveUp() function.

5   Below all the existing code, add the following:

```
function moveUp(e:Event):void {

}
```

Your code so far should read:

```
import fl.ik.*;
import fl.events.SliderEvent;

IKManager.trackAllArmatures(false);
var arm0:IKArmature = IKManager.getArmatureAt(0);
var rt0:IKJoint = arm0.rootJoint;
var jt0:IKJoint = rt0.getChildAt(0).getChildAt(0).getChildAt(0);
var mover0:IKMover = new IKMover(jt0, jt0.position);

snapshot_btn.addEventListener(MouseEvent.CLICK, onSnapshot);

function onSnapshot(e:MouseEvent):void {
    stage.addEventListener(Event.ENTER_FRAME, moveDown);
    snapshot_btn.visible = false;
}

function moveDown(e:Event) {

    if(jt0.position.y < 305) {
        var pt0:Point = new Point(jt0.position.x + 5, jt0.position.y + 5);
        mover0.moveTo(pt0);
    } else {
        stage.removeEventListener(Event.ENTER_FRAME, moveDown);
        stage.addEventListener(Event.ENTER_FRAME, moveUp);
    }
}

function moveUp(e:Event):void {

}
```

6 Test the movie. In the testing environment, press the Take a Snapshot button. The arm graphic should animate down and land on the camera graphic. Notice that even though you added code to control the movement of only one joint, the entire armature moved down and bent at all of its joints.

7 Close the lesson12_start.swf to leave the testing environment.

Now you will add code to the moveUp() function to return the armature to its original position.

Coding the moveUp() function

Once the moveDown() function sends the armature to its target location near the camera graphic, the moveUp() function will return it to its original position.

The code for the moveUp() function is similar to the moveDown() function, but in reverse.

1 Between the braces of the moveUp() function, add code so that the function reads:

```
function moveUp(e:Event):void {
  if(jt0.position.y > 165) {
    var pt0:Point=new Point(jt0.position.x - 5,
     ➥jt0.position.y - 5);
    mover0.moveTo(pt0);
  } else {
    stage.removeEventListener(Event.ENTER_FRAME, moveUp);
    snapshot_btn.visible = true;
  }
}
```

Notice that this function sends the jt0 joint back five pixels on each frame (jt0.position.x - 5, jt0.position.y - 5) until its y location has returned to 165.

When the armature is back in its original position there is no further reason for this function to continue, so it is removed. At this point, the snapshot_btn instance is made visible so that it can be used again.

2   Test the movie. The arm graphic should now move up and down. Notice the snapshot button disappear for the duration of the animation.

You will add additional code to both the moveUp() and moveDown() functions, but first let's use ActionScript to load some sound effects into this project. These will be used to enhance the armature movement.

Creating Sound and SoundChannel instances

The two sound files that accompany this lesson, robotArm.mp3 and click.mp3, will be triggered to play while the armature is animating. The robotArm.mp3 sound will play when the arm is moving up and down. The click will play each time the arm reaches its target location over the camera graphic to create the impression that a snapshot has been taken.

You will create two separate Sound instances so that the two sounds can be controlled independently and overlap a little. A SoundChannel instance will be used for each sound so that it can be stopped and played. If you completed Lesson 9, "Controlling Sound with ActionScript," this code will be familiar to you. Add code to create the Sound and SoundChannel instances and to load the two MP3 files.

1   In the Actions for frame 1 of the actions layer, scroll to locate the line that reads:

```
var mover0:IKMover = new IKMover(jt0, jt0.position);
```

2   Starting on a new line below this line, insert the following code:

```
var fx1:Sound = new Sound();
fx1.load(new URLRequest("robotArm.mp3"));
var channel1:SoundChannel = new SoundChannel();

var fx2:Sound = new Sound();
fx2.load(new URLRequest("click.mp3"));
var channel2:SoundChannel = new SoundChannel();
```

Now that the sounds are loaded and available, you will set them to play and stop as the Armature animation plays. In this lesson, you will assume that the MP3 files will load successfully because the files are local and in the same folder. You should already know how to confirm loading from earlier lessons; in fact, you may want to start doing this in your own online projects.

Playing and stopping the sound effects

The first sound in this animation will begin playing as soon as the user presses the snapshot button. So the code for this will go within the onSnapshot() function.

1   In the onSnapshot() function and below the line that reads:

```
snapshot_btn.visible = false;
```

insert the following line:

```
channel1 = fx1.play();
```

The onSnapshot() function should now read:

```
function onSnapshot(e:MouseEvent):void {
  stage.addEventListener(Event.ENTER_FRAME, moveDown);
  snapshot_btn.visible = false;
  channel1 = fx1.play();
}
```

The robotArm.mp3 sound should play until the arm has completed its descent. At this point the first sound should stop, the click sound should play once, and then the robot arm sound should restart for the ascent of the arm back to its original location. All of the code for this should be inserted at the point where the arm has reached the target over the camera graphic. In your code, this point takes place at the else statement within the moveDown() function. This is where you will add the next bit of code for the sounds.

2   Locate the moveDown() function, and below the line in the moveDown() function that reads:

```
} else {
```

insert the following three lines:

```
channel1.stop();
channel2 = fx2.play();
channel1 = fx1.play();
```

The full moveDown() function should now read:

```
function moveDown(e:Event) {

  if(jt0.position.y < 305) {
    var pt0:Point = new Point(jt0.position.x + 5,
    ➥jt0.position.y + 5);
    mover0.moveTo(pt0);
  } else {
    channel1.stop();
    channel2 = fx2.play();
    channel1 = fx1.play();
    stage.removeEventListener(Event.ENTER_FRAME, moveDown);
```

```
  stage.addEventListener(Event.ENTER_FRAME, moveUp);
 }
}
```

The last Sound control that you will add will stop the sound when the arm has returned to its original position. In your code, this occurs in the `else` statement within the `moveUp()` function.

3   Locate the `moveUp()` function in your code, and below the line that reads:

```
snapshot_btn.visible = true;
```

insert the following line:

```
channel1.stop();
```

The full `moveUp()` function should now read:

```
function moveUp(e:Event):void {
 if(jt0.position.y > 165) {
  var pt0:Point = new Point(jt0.position.x - 5,
    ➡jt0.position.y-5);
  mover0.moveTo(pt0);
 } else {
  stage.removeEventListener(Event.ENTER_FRAME, moveUp);
  snapshot_btn.visible = true;
  channel1.stop();

 }
}
```

4   Test the movie. Press the Take a Snapshot button. Now when the arm animates, the sound effects should play in sync with the movement.

5   Close the lesson12_start.swf to leave the testing environment.

The next sections will add the ability to take an actual snapshot and display it onstage each time the snapshot button is clicked. These snapshots will be taken from a feed from the user's live webcam using ActionScript's `Camera` class.

Accessing the user's webcam or video camera using ActionScript

If your users have webcams or external video cameras connected to their computers, then Flash Player will recognize them, and you can use ActionScript to access a live feed from those cameras to work in Flash. This is done using the `Camera` class in ActionScript. In order for you to test the code you are about to add, you (and your users) must have a video camera connected to your computer. Assuming that a camera is available, the code you will now write will take the feed from the camera and display it within the interface of this project. Later in the lesson, you will write code that can take snapshots from this camera feed.

Using the getCamera() method

● **Note:** Even though ActionScript will let you or your user choose between multiple cameras if there is more than one video source connected, Flash can display the feed from only one camera at a time.

To connect the feed from the user's video camera to your Flash project, you use the `getCamera()` method of the `Camera` class. This accesses the data from a camera but doesn't display it; you create an instance of the `Video` class to display the feed.

Add the code to create an instance of the `Camera` class and access the user's camera.

1   Locate the line of code for frame 1 of the `actions` layer that reads:

```
var channel2:SoundChannel = new SoundChannel();
```

2   On a new line below it, insert the following line:

```
var camera:Camera = Camera.getCamera();
```

Remember that the line you just added will access, but not display, the user's camera.

You'll create a new instance named video to display the camera if one is available.

● **Note:** Instead of being given a specific data type, the variable `video` has a wildcard (*) for a data type. This will allow any type of data to be contained in the variable. You will see the reason for this when you check for the presence of a video camera.

3   Below the line you just typed, add the following code:

```
var video;*
```

Soon you'll use a video object to display the camera, but before you write code to display the input from a video camera, it is a good idea to check if there actually *is* a recognized video camera. You will do this within a conditional statement.

Checking for the presence of a video camera

The instance of the `Camera` class you just created is called `camera`. If there is a video camera or cameras connected to the user's machine, then `camera` will have a value representing that specific camera. If not, it will return `null`. So if the `camera` value is not `null`, you know the user has a camera that Flash can access.

1   On a line below the last code you typed, insert the shell for a conditional statement that checks for a camera's presence:

```
if(camera != null) {

} else {

}
```

If a camera is available, then you want to create a new `Video` object with which to display the camera's input. If there is no camera, you will just trace a message to the Output panel with that information.

2   Add code to the conditional statement so that it now reads:

```
if(camera != null) {
  video=new Video(160, 120);
  video.attachCamera(camera);
  addChild(video);
```

```
} else {
 trace("There is no recognized camera connected to your
 ➡computer.");
}
```

In the line that reads var video=new Video(160, 120), a new camera instance is created and given two properties that represent the size of the video window. In this case, these parameters are set to display the video at 160×120 pixels.

The next line, video.attachCamera(camera), uses the attachCamera() method of the Video class to connect the live camera feed to the video object.

A video instance is a display object. Like movie clips, text fields, and other display objects you've worked with, instances created with ActionScript use the addChild() method to place them in the display list and on stage. The next line, addChild(video);, places the video object with the camera feed on stage.

To take into account that some users may not have a connected video camera, the library of lesson12_start.fla has an alternate video file embedded in a MovieClip named AltVid. Because you did not specify a data type for the video variable, it can contain either a Video instance (if the user has a connected camera) or a MovieClip instance (if there is no camera available) without giving an error message. You'll add code to the else statement so that if there is no connected camera, the clip from the library will play instead, making it possible for users without a camera to use the rest of this lesson's functionality.

3 Add code to the else statement so that the full conditional statement now reads:

```
if(camera! = null) {
 video=new Video(160, 120);
 video.attachCamera(camera);
 addChild(video);
} else {
 trace("There is no recognized camera connected to your
 ➡computer.");
 video = new AltVid();
 addChild(video);
}
```

Your full code so far should read:

```
import fl.ik.*;

var arm0:IKArmature = IKManager.getArmatureAt(0);
var rt0:IKJoint = arm0.rootJoint;
var jt0:IKJoint = rt0.getChildAt(0).getChildAt(0).
 ➡getChildAt(0);
var mover0:IKMover = new IKMover(jt0, jt0.position);
```

(code continues on the next page)

(continued)

```
var fx1:Sound = new Sound();
fx1.load(new URLRequest("robotArm.mp3"));
var channel1:SoundChannel = new SoundChannel();

var fx2:Sound = new Sound();
fx2.load(new URLRequest("click.mp3"));
var channel2:SoundChannel = new SoundChannel();

var camera:Camera=Camera.getCamera();
var video:*;

if(camera! = null) {
 video = new Video(160, 120);
 video.attachCamera(camera);
 addChild(video);
} else {
 trace("There is no recognized camera connected to your
  ➥computer.");
 video = new AltVid();
 addChild(video);
}

snapshot_btn.addEventListener(MouseEvent.CLICK, onSnapshot);

function onSnapshot(e:MouseEvent):void {
 stage.addEventListener(Event.ENTER_FRAME, moveDown);
 snapshot_btn.visible = false;
 channel1 = fx1.play();
}

function moveDown(e:Event) {

 if(jt0.position.y < 305) {
  var pt0:Point = new Point(jt0.position.x + 5,
   ➥jt0.position.y + 5);
  mover0.moveTo(pt0);
 } else {
  channel1.stop();
  channel2 = fx2.play();
  channel1 = fx1.play();
  stage.removeEventListener(Event.ENTER_FRAME, moveDown);
  stage.addEventListener(Event.ENTER_FRAME, moveUp);
 }
}
```

```
function moveUp(e:Event):void {
 if(jt0.position.y > 165) {
   var pt0:Point = new Point(jt0.position.x - 5,
    ➥jt0.position.y - 5);
   mover0.moveTo(pt0);
 } else {
   stage.removeEventListener(Event.ENTER_FRAME, moveUp);
   snapshot_btn.visible = true;
   channel1.stop();
 }
}
```

4 Test your movie to see the results of this camera code.

In the testing environment, you should see either a message telling you that no video camera is connected to your machine (or that Flash is not recognizing your camera) or a Flash Player Settings dialog box requesting access to the camera that has been recognized.

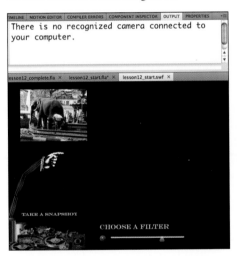

About the camera and microphone settings

If a SWF file contains ActionScript, like the getCamera() method you used in this lesson, that requests access to a user's camera or microphone, then the security that is built into Flash Player will display a screen giving the user the option of permitting or denying this access. As a developer, there is nothing you can do to override this security, but you can write code that will inform your application as to whether or not the user granted permission, so that you can then write alternate content in case the user denies camera access.

5 Assuming you see the dialog box, click Allow to grant Flash Player access to your camera. You should see the live video feed in the upper-left corner of the stage.

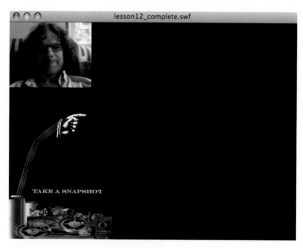

The live video camera reveals that the diligent author is sleep deprived and needs a shave.

6 Close the lesson12_start.swf file to leave the testing environment.

You will doubtless think of many creative and fruitful uses for the Camera class in your own projects. In this project, you will use the snapshot button to create still images from the video feed. To do this, you'll use some very robust ActionScript classes for creating and manipulating bitmap images. After that, you'll use some new tools that ship with Flash CS4 to manipulate the snapshots.

Using the Bitmap and BitmapData classes

If you wish to create and manipulate bitmap graphics with ActionScript, you'll want to get to know the Bitmap and BitmapData classes well. In this lesson, we will introduce and use a few features of these classes.

The BitmapData and Bitmap classes work together in a manner not unlike the way that the Camera class and the Video class were used in the previous section. Typically, a BitmapData instance is used to store the pixel information for a bitmap image, and that data is passed to an instance of the Bitmap class to be displayed on stage.

A method of the BitmapData class called draw() lets you draw a bitmap copy of any display object in Flash and display it in a Bitmap instance. You will use this draw() method to take snapshots from the video feed.

First, however, you will create a new variable to store a bitmap image.

1 Near the top of the Actions panel for frame 1, locate the line that reads:

```
var mover0:IKMover = new IKMover(jt0, jt0.position);
```

2 On a new line below this code, create a new variable with the data type `Bitmap`:

```
var bmp:Bitmap;
```

When the snapshot button has been clicked and the armature reaches its bottom target, you have already set a "click" sound to play. It is at this point that a snapshot should be taken and displayed. This functionality all belongs in the `else` portion of the `moveDown()` function. You will add this snapshot functionality now.

3 Locate the `else` statement of the `moveDown()` function in the Actions panel.

4 Below the line of code that reads:

```
channel1 = fx1.play();
```

insert the following code:

```
var bData:BitmapData = new BitmapData(camera.width, camera.
 ➥height);
```

This line creates a new instance of the `BitmapData` class. The two parameters are for the `width` and `height` of the new bitmap data; here, they are set to match the size of the onstage camera feed. Next, you will use the `draw()` method of the `BitmapData` class to capture a still from the camera feed.

5 On the line below the code that you added, insert the following:

```
bData.draw(video);
```

The parameter of the `draw()` method indicates which display object will be drawn into the `BitmapData` instance. In this case, the `video` instance is being drawn. As mentioned earlier, the `BitmapData` instance doesn't display the bitmap data; to do this, you create a `Bitmap` instance in the variable you set up for this purpose.

6 On the line below the code you just added, type the following:

```
bmp = new Bitmap(bData);
addChild(bmp);
```

The new `Bitmap` instance takes the `BitmapData` instance as its parameter. The subsequent line (`addChild(bmp)`) adds the new `bitmap` instance to the display list and puts it onstage.

When things are added to the stage using `addChild()`, they are given the default position of the stage's upper-left corner (0,0). Since this is already the location of the camera feed, you need to move the Bitmap object.

7 Below the last line you added, type the following lines:

```
bmp.x = 220;
bmp.y = 20;
```

As you can easily surmise, this shifts the object 220 pixels to the right and 20 pixels down.

Before you test the movie, scale the bitmap up a little by setting its scaleX and scaleY properties.

8 Add this line below the last code you entered:

```
bmp.scaleX = bmp.scaleY = 2;
```

The full moveDown() function should now read:

```
function moveDown(e:Event) {

  if(jt0.position.y < 305) {
   var pt0:Point = new Point(jt0.position.x + 5,
    ➥jt0.position.y + 5 );
   mover0.moveTo(pt0);
  } else {
   channel1.stop();
   channel2 = fx2.play();
   channel1 = fx1.play();


    var bData:BitmapData=new BitmapData(camera.width, camera.
     ➥height);
    bData.draw(video);
    bmp = new Bitmap(bData);
    addChild(bmp);
    bmp.x = 220;
    bmp.y = 20;
    bmp.scaleX = bmp.scaleY=2;


    stage.removeEventListener(Event.ENTER_FRAME, moveDown);
    stage.addEventListener(Event.ENTER_FRAME, moveUp);
  }
}
```

● **Note:** Beyond the basic methods you've learned here, the Bitmap and BitmapData classes contain many additional methods and properties that offer a wide range of possibilities for code-driven graphics.

9 Test the movie. After you click the Allow button to grant permission to access the camera, the video feed should appear (if there is not a connected camera then the *AltVid* clip will play instead). When you click the Take a Snapshot button, the arm lowers, and a still image of the current video image should appear on the right.

There are already a lot of cool things going on in this project, but we'll discuss one final set of features that will take advantage of some tremendous new creative possibilities in Flash CS4. The new Shader classes in ActionScript 3.0 work with the Adobe Pixel Bender technology to let you write your own image-manipulating filters and apply them dynamically in your Flash projects. The Pixel Bender Toolkit lets you write, test, and compile these filters. It is beyond the scope of this book to cover these processes in detail, but it is worth taking a brief look at these tools to get a feel for how they work.

Examining the Pixel Bender Toolkit

When you install Flash CS4 on your machine with the default installer, the Pixel Bender Toolkit is also installed. (If it is not, you can install it from the original install disk or download it from www.adobe.com.) On the Macintosh, this application can be located at Applications/Utilities/Adobe Utilities/Pixel Bender Toolkit. On Windows, it is located under /Program Files/Adobe/Adobe Utilities/ Pixel Bender Toolkit. You can launch it on Windows by selecting Start/Programs/ Adobe/Adobe Pixel Bender Toolkit.

1 Locate or install the Pixel Bender Toolkit application on your machine, and then launch it.

   The Pixel Bender Toolkit lets you create filters using a relatively easy-to-learn language and save them to be used in Flash. It also lets you import, modify, and test existing filters. This is good way to get a sense of how Pixel Bender Toolkit works.

   To work with the Pixel Bender Toolkit, you need to create or open an existing filter and load an image to test the filter. Start by loading an image.

Note: In Flash, Pixel Bender filters can be applied to MovieClips, buttons, video, text fields, or BitmapData using ActionScript. However, in the Pixel Bender Toolkit they can only be tested on JPG and PNG files.

2   In the Pixel Bender Toolkit, choose File > Load Image 1.

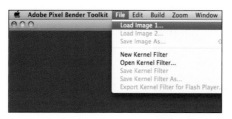

The Open Image File dialog box displays a default folder of sample images. Select one of these, or navigate to select any JPEG or PNG image on your computer, and click OK.

The next step is to load a filter.

3   Choose File > Open Kernel Filter.

Navigate to the Lessons > Lesson12 > filters4PixelBenderToolkit folder, select twirl.pbk, and click Open. (The twirl.pbk filter is one of the many filters that come with the Pixel Bender Toolkit; many more are available online at www.adobe.com and other locations.)

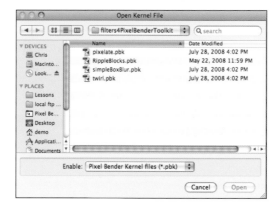

4 Choose Build > Run to see this filter applied to your selected image.

When the filter runs, it is compiled and applied to the selected image. The parameters for the loaded filter can be controlled using the sliders on the right.

You can export these filters for use in Flash by choosing File > Export Kernel Filter for Flash Player.

You will not need to do this right now, since you will be working with precreated filters in this lesson, but digging deeper into the possibilities available with this application via Flash Help and resources at Adobe.com would be time well spent.

For now, quit the Pixel Bender Toolkit and return to Flash, where you will use a provided ActionScript file to add Pixel Bender capabilities to your lesson file.

Examining the PBFilter.as file

In the interest of keeping the timeline code in the lesson file from getting too long, an external ActionScript file has been provided that you will integrate into the lesson project to let users select and use the Pixel Bender filter of their choice. It is beyond the scope of this lesson to go through every line in the PBFilters class, but it is worth taking a look at the code in this file and noting a couple of significant points.

1 In Flash CS4, choose File > Open, and navigate to the Lessons > Lesson12 > Start folder.

2 Open the PBFilter.as file.

3 Notice lines 12 through 16. These variable declarations indicate much of what this class will do.

This file contains an instance of the FileReference class. This class is used to let users upload files to a server and browse to locations on their hard drives. In this project, it will allow users to choose the location of a Pixel Bender filter on their computers.

```
12        private var fr:FileReference;
13        private var shader:Shader;
14        private var shaderFilter:ShaderFilter;
15        public var filterValue:Number;
16        public var filterName:String;
```

Line 13 creates a variable to store an instance of the Shader class, which is used to represent a Pixel Bender filter in ActionScript.

Line 14 references the ShaderFilter class, which is used to apply a Pixel Bender filter using ActionScript.

Notice that lines 15 and 16 create public variables called filterValue and filterName. These variables are both set to public so they can be referenced in external files. You will work with both these variables soon in this lesson's project.

4 Examine line 18. Since this function (PBFilter) has the same name as the file (PBFilter.as), it is clearly the constructor function (see Lesson 4, "Creating ActionScript in External Files," for a review of constructor functions). Notice that this function takes two parameters. The first one has a data type of Bitmap, and the second a data type of Number. This means that when an instance of the class is created, it can pass a Bitmap reference and a number. You will use these parameters in your Flash file to tell this class which bitmap image will receive the filter selected by the code in this file. The numeric value will set an initial property of that filter.

```
18          public function PBFilter(image:Bitmap=null, val:Number = 0):void
19          {
20              filterValue = val;
21              image2Filter = image;
22              fr = new FileReference();
23              fr.addEventListener(Event.SELECT, onSelect);
24              fr.addEventListener(Event.COMPLETE, onComplete);
25              fr.browse();
26          }
27
```

5 Scroll down to line 35 and examine the onComplete() function. Notice that
   this function is set to be public. This function will be called once each time the
   user selects a filter to apply to an image, but it will also be called from the Slider
   instance in the lesson file to manipulate the filter's parameters. Since each Pixel
   Bender filter can have many parameters with various names, this function looks
   to see if the selected filter has one of the most common parameter names; if
   it does, it will let the user adjust that parameter. You will work with the Slider
   component in the lesson file to give the user the ability to adjust whichever of
   these parameters is available.

```
35          public function onComplete(e:Event=null):void
36          {
37              shader = new Shader(fr.data);
38              filterName = fr.name;
39              if(shader.data.radius!= undefined){
40              filterName += ": radius";
41              shader.data.radius.value = [filterValue];
42              }else if(shader.data.amount != undefined){
43                  filterName += ": amount";
44                  shader.data.amount.value = [filterValue];
45              }else if(shader.data.amplitude != undefined){
46                  filterName += ": amplitude";
47                  shader.data.amplitude.value = [filterValue];
48              }else if(shader.data.Radius!= undefined){
49                  filterName += ": Radius";
50              shader.data.Radius.value = [filterValue];
51              }
52              shaderFilter = new ShaderFilter();
53              shaderFilter.shader = shader;
54              image2Filter.filters = [shaderFilter];
55          }
56      }
```

You may want to come back to this file and use it as a starting point for your own
experiments, but for now, close the PBFilter.as file. You will import it into your
project file for this lesson.

Working with the PBFilter class

There are three interface elements on the stage of the lesson12_start.fla file that you
have not yet used. These will work with the PBFilter class you just examined to
add live filtering to the snapshots taken using this project.

1   If it's not still open, reopen the Lessons > Lesson12 > Start > lesson12_start.fla file.

2   Select frame 1 of the `actions` layer in the timeline, and make the Actions panel visible.

You will soon be working with the Slider instance that is onstage. If you recall from previous lessons, the `SliderEvent` class needs to be imported in order to work with its events in ActionScript.

3   Below the first line of the Actions panel that reads:

```
import fl.ik.*;
```

insert an `import` statement for the `SliderEvent` class:

```
import fl.events.SliderEvent;
```

Now create a new variable that will be used to store an instance of the `PBFilter` class you just examined.

4   Locate the line that reads:

```
var bmp:Bitmap;
```

5   Below this line, add the following code:

```
var filter:PBFilter;
```

Using the onstage interface elements to add filters

Three interface elements onstage give the user control over applying filters to their snapshots. The filter_btn instance will be used to let the user select a filter. The valueText field will give the user textual feedback on the filters. The `fSlider` instance will be used after the user has applied a filter to alter a parameter of the filter.

Your users will not need the ability to place a filter on a snapshot until they have actually taken a snapshot, so when the file first launches you will hide all three of the interface elements, and subsequently make them visible as needed.

1   On the line below the code you added in the previous step, insert these lines:

```
valueText.visible = false;
fSlider.visible = false;
filter_btn.visible = false;
```

The code you just added will make the text field, the slider, and the button invisible when the project starts up. Remember that snapshots are taken within the `else` statement of the `moveDown()` function, so that is also the place where the user will need to use the button and see the text field.

Insert code into this function to make the button and text field visible. You will also insert text into the text field to instruct the user to select a filter.

2 Locate the `else` statement of the `moveDown()` function, and below the line that reads:

```
bmp.scaleX = bmp.scaleY = 2;
```

insert the following lines:

```
valueText.visible = true;
valueText.text = "\n" + "Choose a Filter";
filter_btn.visible = true;
fSlider.visible = false;
```

With this code in place, when a snapshot has been taken, the user will see the button and text that will instruct them to select a filter.

The full (and final) `moveDown()` function should now read:

```
function moveDown(e:Event) {

  if(jt0.position.y<305) {
   var pt0:Point = new Point(jt0.position.x + 5,
     ➥jt0.position.y + 5);
   mover0.moveTo(pt0);
  } else {
   channel1.stop();
   channel2 = fx2.play();
   channel1 = fx1.play();

   var bData:BitmapData = new BitmapData(camera.width, camera.
     ➥height);
   bData.draw(video);
   bmp = new Bitmap(bData);
   addChild(bmp);
   bmp.x = 220;
   bmp.y = 20;
   bmp.scaleX = bmp.scaleY = 2;


   valueText.visible = true;
   valueText.text = "\n" + "Choose a Filter";
   filter_btn.visible = true;
   fSlider.visible = false;

   stage.removeEventListener(Event.ENTER_FRAME, moveDown);
   stage.addEventListener(Event.ENTER_FRAME, moveUp);
  }
}
```

Adding a function to the filter_btn

The filter_btn instance will give users the ability to select a filter and apply it to the snapshots they have taken. Most of the work to accomplish this will be done by an instance of the PBFilter class that will be created when the user clicks this button.

1 Below all the existing code in this file, add an event listener for the filter_btn with the following code:

```
filter_btn.addEventListener(MouseEvent.CLICK, onFilter);
```

2 Below the line you just typed, add the shell for the onFilter() function that the filter_btn will call:

```
function onFilter(e:MouseEvent):void {

}
```

The first thing this function will do is create a new instance of the PBFilter class.

3 Within the braces of the onFilter() function, add this line:

```
filter = new PBFilter(bmp, fSlider.value);
```

If you recall, the constructor function of the PBFilter class takes two parameters, the first being a Bitmap. Here you send it the onstage bitmap (bmp) that contains the current snapshot. The second parameter that is passed comes from the number currently stored as the value of fSlider.

When this filter_btn instance is clicked, the PBFilter instance opens a dialog box that lets the user select a filter to apply to the current snapshot.

Next, you'll add code to this function to enable the slider.

4 Below the line you just typed, add the following two lines:

```
fSlider.visible = true;
valueText.text = "\n" + "Choose a Value";
```

The first of these lines makes the slider visible. Now that a filter has been selected, the fSlider should be available to change its parameters.

The second line changes the text in the text field to instruct the user to choose a value with the slider.

5 Test the movie. Notice that when the movie launches, the button, text field, and slider are not visible.

6 Click the Take a Snapshot button. When the snapshot appears, the Choose a Filter button and text field become visible.

7 Click the Choose a Filter button. A dialog box opens to let you select a filter.

8   Browse to the Lessons > Lesson12 > filters4Flash folder, and select one of the filters.

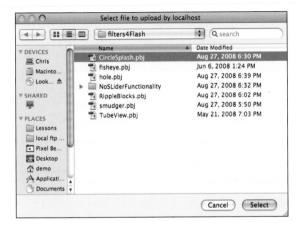

The filter you selected should be applied to your snapshot. Experiment with some of the other filters in the filters4Flash folder. If you create your own Pixel Bender filters or download filters from the web, they can also be used with this project.

9   Notice that even though the slider is now visible, moving it has no effect.

10 Close the lesson12_start.swf file to leave the testing environment.

The final step of this project is to program the `fSlider` instance to manipulate a filters parameter.

Manipulating a filter parameter with the Slider

In previous lessons, you have used the Slider component a number of times. In those lessons, you have used the CHANGE event of the `SliderEvent` class to do something when the user drags the slider. The CHANGE event fires only when the user stops dragging, so it occurs only once for each drag. To get real-time updates of a filter while the user drags the `fSlider`, you will use a different Slider event. This one is called the THUMB_DRAG event (the little *thingy* that the user slides around is known as the *thumb*), and it occurs repeatedly while the slider is being dragged.

1   Below all the existing code for this file, add an event listener for the THUMB_DRAG event:

```
fSlider.addEventListener(SliderEvent.THUMB_DRAG, valueChange);
```

The `valueChange()` function communicates with the `PBFilter` instance to change the values of the loaded filter.

2 Add the shell for this function:

```
function valueChange(e:SliderEvent):void {

}
```

If you recall, the PBFilter class had a `public` property called `filterValue`. Because that property is public, it can be set using the value of the slider.

● **Note:** Many developers frown upon the practice of allowing properties in a class file to be set from outside the file. They deem it desirable, in many situations, to keep the classes independent of any other files, so they can be reused. To accomplish tasks like the one you're doing here, you could use getter and setter functions instead of setting the class files properties directly. This is probably something you don't need to worry about too much now, but may want to keep in mind for the future. For more information, see Colin Moock's *Essential ActionScript 3.0*.

3 Insert the following line between the curly braces of the `valueChange()` function:

```
filter.filterValue = fSlider.value;
```

Now you'll add code to change the text in the valueText field to show the name of the selected filter as well as the current value of the fSlider.

4 On the next line, add the following code:

```
valueText.text = filter.filterName + " \n" + "Value: " +
➡filter.filterValue;
```

The final step is to call the public function named `onComplete()` in the PBFilter instance. If you recall, this function scans through a number of common filter parameters, and if it finds one that's contained in the currently applied filter, it will take the slider's value as that parameter value. Most of the supplied filters have a parameter that this function will recognize.

5 On the line below the code you just entered, add this code:

```
filter.onComplete();
```

The final `valueChange()` function should read:

```
fSlider.addEventListener(SliderEvent.THUMB_DRAG, valueChange);

function valueChange(e:SliderEvent):void {
  filter.filterValue = fSlider.value;
  valueText.text = filter.filterName + " \n" + "Value: " +
    ➡filter.filterValue;
  filter.onComplete();
}
```

The completed code for the entire file is:

```
import fl.ik.*;
import fl.events.SliderEvent;

var arm0:IKArmature = IKManager.getArmatureAt(0);
var rt0:IKJoint = arm0.rootJoint;
var jt0:IKJoint = rt0.getChildAt(0).getChildAt(0).
➡getChildAt(0);
var mover0:IKMover = new IKMover(jt0, jt0.position);

var bmp:Bitmap;
var filter:PBFilter;
```

```
valueText.visible=false;

fSlider.visible = false;
filter_btn.visible = false;

var fx1:Sound = new Sound();
fx1.load(new URLRequest("robotArm.mp3"));
var channel1:SoundChannel = new SoundChannel();

var fx2:Sound = new Sound();
fx2.load(new URLRequest("click.mp3"));
var channel2:SoundChannel = new SoundChannel();

var camera:Camera = Camera.getCamera();
var video:*;

if(camera != null) {
 video=new Video(160, 120);
 video.attachCamera(camera);
 addChild(video);
} else {
 trace("There is no recognized camera connected to your
  ➥computer.");
 video = new AltVid();
 addChild(video);
}

snapshot_btn.addEventListener(MouseEvent.CLICK, onSnapshot);

function onSnapshot(e:MouseEvent):void {
 stage.addEventListener(Event.ENTER_FRAME, moveDown);
 snapshot_btn.visible = false;
 channel1 = fx1.play();
}

function moveDown(e:Event) {

 if(jt0.position.y < 305) {
  var pt0:Point = new Point(jt0.position.x + 5,
   ➥jt0.position.y + 5);
  mover0.moveTo(pt0);
 } else {
  channel1.stop();
  channel2 = fx2.play();
  channel1 = fx1.play();
  var bData:BitmapData = new BitmapData(camera.width, camera.
   ➥height);
```

(code continues on the next page)

(continued)

```
    bData.draw(video);
    bmp = new Bitmap(bData);
    addChild(bmp);
    bmp.x = 220;
    bmp.y = 20;
    bmp.scaleX = bmp.scaleY = 2;

    valueText.visible = true;
    valueText.text = "\n" + "Choose a Filter";
    filter_btn.visible = true;
    fSlider.visible = false;

    stage.removeEventListener(Event.ENTER_FRAME, moveDown);
    stage.addEventListener(Event.ENTER_FRAME, moveUp);
   }
  }

  function moveUp(e:Event):void {
   if(jt0.position.y > 165) {
    var pt0:Point = new Point(jt0.position.x - 5,
     ➥jt0.position.y - 5);
    mover0.moveTo(pt0);
   } else {
    stage.removeEventListener(Event.ENTER_FRAME, moveUp);
    snapshot_btn.visible = true;
    channel1.stop();
   }
  }

  filter_btn.addEventListener(MouseEvent.CLICK, onFilter);

  function onFilter(e:MouseEvent):void {
   filter = new PBFilter(bmp, fSlider.value);
   fSlider.visible = true;
   valueText.text = "\n" + "Choose a Value";

  }

  fSlider.addEventListener(SliderEvent.THUMB_DRAG, valueChange);

  function valueChange(e:SliderEvent):void {
   filter.filterValue = fSlider.value;
   valueText.text = filter.filterName + " \n" + "Value: " +
    ➥filter.filterValue;
   filter.onComplete();
  }
```

6   Test the movie. Go through the process of taking a snapshot and selecting a filter. When a filter is selected, the slider should appear, and if that filter has one of the coded properties in the onChange() function, you should be able to manipulate that property of the filter live.

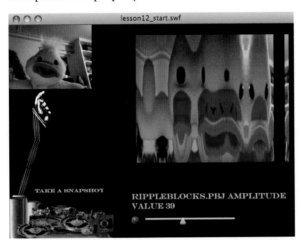

● **Note:** Some of the filters tend to be very processor-intensive. They work beautifully on Intel Macs and newer Windows machines but may perform more slowly for you if you use a PowerPC Mac or an older PC.

Whew! If you made it successfully through this lesson, you are probably starting to get comfortable with ActionScript 3.0. You've just covered a lot of very formidable new material. Again, it is important to remember that most all the classes used in this lesson have many capabilities that were not even touched on. To make full use of them, it is worth taking time to look up each class in Flash Help and see what else it can do.

When you have time, experiment with the many topics introduced in this lesson, and when you feel ready, try to work some of these features into your real-world projects.

Suggestions to try on your own

There are an infinite number of ways that the project in this lesson could be enhanced. Here are just a few:

*   In a copy of the lesson project, try to alter the graphics in the library that are used in the Armature layer.

*   Make your own IK armatures with authoring (timeline) animation, and integrate them into the project as design elements.

*   Change the parameters of the moveTo() methods and experiment with runtime IK animation.

- Set the `jt0` variable to refer to different joints in the armature and check out the resulting animations.

- Use the `draw()` method of the `BitmapData` instance to draw other display objects in the file, and then modify the lesson to add filters to those objects.

- Experiment with the Pixel Bender Toolkit. Try making your own filters or modifying existing ones. Load them into the lesson file.

Review questions

1 What step is necessary in the Flash interface to indicate that an IK armature will be controlled with ActionScript?

2 What are the two IK classes that are created automatically when an armature is created in Flash?

3 Describe the process in ActionScript of displaying the feed from a user's video camera on the Flash stage.

4 Describe the process of creating a bitmap graphic in ActionScript that draws a copy of another display object.

5 What is an event that can be used with the Slider component to do live tracking as the user moves a slider's thumb around?

Review answers

1 An IK armature that will be controlled by ActionScript must have its options in the Properties panel set to Runtime.

2 When an IK Armature is created in the Flash authoring environment, an instance each of the IKManager class and the IKArmature class are created automatically.

3 To display a feed from a camcorder or webcam, an instance of the Camera class is created in ActionScript that uses the getCamera() method to connect to a video camera. An instance of the Video class is created to display the camera feed. The Video instance is connected to the Camera instance using the attachCamera() method of the Video class, and then the Video instance is placed onstage using an addChild() method.

For example:

```
var camera:Camera = Camera.getCamera();
var video = new Video(160, 120);
video.attachCamera(camera);
addChild(video);
```

4   To create a bitmap in ActionScript that is drawn from another display object, you create an instance of the BitmapData class, and then use the draw() method of that class to draw an existing display object to the BitmapData instance. Next, an instance of the Bitmap class is passed the BitmapData, and finally the Bitmap instance is displayed onstage with the addChild() method.

For example:

```
var bd:BitmapData = new BitmapData(400, 300);
bd.draw(someDisplayObject);
bmp = new Bitmap(bd);
addChild(bmp);
```

5   The SliderEvent named THUMB_DRAG will fire continuously while a Slider instance is being dragged around. This can be used to do live tracking of the Slider's value.

13 PRINTING AND SENDING EMAIL WITH ACTIONSCRIPT

Lesson overview

In this lesson, you will learn to do the following:

- Send email from a Flash project.

- Work with a PHP script that will receive email information from ActionScript.

- Send data from Flash to a PHP script using the `URLVariables` class.

- Create new variables in a `URLVariables` instance.

- Print content from a Flash file using the `PrintJob` class.

- Control printing using the methods and properties of the `PrintJob` class.

- Catch errors that may occur while attempting to print using a `try/catch` statement.

 This lesson will take approximately 2.5 hours.

One of the great things about ActionScript is the ease with which it can send and receive data from external sources. You have already taken advantage of this in a number of ways in earlier lessons. In this lesson, you will use ActionScript to control the printing and sending of email from a Flash application. You will learn two different techniques for sending email from Flash and explore the basics of the ActionScript `PrintJob` class, which is used to communicate with the printing capabilities of the user's operating system.

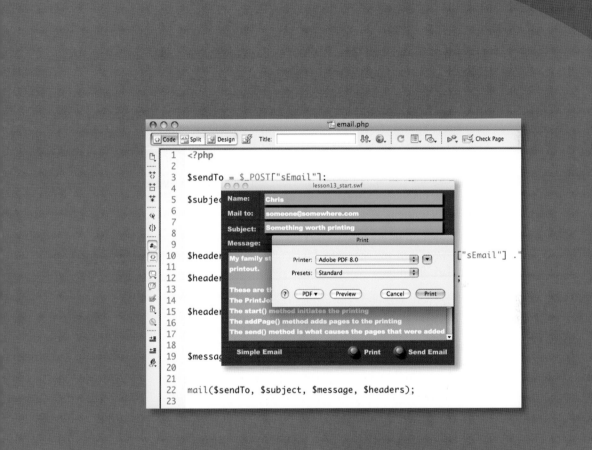

A Flash project can contain powerful printing and emailing capabilities.

Examining the starting file

The starting file for this lesson is actually very simple. It consists of a few text fields and buttons that will be used to type text that can then be printed or sent as an email. By successfully accomplishing this task, you'll have learned how to add email capability and a wide range of printing options to your projects.

1   Open the lesson13_start.fla file from the Lessons > Lesson13 > Start folder.

    The timeline for this lesson has four layers. The `static text` and `background` layers have graphic elements that will be unaffected by ActionScript. The `actions` layer, of course, is where you will place the code for this lesson. The `Interactive Content` layer has a collection of text fields and a pair of buttons that you will use in this lesson.

2   With the Properties panel visible, one at a time select each of the five empty text fields that are on the stage, and notice their instance names and types. There are four input text fields, sporting the instance names of name_text, email_txt, subject_txt, and note_txt. Because the note_txt field is intended to let users type as much text as they want, there's a UIScrollBar component, to make that text field scrollable. There is also one dynamic text field called feedback_txt. The static text field in the lower-left, Simple Email, is also in this layer. You will use this text very soon.

3   Select the buttons in the lower-right, and notice that they have the instance names print_btn and send_btn. Much of the code for this file will be written to take place when these buttons are clicked.

The first features you will add to this project will let the user send email from this file. You will add two different types of email capability—one that is simple but limited and one that is more robust but requires an external server script. By understanding both options, you can use whichever technique is appropriate in your own projects.

Adding a simple email link

You can add a simple link to any text field in Flash using the Properties panel; no ActionScript required. Typically, you would use this technique to create a simple hyperlink to a URL in a browser. You can also use this feature as a simple way of prompting the user to send email. Try this now by adding an email link to a static text field.

1   Select the text field in the lower-left of the stage that reads Simple Email.

2   In the Properties panel, locate the Link field for the Simple Email text field.

3   Populate the Link field to create a mailto link similar to the following (with your own address, of course):

```
mailto:yourName@yourISP.com?subject=From Lesson 13 link&Body=
➥This message was sent from Flash
```

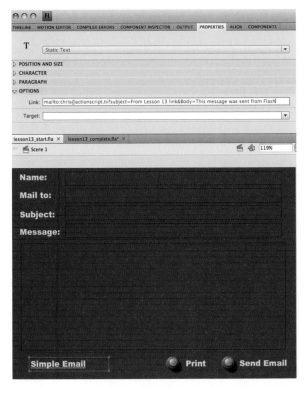

▶ **Caution:** You may have noticed that ActionScript is very forgiving about spaces between names and values. For example, in ActionScript, "clip.x=30;" and "clip.x = 30;" would be treated the same. The spaces are ignored; you can choose whether or not to use spaces based on your personal preference. However, when you create code that will be sent as a URL, as you are doing here for this email link, it is important not to use any spaces at all between names and values.

If you have worked with `mailto:` syntax in HTML pages, then you are familiar with this type of link. After the email address, a question mark is used to indicate the addition of parameters such as subject and body. Each parameter is separated by an ampersand (&). You can change the value of the subject and body parameters to anything you wish.

4 Test the movie. When the text that contains the link is clicked, your default mail application will open and come to the foreground with the address, subject, and body filled in from the link.

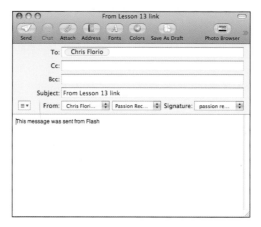

5 Close your mail application.

6 Return to Flash, and close the lesson13_start.swf file to leave the testing environment.

This technique is very simple. However, it relies on an external mail application and requires the user to manually complete the process of sending and potentially altering, the email. There are times when you may want to assure that an email is sent automatically to the user with specific information included. That's when you'd want to have a more sophisticated alternative that uses a server script.

Sending email from Flash

To send email directly from Flash without using the user's mail application as an intermediary involves posting the email data directly from Flash to a server script. The server script can then send the mail directly to the email address(es). There are many server-side languages you could use to process an email address; in this example, you will use a simple PHP script. This script will reside on a PHP-supported server. The PHP script will receive ActionScript variables and use them to create an email that it will then send to an address supplied in the Flash data. For this lesson, a PHP file has been created for you. The one that you will actually use to test this lesson is installed on a server at www.actionscript.tv/email.php. A copy of this file is in the Lesson13 folder.

First, let's examine this file. Open the email.php file from the Lessons > Lesson13 folder.

The PHP file contains a simple mail function. For this lesson, you don't need to have had any experience with PHP; you just need to know that all the references in this file to variables that begin with the "s" prefix represent variable names that will be passed from your Flash project. You will write ActionScript to create and pass values for these variables based on the information your users type in. The PHP file will take care of the rest.

Sending values using the URLVariables class

When you wish to send variables and their values from Flash to an external URL, you can use the ActionScript URLVariables class. You can create an instance of this class and assign variables as properties of the instance. You can then use the instance of the URLVariables class as the data parameter of a URLRequest. When you use the sendToURL() or navigateToURL() method, all the variables that were appended to the URLRequest are sent to that URL. If the description of this technique left you scratching your head at all, it will likely make more sense when you go through it yourself. So the first ActionScript you will add to this project will create instances of the URLVariables and URLRequest classes.

With frame 1 of the actions layer selected and the Actions panel visible, add the following code to the top of the Actions panel:

```
var variables:URLVariables = new URLVariables();

var mailAddress:URLRequest = new
➥URLRequest("http://www.actionscript.tv/email.php");
```

The parameter for the mailAddress instance is the online location of the email. php script you just examined.

The text fields onstage will be the source of the text to be emailed. Before you add code to create the email data, you will first set a few properties for these text fields in your code.

Setting textColor and backgroundColor

As you have seen, many of the properties of a text field can be set either in the interface using the Properties panel or with ActionScript using the properties of the `TextField` and `TextFormat` classes. Oddly enough, one property that cannot be set in the interface is the background color of a text field. In the Properties panel, you have the choice of only a transparent background or an opaque white background. In this case, neither would be appropriate for the input text fields onstage. If the background were transparent, the user would not know where to type, and since the text fields are set to use white text, a white background would make the text impossible to read.

You will add ActionScript that will set the background to be visible for all the input text fields onstage and set their background to a golden color.

1 In the Actions panel, add the following lines below the existing code:

```
note_txt.background = true;
note_txt.backgroundColor = 0xCCAA00;

name_txt.background = true;
name_txt.backgroundColor = 0xCCAA00;

email_txt.background = true;
email_txt.backgroundColor = 0xCCAA00;

subject_txt.background = true;
subject_txt.backgroundColor = 0xCCAA00;
```

2 Test the movie to confirm that the text fields now have background colors.

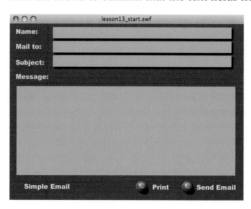

3 Close the lesson13_start.swf file to exit the testing environment.

Sending URLVariables to the PHP file

The text the user types into the onstage text fields will be stored as variables in the URLVariables instance you created named `variables`. Those variables will be set and sent any time the user clicks the send_btn instance (the Send Email button onstage).

Start by adding an event listener to this button.

1 Below the existing code in the Actions for frame 1, add the following line:

```
send_btn.addEventListener(MouseEvent.CLICK, onSubmit);
```

2 On a new line below what you just added, create the shell for the onSubmit() function:

```
function onSubmit(e:Event):void {

}
```

If you recall from Lesson 7, "Using Arrays and Loops in ActionScript 3.0," a dynamic class is one that can have properties and methods added to its instances from external files. The URLVariables class is a dynamic class. Properties added to instances of the URLVariables class are the variables that will be sent when that instance is used as the data for a URLRequest.

In the onSubmit() function, you will create a few properties for the `variables` instance that will store the text that the user types into the input text fields.

3 Within the curly braces of the onSubmit() function, add the following lines:

```
variables.sName = name_txt.text;
variables.sEmail = email_txt.text;
variables.sSubject = subject_txt.text;
variables.sMessage = variables.userName + " has sent this
➥note:" + "\n\n" + note_txt.text;
```

Note the values of these properties (variables) are set similarly to the way that normal string variables are set. The first three lines simply take text from the onstage text fields. The sMessage property joins, or concatenates, the text from two text fields with some literal text. The sMessage property (variable) will be used as the email message.

Now you will set all these URLVariables to be the data property for the URLRequest instance that you created earlier called mailAddress. The data property is used to contain data that is sent to the URL stored in a URLRequest.

4 Above the closing brace of the onSubmit() function, add this line:

```
mailAddress.data = variables;
```

The URLRequest class's method property determines the HTTP form-submission type. Typically this is set to either GET or POST. You will send the variables using the POST method. Set that property now.

5   Add this code below the line you just added:

```
mailAddress.method = URLRequestMethod.POST;
```

Now that all the URLVariables are appended to the URL that you stored in mailAddress (remember that this URL was the location of the PHP file), you can send those variables to this address using the sendToURL() method.

6   Below the last line you typed, add the following code:

```
sendToURL(mailAddress);
```

The final line of this function gives the user some feedback by putting text in the feedback_txt field. In a more robust application, you might want to get confirmation from the PHP file that the email was successfully delivered. In this example, you are just confirming the data was sent to the PHP file.

7   Add the following line above the closing brace of the onSubmit() function:

```
feedback_txt.text = "Your mail has been sent";
```

The final onSubmit() function should now read:

```
send_btn.addEventListener(MouseEvent.CLICK, onSubmit);

function onSubmit(e:Event):void {

    variables.sName = name_txt.text;
    variables.sEmail = email_txt.text;
    variables.sMessage = variables.sName + " has sent this note:" + "\n\n"+note_txt.text;
    variables.sSubject = subject_txt.text;
    mailAddress.data = variables;
    mailAddress.method = URLRequestMethod.POST;
    sendToURL(mailAddress);

    feedback_txt.text = "Your mail has been sent";
}
```

8   Test your movie. Fill out the text fields using your own email address in the Mail To field.

9   Click the Send Email button. The feedback_txt field should inform you that the mail was sent.

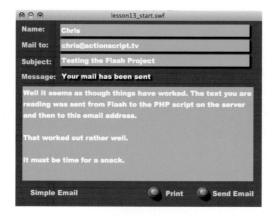

10 Open your default email application and check your email. It may take a few
moments, but an email should arrive with the information that you typed in
Flash.

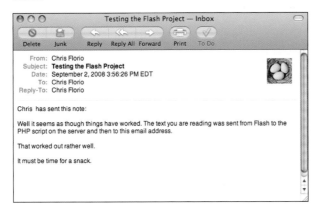

You can use and modify the email.php file and place it on your own server to add
email functionality to your projects.

Now you will add printing capabilities using the `PrintJob` class.

Adding printing capabilities
with the PrintJob class

The `PrintJob` class allows Flash projects to communicate with the printing capabilities of the user's operating system. It can initiate printing, confirm the user's
printing settings, and send multiple pages of specified content to the user's printer.
However, Flash cannot directly control the user's printer, and the success of a
print job from Flash will depend not only on the user having (of course) a properly
connected printer, but also on the user clicking to confirm the print dialog box as
presented by the operating system.

Once a `PrintJob` instance is created, the process of printing proceeds in three
steps, using three methods of the `PrintJob` class. The `start()` method opens the
operating system's Print dialog box. At this point, the ActionScript will pause until
the user either confirms or cancels the printing. If the user confirms the printing,
then the `start()` method will return `true`; if not, it will return `false`.

Assuming that the user has allowed the printing to proceed, the second step of the
process is to use the `addPage()` method of the `PrintJob` class. This method can
send any sprite or frame of a MovieClip to the printer. You can add as many pages
as you wish to a print job by calling the `addPage()` method multiple times.

You have tremendous control over the properties of what to print and how to print it (we will touch on only few of those properties, so consult Flash Help for more information). Finally, when the pages have been added, the send() method of the PrintJob class initiates the printing of the added pages.

In this lesson, you give the user the option of printing the information that they have filled out in the text fields with some additional text added in your ActionScript. On your own projects you have complete control over what is sent to the printer from Flash. As an example, in Lesson 14, "Creating Adobe AIR Applications with Flash and ActionScript," you will add a bitmap image to the document that is sent to the printer.

The printing process will be initiated when the user clicks the print_btn, so start by adding an event listener to that button.

1 On the line below all your ActionScript for frame 1, add this line:

```
print_btn.addEventListener(MouseEvent.CLICK, onPrint);
```

If you guessed that the next step is the shell for the onPrint() function, you guessed right.

2 Add the shell for the onPrint() function below the last line:

```
function onPrint(e:MouseEvent):void {

}
```

Capturing the current date and time with the Date class

It's become a standard convention in email client software that printed emails include some automated header or footer indicating the recipient and the date and/or time it was printed or sent. To achieve this functionality in this project, you will take advantage of the constructor function of the Date class. This class offers many versatile methods and properties for working with time and date-related information. In this case, you will use the Date class in a very simple way: You'll create an instance of the Date class that will return the current date and time, which will then be placed at the top of documents that the user prints.

Creating an instance of the Date class is the same as with other classes you have used.

1 Within the curly braces of the onPrint() function, add this line:

```
var now:Date = new Date();
```

You will use the Date instance you just created in documents that the user prints.

This is an example of a place where tracing the code you just typed might be useful. Remember, tracing is just a developer tool to help you get feedback on your ActionScript as you work. In this case, if you haven't worked with the Date() constructor before, it might be helpful to see what it returns.

2 Add this line below the previous one:

```
trace(now);
```

3 Test the movie. When you press the Print button, the Output panel will present the current date and time in its default format.

```
Sep 2 18:06:23 GMT-0400 2008
```

Get in the habit of tracing code as you work whenever you're not sure what the results of a specific action might be. You will probably encounter many situations where `trace()` statements can be helpful.

4 Close the lesson13_start.swf to leave the testing environment.

5 The `trace()` statement has served its purpose, so if you like, you can delete it or comment it out by placing two forward slashes at the beginning of the line:

```
//trace(now);
```

Creating the content to print

When the user clicks the Print button, his or her name, the date, and whatever text was typed in the note_txt field will be printed. Remember that the `PrintJob` class will be looking for a Sprite or MovieClip instance to print. You will store all the text to be printed in a variable, place that variable in a new Sprite instance, and then print that Sprite. All of this will go in the `onPrint()` function.

Start by creating the string of text that will be sent to the printer. This will go in a new variable named `note`.

1 Above the closing brace of the `onPrint()` function, add the following line:

```
var note:String = name_txt.text + " has sent this note on:" +
➥"\n" + String(now) + "\n\n" + note_txt.text;
```

As already described, this line combines the name that the user typed in the Name field with the date and time from the `Date` instance and the message they typed into the note_txt field.

Soon you will place this text in a new `TextField` instance, but first you'll create the `PrintJob` instance.

2 On a line below the previous line you typed, add the following:

```
var printNote:PrintJob = new PrintJob();
```

As mentioned earlier, when a print job is started, it will return either `true` or `false`, depending on whether the user chose to print (`true`) or cancel (`false`). Therefore, it is a good idea to confirm that the `start()` method returns `true` before proceeding with processing the `PrintJob`. You will do this with a conditional statement.

3 Below the last line that you typed, create the shell for a new conditional statement that checks to see if the `start()` method returns the value `true`:

```
if(printNote.start()) {

}
```

Remember that the code in Flash stops until the `printNote.start()` method returns either `true` or `false`. If it returns `true`, the conditional statement runs, and if not, it ends. Whatever code you type in the `if` statement will run only when the user clicks to confirm the printing.

This all seems fairly predictable and straightforward, and in most cases, the printing should proceed uneventfully at this point. However, anyone who has ever used a printer before knows that even when the user confirms a print job, there are still any number of potential problems that could cause an error in the printing. If any one of these potential problems occurs, it could cause a runtime error in your Flash project that would stop the Flash project from running altogether. There is nothing you can do in ActionScript to fix a problem with the user's printer, but you can prevent printer problems from stopping your Flash movie. You will do this next, with a `try/catch` statement.

Using try/catch statements in ActionScript

You can use a `try/catch` statement in ActionScript any time there is potential for a runtime error that could halt your application. A `try/catch` statement is used for errors similarly to the way an `if/else` statement is used for conditions. In a `try/catch` statement, if no errors take place, then the code within the `try` block of the statement executes. If there is an error, then the `catch` block of the code runs; that is, it handles the error. The act of "catching" the error prevents the file from being halted by the error.

1 Below the line that reads:

```
if(printNote.start()) {
```

add the shell for a `try/catch` statement with this code:

```
try {

} catch(e:Error) {

}
```

Notice that the shell of the `try/catch` statement resembles the basic syntax of an `if/else` statement.

The `try` statement contains the code that will execute if there are no errors in the printing. The first things you will create in the `try` statement are the TextField instance to contain the text to be printed and a new Sprite instance to contain the TextField.

2   Beneath the code that reads:

```
try {
```

create two new instances with these lines:

```
var pageSprite:Sprite = new Sprite();
var noteText:TextField = new TextField();
```

When the user clicks OK in the Print dialog box, the current printer settings are sent to Flash. These settings can be accessed as properties of the `PrintJob` instance. The `paperWidth` and `paperHeight` properties tell you the printable area of the selected paper size on the user's printer. You can use these properties to set the size of the text field to match the printable area. Do this now.

3   Beneath the previous line that you added, place this code:

```
noteText.width = printNote.paperWidth;
noteText.height = printNote.paperHeight;
```

Now place the text from the `note` variable into the new text field.

4   On the line below what you just typed, add the following line:

```
noteText.text = note;
```

Now that the text field and Sprite are ready to go, place the Sprite in the display list and the text field in the Sprite. (You will leave them in the display list only long enough to print, so the user will never see these objects onstage.)

5   Add this code below the last line you typed:

```
addChild(pageSprite);
pageSprite.addChild(noteText);
```

Now that the `pageSprite` is set to print, add it to the `PrintJob` instance using the `addPage()` method.

6   On the line below the code you just added, type this code:

```
printNote.addPage(pageSprite);
```

This completes the code that executes in the `try` statement. You will just add a simple `trace` statement in the `catch` block to report an error if it occurs.

7 Below the line that reads:

```
} catch(e:Error) {
```

insert this line:

```
trace("There was an error");
```

This completes the try/catch statement. There should be a single closing brace below the line you just typed, and two more closing braces below that: one for the if statement and for the entire onPrint() function.

...and now to the printer

The last two lines you'll add to this project will send the pageSprite to the printer and then remove it from the display list.

1 Below the first of the three closing braces (the one for the try/catch statement), add these two lines:

```
printNote.send();
removeChild(pageSprite);
```

The entire onPrint() function should now read:

```
function onPrint(e:MouseEvent):void {
 var now:Date = new Date();

 var note:String = name_txt.text + " has sent this note
➥on:" + "\n"+String(now) + "\n\n" +  note_txt.text;

 var printNote:PrintJob = new PrintJob();

 if(printNote.start()) {
  try {
   var pageSprite:Sprite = new Sprite;
   var noteText:TextField = new TextField();
   noteText.wordWrap = true;
   noteText.width = printNote.paperWidth;
   noteText.height = printNote.paperHeight;
   noteText.text = note;
   addChild(pageSprite);
   pageSprite.addChild(noteText);
   printNote.addPage(pageSprite);
  } catch(e:Error) {
   trace("There was an error");
  }
  printNote.send();
  removeChild(pageSprite);
 }
}
```

Don't forget to double-check that you have the right number of braces.

The code for the entire file should read:

```
var variables:URLVariables = new URLVariables();
var mailAddress:URLRequest = new URLRequest(
➥"http://www.actionscript.tv/email.php");


note_txt.background = true;
note_txt.backgroundColor = 0xCCAA00;

name_txt.background = true;
name_txt.backgroundColor = 0xCCAA00;

email_txt.background = true;
email_txt.backgroundColor = 0xCCAA00;

subject_txt.background = true;
subject_txt.backgroundColor = 0xCCAA00;


submit_btn.addEventListener(MouseEvent.CLICK, onSubmit);

function onSubmit(e:Event):void {
 variables.sName = name_txt.text;
 variables.sEmail = email_txt.text;
 variables.sSubject = subject_txt.text;
 variables.sMessage = variables.userName + " has sent this
  ➥note:" + "\n\n" + note_txt.text;
 mailAddress.data = variables;
 mailAddress.method = URLRequestMethod.POST;
 sendToURL(mailAddress);

 feedback_txt.text = "Your mail has been sent";

}

print_btn.addEventListener(MouseEvent.CLICK, onPrint);


function onPrint(e:MouseEvent):void {
 var now:Date = new Date();

 var note:String = name_txt.text + " has sent this note
  ➥on:" + "\n" + String(now) + "\n\n" + note_txt.text;
```

(code continues on the next page)

(continued)

```
var printNote:PrintJob = new PrintJob();

if(printNote.start()) {
 try {
  var pageSprite:Sprite = new Sprite;
  var noteText:TextField = new TextField();
  noteText.wordWrap = true;
  noteText.width = printNote.paperWidth;
  noteText.height = printNote.paperHeight;
  noteText.text = note;
  addChild(pageSprite);
  pageSprite.addChild(noteText);
  printNote.addPage(pageSprite);
 } catch(e:Error) {
  trace("There was an error");
 }
 printNote.send();
 removeChild(pageSprite);
}

}
```

2 Test your movie. Fill in all the fields on the stage.

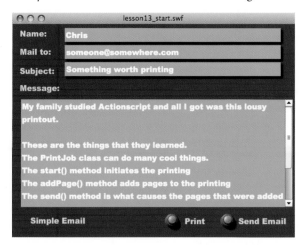

3   Click the Print button. The normal Print dialog box of your operating system will appear.

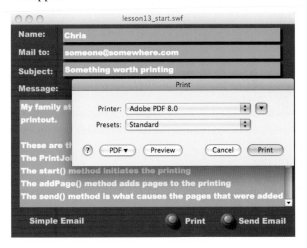

4   Click to Print. If you have a printer connected to your computer, the text you typed in the name and note fields, along with the date, will print.

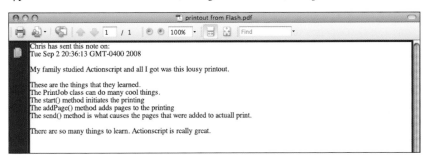

For everything from game scores to product receipts and test results, being able to print and send email from Flash offers countless creative options for your projects. Bear in mind that you do not have to create a sprite specifically for printing, as you did in this lesson, but could instead print any existing sprite, any frame of any movie clip, or the root timeline of any Flash file. Remember you determine what is printed with a parameter in the addPage() method.

In the next lesson, you'll see that by using the new Adobe AIR technology you can have even more interaction with the user's operating and file systems.

Some suggestions to try on your own

A number of features were introduced in this lesson that you may want to pursue more deeply, particularly the method and properties of the `PrintJob` and `Date` classes. You can also try some of these ideas:

- Try uploading the email.php file to your own server. Experiment with the code in this file to format the email in other ways.

- Add additional text fields to the screen. Create corresponding variables in the `URLVariables` instance to add this text from the new text fields to your emails.

- Study the methods and properties of the `Date` class in Flash Help, and format the date and time in your emails any way you like.

- Study the parameters of the `addPage()` method of the `PrintJob` class and modify the way the document is printed.

- Add graphics to the sprite that will print. Use techniques covered in earlier chapters to include images in your printing.

- Create a TextFormat object to set the style or size of the text that is printed.

Review questions

1 What are the limitations of sending email using a text-field link?

2 Name a `TextField` property that cannot be set in the Flash interface.

3 Which class is used to send variables to a URL?

4 What three methods of the `PrintJob` class are used to control printing from ActionScript?

5 What is a process used in ActionScript to prevent a runtime error from halting playback?

Review answers

1 While an email link on a text field is very convenient, it has the limitations of relying on the user and the user's default email application to assure that the email is sent. It also gives the user the opportunity to delete or alter data that was included in the email from Flash.

2 The background color of a text field cannot be set in the Flash interface; it can only be controlled using the `backgroundColor` property of the `TextField` class in ActionScript.

3 The `URLVariables` class is used to create variables for sending to a URL.

4 The `start()` method opens the operating system's Print dialog box to initiate printing. The second step (assuming the user has allowed the printing to proceed) adds pages to print using the `addPage()` method. Finally, the `send()` method sends the page(s) to the printer.

5 A `try/catch` statement is used in ActionScript to catch potential runtime errors that could halt the application. In a `try/catch` statement, the `try` block of code is executed with code that has the potential to cause an error. If no error occurs, the code in the `try` statement proceeds normally. If an error does occur, however, the code in the `catch` block of the statement occurs instead. The basic syntax of a `try/catch` statement is:

```
try {
  something that could produce an error();
}
catch(errObject:Error) {
  someReponseToError()
}
```

14

CREATING ADOBE AIR APPLICATIONS WITH FLASH AND ACTIONSCRIPT

Lesson overview

In this lesson, you will learn how to do the following:

* Use Flash to create cross-platform desktop applications.

* Assign the Flash publish settings for Adobe AIR applications.

* Customize the AIR application and installer settings.

* Set custom icons for an AIR application.

* Create a digital signature for an AIR application.

* Use AIR classes in ActionScript to create interaction with the user's operating system.

* Publish and install an AIR application.

* Create drag-and-drop functionality in an AIR application using ActionScript.

* Use the `File` and `FileStream` classes to read data from external files.

This lesson will take approximately 2 hours.

Although Flash has always been used to create content for both online and offline work, it has traditionally been considered primarily a web tool. Most Flash developers typically create Flash content designed to be played back as SWF files in the user's browser.

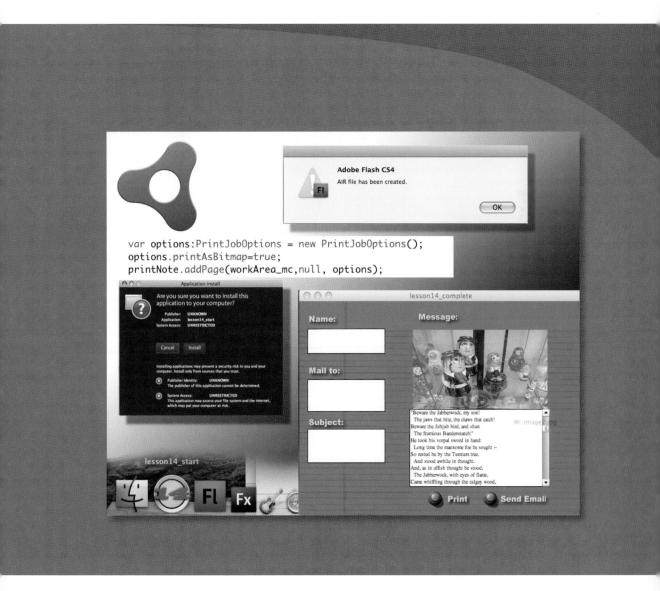

```
var options:PrintJobOptions = new PrintJobOptions();
options.printAsBitmap=true;
printNote.addPage(workArea_mc,null, options);
```

Standard Flash development tools can now make
desktop AIR applications.

Adobe has recently introduced a new technology called AIR (Adobe Integrated Runtime) that lets you leverage your existing Flash skills to create desktop applications.

AIR applications can be created within Flash using the same toolset you use for creating traditional Flash projects. Instead of publishing the finished project for Flash Player, you publish the project as a stand-alone AIR application. This resulting file plays as a true desktop application on Macintosh, Windows, or Linux machines as long as the AIR runtime is installed. Users who do not have the AIR runtime and try to view an AIR application are prompted to download and install the runtime for free.

AIR applications can be built with standard web tools like Flash, Flex, and Dreamweaver using languages including ActionScript, JavaScript, and HTML. All the design and interactive tools in Flash can be incorporated into an AIR application, and the entire ActionScript 3.0 language is supported in AIR applications. This means that you can immediately incorporate all your existing Flash skills and ActionScript knowledge as you start to create desktop applications.

In addition to using your existing skills in AIR, applications created in Flash for distribution as AIR applications can add functionality not available to Flash projects intended to play as SWF files in a browser. For security reasons, online Flash projects have very limited access to your user's operating system, but AIR applications have the same access as other desktop applications, including the ability to read and write files to the user's machine, copy and paste to the clipboard, and drag and drop into and out of other applications. In addition, AIR applications can include browser capabilities, integrate pdf files, and can create local databases on the user's machine using built-in SQLite capabilities.

This lesson is not intended as a full overview of the capabilities of Adobe AIR, rather to give you a sense of how Flash can be used to create AIR applications and to see some of the features in ActionScript available for AIR projects. If you are interested in pursuing development for Adobe AIR, there are a number of good books on the subject as well as plenty of information at Adobe AIR Developer Center for Flash, found at www.adobe.com/devnet/air/flash/.

In this lesson, you will set up a Flash project to create an AIR application. You will use a variation of the project from Lesson 13, "Printing and Sending Email with ActionScript," convert it to an AIR application, and then add some AIR-specific ActionScript to give the project drag-and-drop capabilities. The resulting file from this lesson will be a stand-alone, cross-platform AIR application.

AIR-specific ActionScript

As mentioned, AIR applications can take advantage of the entire ActionScript 3.0 language, but there is quite a bit of ActionScript that is created specifically for AIR and cannot be used in normal Flash web projects.

The ActionScript 3.0 Language and Components Reference, which can be found within Flash Help as well as online at Adobe.com, has information about every class in the ActionScript language. If you go through the list of classes in this reference, you will notice that a number of them have the red AIR logo next to the class name.

The classes that display this logo contain ActionScript that will work in an AIR application but should not be used in a normal Flash SWF file.

Note: Notice that reference information for NativeWindowType in the ActionScript 3.0 Language and Components Reference indicates that this is an AIR-only class.

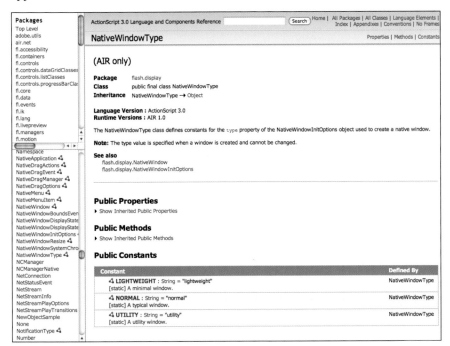

Looking briefly at this list, you will see that there are many AIR-specific classes to explore that can add quite a lot of features to your applications. Many developers are creating applications in AIR or creating projects that are a combination of online Flash applications and offline AIR applications. For examples of work created in AIR, you can visit Adobe AIR showcase at www.adobe.com/products/air/showcase/.

Before you start writing AIR-specific ActionScript, let's look at the settings in Flash for turning a Flash project into an AIR application.

Flash publish settings for an AIR project

In order to turn a Flash project into an AIR application, you need to set the Flash publish settings to indicate that your file should be published for AIR. You will do this for the Lesson 14 project file.

1   From the Lessons > Lesson14 > Start folder, open the lesson14_start.fla file.

This file is a variation on the completed file from Lesson 13. You will take a closer look at its content and code soon, but first you'll set its publish settings to turn it into an AIR project.

2   From the File menu, choose Publish Settings.

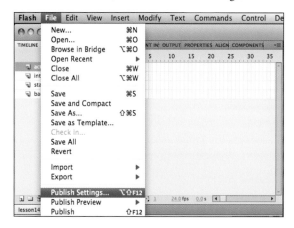

3   In the Publish Settings dialog box, select the Flash tab. The Player menu is currently set to Flash Player 10, indicating that publishing will create a SWF file for that version. From the Player menu, switch to Adobe AIR 1.1. (That's the latest version at the time of writing, but if you have a more recent version, choose that.)

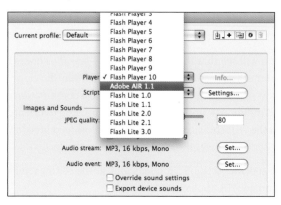

Now that you have selected to publish as an AIR application, you can adjust the settings for this AIR file using (how appropriate) the Settings button to the right of the Player menu.

Setting the AIR descriptor file options

When an AIR file is created, it uses an XML descriptor file to determine many of its settings, including how the AIR application's default window will be displayed and what icons will be used by the operating system to represent the application. This file is created, and the settings chosen, via the AIR - Application & Installer Settings dialog box in Flash. Alternatively, in this dialog box you can point to an existing descriptor file to determine these settings.

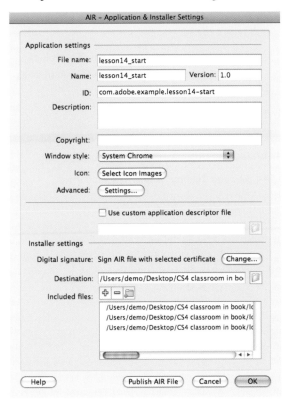

It is beyond the scope of this book to go through all of these application and installer settings in detail, and you'll leave most of them at their defaults for this project. You will, however, use a few to set some custom icons, create a digital signature, and set an included image for the project.

Setting custom icons

Because AIR applications are true desktop applications, they are represented in the operating system with icons the same way as any other application. You can choose your own graphics to be used as icons, creating or fine-tuning them in Photoshop or any other graphics application. Up to four files can be used for any one icon: They must be PNG format, and they must be in the specific sizes of 128×128, 48×48, 32×32, and 16×16 pixels. The user's operating system will use the different sized icons under different circumstances. For example, the larger icons might appear in the Macintosh Dock and in the Windows System Tray. The Lesson14 folder has some graphics provided in the correct format for icons. You'll assign those files to be the icons for your AIR application.

1   In the AIR - Application & Installer Settings dialog box, click the Set Icon Images button.

    Here you will see the default icons provided for AIR applications. To replace these defaults, you'll select the browse folder next to each of the four icon sizes. (Remember that the sizes have to match exactly.)

2   Select the folder icon next to the 128×128 image.

3   Browse to the Lessons > Lesson14 > Icons folder, and select the file named AIRicon128.png to assign the first icon.

4   Repeat Steps 2 and 3 for the 48-, 32-, and 16-pixel icons. The filenames correspond to the icon sizes.

5   Click OK when you are finished.

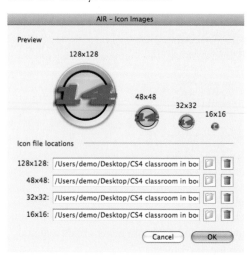

Soon you will test the AIR application and view the icons, but first you will create a digital signature.

Creating a digital signature

An AIR application requires a digital signature. The purpose of a digital signature in an AIR application, or any application, is to provide your users with some assurance as to the creator of the application. For a high level of security, you can provide a verified digital signature for your application by purchasing one from an authorized certificate authority. You can find more information about this at the Adobe AIR Developer Center (www.adobe.com/devnet/air/). In less critical situations, you can create unverified signatures in Flash that work fine. You will do that now.

1   In the AIR - Application & Installer Settings dialog box, click the Set button next to the Digital signature settings.

2   In the Digital Signature dialog box, click the Create button.

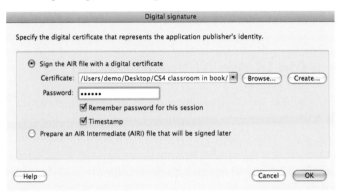

3   Fill out the project information in the Create Self-Signed Digital Certificate dialog box however you like. Since security is not a priority for this file, choose a password that is short and easy to remember. You can leave the default encryption of 1024-RSA (2048-RSA is more secure, but again, this is not a high-security situation).

4   Browse to the Lessons > Lesson14 folder to indicate the location to store the digital certificate.

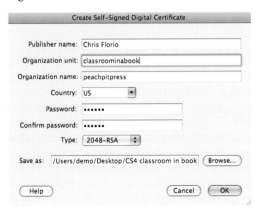

5 Click OK.

You should see a simple dialog box telling you the certificate has been created.

6 Click OK again. This will return you to the Digital Signature dialog box.

7 Enter the password you just created in the Password field.

8 Select "Remember password for this session," and click OK to return to the AIR - Application & Installer Settings dialog box.

Including a file in the AIR application

By default, when you publish an AIR application, the Flash project from which it was made and the XML descriptor file that contains its settings are automatically included in the AIR application. If there are other files that are required by the application such as media that is loaded at runtime, those files can be included in the AIR application as well. You will do this with the JPG file that is loaded into the UILoader component in this project.

1 Locate the Included files area at the bottom of the AIR - Application & Installer Settings dialog box.

2 Click the Add (+) button to include a file in the AIR application.

3 In the dialog box that appears, navigate to the Lessons > Lesson14 > Start folder and select the image5.jpg file.

4 Click to include the image and leave the dialog box.

Leave the rest of the AIR settings at their defaults.

Next, you will use the settings you just applied to publish an AIR application from this project.

Creating an AIR application

When you publish an AIR project, an AIR file (.air) is created. This is an installer file which, when opened, steps the user through a fairly standard process of installing the application on a local hard drive. You do not need to go through this publishing process every time you want to test your AIR file—the Flash testing environment and Test Movie command work fine with AIR projects—but it is worth publishing at least once to see what to expect from the process and to see in action the custom icons that you installed.

Continuing from the previous steps, you should still be in the AIR - Applications & Installer Settings dialog box preparing to create an AIR application from the lesson14_start.fla.

1 In the AIR - Application & Installer Settings dialog box, choose the browse folder next to the Destination field.

2 Browse to select the Lessons > Lesson14 folder, and click Save.

3 At the bottom of the AIR - Application & Installer Settings dialog box, click the Publish AIR File button.

4 Click OK to the dialog box that appears, telling you the AIR file has been created.

5 Navigate to the Lessons > Lesson14 folder, locate the lesson14_start.air file, and double-click it. This is the installer file for the project that you just created.

6 An Application Install dialog box appears. Notice that because the digital signature is unverified, the publisher is listed as unknown. Click the Install button.

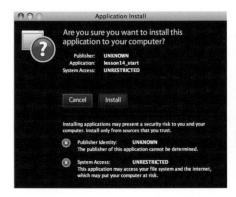 

7 Click the browse folder next to the Installation Location field, and choose the location on your hard drive where you wish to install the application. The default location is in the Applications (Mac) or Program Files (Windows) folder. You may wish to change this to the Lessons > Lesson14 folder.

8 Make sure that the "Start application after installation" option is selected, and click Continue.

Your AIR application is installed in the location that you selected and launches automatically.

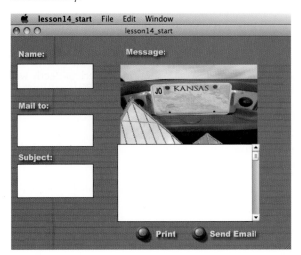

Notice that this is a true application with standard window controls for maximizing, minimizing, and closing that are appropriate to your operating system. If you are on a Mac, you should also see the default File, Edit, and Window menus.

Application menus in AIR

If you wish to experiment with ActionScript for AIR, you will find AIR classes in the ActionScript 3.0 Reference Guide that let you code your own custom menus and write functions that respond when menu items are selected. You can also create contextual menus for interactive objects, and even create custom menus for the Dock or Taskbar icons. There are many other ways that AIR applications can be customized with ActionScript to behave like other applications you have worked with.

9 Before closing the application, notice your Dock (Mac) or Taskbar (Windows). You should see the custom icon that you assigned showing that the application is running.

10 Notice that the features in this application are the same as what you added to the Lesson 13 project. The email and print functionality still works. An image has been added in a `UILoader` instance and a few graphical changes have been made, but otherwise this is the same basic file and code that you have already worked with. You will add some AIR-specific ActionScript to this file to give it some functionality that would not be available to SWF files.

11 Quit the application and return to Flash.

Examining the starting file

As mentioned earlier, the lesson14_start.fla file is a slightly modified version of the completed Lesson 13 file. As the project stands now, it would work perfectly well in Flash Player as a SWF file, and as you just saw, this file was also easily turned into an AIR application.

Soon you will add some drag-and-drop functionality to this file that will work only in AIR, but first take a moment to familiarize yourself with a few differences between this file and the Lesson 13 file.

If you completed Lesson 13, you should notice changes to the layout and color of the graphics and text onscreen. The layout changes are mainly in order to accommodate the additional `UILoader` instance in the upper-right of the stage. This UILoader component and the preexisting note_txt field have both been embedded in a MovieClip symbol.

1 With the Properties panel visible, select either the UILoader or the large text field below it on the stage. You will see in the Properties panel that they are both part of a MovieClip with an instance name of *workArea_mc*.

2   With this clip still selected, choose Edit > Edit Symbols.

You will see that this clip stores a UILoader component with an instance name of `imgLoader`, an input text field named note_txt, and a UIScrollBar component with an instance name of `scroller`.

Soon you will use the AIR classes in ActionScript to allow the user to drag text documents into the note_txt field and image files from their desktop or other open applications into the imgLoader component. The reasons for containing these clips together in a movie clip are so that they can both be part of the same drag operation and so that the image and text can be printed together. If you recall from the previous lesson, the `addPage()` method of the `PrintJob` class lets you easily send the contents of a `MovieClip` to the printer.

3   Return to the Edit menu, and choose Edit Document to return to the main Flash Timeline.

A closer look at the ActionScript file

In addition to the layout and color changes to the Lesson 13 file mentioned, a few modifications to the completed code have also been made to this file. Examine these changes before adding AIR functionality to this project.

Select frame 1 of the `actions` layer in the timeline, and view the ActionScript in the Actions panel.

If you completed the Lesson 13 project, most of this code should be very familiar. If you compare it to the completed Lesson 13 file, you will see that the code that formatted the background of the text fields has been removed. This is solely for the sake of simplifying the code. Feel free to add your own text-formatting code.

The code in the `onSubmit()` function that is used to send email is identical to what you saw in Lesson 13.

The main changes to the code are in the `onPrint()` function, to accommodate the new UILoader and the *workArea_mc* clip and to make sure that this clip prints accurately when the user clicks the Print button.

One change worth pointing out is on lines 42–44. These lines create a new instance of a class called `PrintJobOptions`. One of the properties of this class allows a `PrintJob` to be sent to the printer as bitmap graphics rather than as default vector graphics. Since this project sends text and images to the printer, this property is set to `true`. In line 44, these `PrintJobOptions` are added as the third parameter when the `addPage()` method sends the page to the printer. The rest of the `PrintJob` instance's ActionScript here should be familiar from the previous lesson.

```
42          var options:PrintJobOptions = new PrintJobOptions();
43          options.printAsBitmap = true;
44          printNote.addPage(workArea_mc, null, options);
```

You will not need to make any changes to the printing and email functions that are already here. Instead, you will add two new functions to this file that will add drag-and-drop capabilities to the project. This will let users drag external text and image files into your AIR application. You will take advantage of a number of ActionScript AIR classes to do this, including the `NativeDrag` class, the `File` class, and the `Clipboard` class. The first class you will add to the project is the `NativeDragEvent` class, but first you will import the AIR classes that you will use.

Listening for drag events

The `NativeDragEvent` class is used to keep track of drag-and-drop events in AIR applications. In this project, you will use events in this class to respond when a file is initially dragged over the *workArea_mc* clip and when a file is dropped on this clip. The two events you will use are called `NATIVE_DRAG_ENTER` and `NATIVE_DRAG_DROP` respectively. As you might guess, they work in the same basic way as all the other ActionScript events you have used.

1   Below all the existing code on frame 1 of the `actions` layer, add listeners for these two events with this code:

```
workArea_mc.addEventListener(NativeDragEvent.
➡NATIVE_DRAG_ENTER, onDragEnter);
workArea_mc.addEventListener(NativeDragEvent.NATIVE_DRAG_DROP,
➡onDragDrop);
```

2   Next, add the shells for the two functions that these events will trigger:

```
function onDragEnter(e:NativeDragEvent):void {

}

function onDragDrop(e:NativeDragEvent):void {

}
```

Using ClipboardFormats

Drag-and-drop capabilities (and copy and paste capabilities) in AIR projects use the operating system's clipboard to perform their tasks. There are ActionScript classes that let AIR applications take advantage of nearly all the native operating system's clipboard functionality, including drag and drop.

One useful clipboard feature is the ability to check what type of data has been stored on the clipboard. When a file is dragged, copied, or cut to the clipboard, you can determine if the data on the clipboard is text, bitmap, HTML, or some other type of data. Being able to check what is on the clipboard is useful when writing ActionScript that will determine how and if the clipboard's contents are used.

Often, a single file on the clipboard has multiple types of data. When one or more files are placed on the clipboard, one of the types of data is *file data*, which contains a list of the files placed on the clipboard. The onDragEnter() function will check to see if there is file-list data on the clipboard. If the clipboard does contains file information, then a method of the NativeDragManager class called acceptDragDrop() is used to allow the *workArea_mc* to receive files that are dropped on it.

Add code to the onDragEnter() function so that the full function now reads:

```
function onDragEnter(e:NativeDragEvent):void {
  if(e.clipboard.hasFormat(ClipboardFormats.FILE_LIST_FORMAT)) {
    NativeDragManager.acceptDragDrop(workArea_mc);
  }
}
```

Now that the *workArea_mc* clip is set to receive files that are dropped on it, you will use the onDragDrop() function to determine what is done with those dropped files.

Adding the onDragDrop() function

In the onDragEnter() function, you added code that checked if file-list data had been dragged over the *workArea_mc* clip. Now, if the user drops the items over the *workArea_mc* clip, the first thing you want to have happen is to store (in a local array) the names of the file or files that were dropped.

1 Between the curly braces of the onDragDrop() function, add this code to create a new array:

```
var cbFiles:Array = e.clipboard.getData(
  ➥ClipboardFormats.FILE_LIST_FORMAT,
  ➥ClipboardTransferMode.CLONE_ONLY) as Array;
```

The clipboard.getdata() method retrieves the data on the clipboard only if it's in the format indicated in its first parameter. In this case, the data is of the type clipboardFormats.FILE_LIST_FORMAT. The second parameter indicates whether a reference to the original file(s) or a copy of the file(s) is retrieved. CLONE_ONLY indicates that a copy of the file data is retrieved.

Recall that you want to load compatible images into the imgLoader instance and text files into the note_txt field. To accomplish this, you will create two arrays. The first will contain the possible suffixes for compatible image files, the second for text files. Then you will create two for loops, which will be used to see if the file dropped on the *workArea_mc* clip has any of the suffixes stored in the arrays and determine what to do with the data.

First, you'll create the two arrays of file types.

2   Above the closing brace of the onDragDrop() function, add these lines:

```
var imageTypes:Array = new Array("jpg", "jpeg", "png", "gif");
var textTypes:Array = new Array("txt", "html", "htm", "xml",
➥"as", "php", "rtf");
```

Next you will store a reference to the first file that was dropped on the *workArea_mc* clip and to that file's name. These references will check if it is one of the file types stored in the imageTypes and textTypes arrays.

3   Add this code below the last lines that you typed:

```
var file:File = cbFiles[0];
var str:String = cbFiles[0].name;
```

About the File and FileStream classes

The file variable you just created stores an instance of the File class. Soon you will use the FileStream class to read the data in that file.

The File and FileStream classes are two of the most useful AIR-specific ActionScript classes. They can be used to open, create, and save files and write data to existing files. If you plan to create your own AIR applications, it would be valuable to make a thorough study of these two classes.

At this point, the onDragDrop() function should read:

```
function onDragDrop(e:NativeDragEvent):void {
  var cbFiles:Array = e.clipboard.getData(
    ➥ClipboardFormats.FILE_LIST_FORMAT,
    ➥ClipboardTransferMode.CLONE_ONLY) as Array;

  var imageTypes:Array = new Array("jpg", "jpeg", "png", "gif");
  var textTypes:Array = new Array("txt", "html", "xml", "as", "php",
    ➥ "rtf");

  var file:File = cbFiles[0];
  var str:String = cbFiles[0].name;
}
```

Looping through the file type arrays

Next, you will add two separate `for` loops within the `onDragDrop()` function. The first will cycle through all the suffixes in the `imageTypes` array to see if any of those suffixes are in the name of the file that was dragged in. The second loop will do the same for the `textTypes` array.

1   Above the closing brace of the `onDragDrop()` function, add this `for` loop:

```
for(var i:int = 0; i < imageTypes.length; i++) {

}
```

Within the braces of this `for` loop, you will add a conditional statement to check each element in the `imageTypes` array against the name of the file that was dragged in. The `indexOf()` method of the `String` class will search for the file suffixes in the `imageTypes` array.

2   Within the braces of the `for` loop you just created, add code so that the loop reads:

```
for(var i:int = 0; i < imageTypes.length; i++) {
  if(str.indexOf(imageTypes[i], 0) != -1) {
    workArea_mc.imgLoader.source = file.url;
  }
}
```

The first parameter of the `indexOf()` method represents the characters that are being searched for. Each time the loop repeats, it will search for a different string from the `imageTypes` array. The second parameter represents the first character in the string to begin searching. In this case, the search starts at the first character in the `str` instance and searches the whole string for the `imageType` elements. If the search finds the characters it is looking for, then a number will be returned representing the location of the string that was found. If the string is not found, the method will return -1. So, the `if` statement checks to see if `indexOf()` does not return -1.

If there is a match, it will mean that the file that was dragged onto the *workArea_mc* clip is one of the image types that the `UILoader` supports, in which case that `UILoader` instance's (`workArea_mc.imgLoader`) `source` property is set to the file that was dropped. This will cause the dropped image to appear in the `UILoader` instance.

Finally, a second `for` loop will be added to do a similar thing with the area for the text file types.

3　Below the closing brace of the `for` loop you just typed and above the closing brace of the `onDragDrop()` function, add the second `for` loop with this code:

```
for(var j:int = 0; j < textTypes.length; j++) {

}
```

Like the first `for` loop, this one will use a conditional statement to see if the name of the dropped file contains one of the strings stored in an array, only this time it will be the `textTypes` array.

4　Between the braces of the new `for` loop, add a conditional statement so that the `for` loop now reads:

```
for(var j:int = 0; j < textTypes.length; j++) {
  if(str.indexOf(textTypes[j], 0) != -1) {

  }
}
```

If the conditional statement that you just added returns `true`, then you know that the user dropped a file that contains text onto the *workArea_mc* clip, in which case you use the `FileStream` class to stream the byte data from the text file into Flash. You will then store this data in a new variable named `data`, and display that string in the note_txt text field.

5　Add code to the current `for` loop so that it reads:

```
for(var j:int = 0; j < textTypes.length; j++) {
  if(str.indexOf(textTypes[j], 0) != -1) {

    var fs:FileStream = new FileStream();
    fs.open(file, FileMode.READ);
    var data:String = fs.readUTFBytes(fs.bytesAvailable);
    fs.close();

    workArea_mc.note_txt.text = data;
  }
}
```

The line that reads:

```
var fs:FileStream = new FileStream();
```

creates a new `FileStream` instance. The next line:

```
fs.open(file, FileMode.READ);
```

uses the `open()` method to open the data in a File object. The first parameter points to a `File` instance; the second parameter determines how the data will be used. In this case, the data will be read. This method can also be used to write data, which is how files can be both created and saved in AIR applications.

The next line:

```
var data:String = fs.readUTFBytes(fs.bytesAvailable);
```

stores all of the byte data from the text file in a new local variable, named data, as a string.

Once the data has been stored, the close() method is used to close the FileStream.

Finally, the text data from the dropped file is placed onstage in the note_txt field:

```
workArea_mc.note_txt.text = data;
```

The full onDragDrop function should read:

```
function onDragDrop(e:NativeDragEvent):void {
 var cbFiles:Array = e.clipboard.getData(
  ➥ClipboardFormats.FILE_LIST_FORMAT,
  ➥ClipboardTransferMode.CLONE_ONLY) as Array;
 var imageTypes:Array = new Array("jpg", "jpeg", "png",
  ➥"gif");
 var textTypes:Array = new Array("txt", "html", "htm", "xml",
  ➥"as", "php", "rtf");

 var file:File=cbFiles[0];
 var str:String=cbFiles[0].name;

 for (var i:int = 0; i < imageTypes.length; i++) {
  if (str.indexOf(imageTypes[i],0) != -1) {
   workArea_mc.imgLoader.source = file.url;
  }
 }

 for (var j:int = 0; j < textTypes.length; j++) {
  if (str.indexOf(textTypes[j],0) != -1) {
   var fs:FileStream = new FileStream();
   fs.open(file, FileMode.READ);
   var data:String = fs.readUTFBytes(fs.bytesAvailable);
   fs.close();
   workArea_mc.note_txt.text = data;
  }
 }
}
```

6 Test your movie in the normal manner. (When the publish settings are set to create an AIR application, the Test Movie command creates an AIR application instead of a SWF file in the testing environment.)

The file should look about the same as the last time you tested it.

7   Try dragging a JPG, GIF, or PNG file from the desktop or any open application over the UILoader instance in your project. Drag and drop a text file (in one of the formats stored in the textTypes array). The text should appear in the note_txt field. When you click the Print button, the most recent image and text that you selected (along with the date and user name) will print.

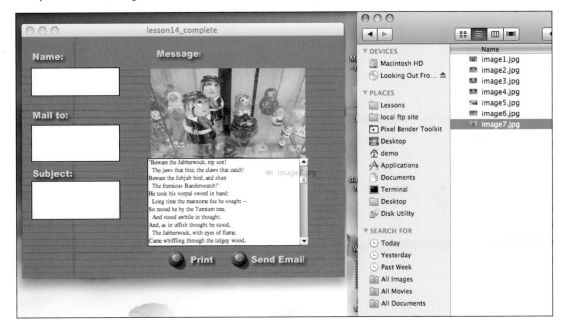

If you publish the file, you could create and distribute an installer that includes your file with the settings and icons you set earlier in the lesson. This file would install and run on Macintosh, Windows, and Linux computers.

As mentioned at the beginning of the lesson, this is just a taste of the capabilities available for AIR applications using ActionScript. Hopefully, it will lead you to a deeper study of the creative possibilities that this technology offers.

Some suggestions to try on your own

There are countless possible ways you could expand on the file from this lesson. Here are few ideas:

* Create your own custom icons in your favorite graphics application and set them to be the icons for the AIR application.

* Use the filter techniques covered in Lesson 12, "Delving Deeper into Graphics and Animation with ActionScript," to apply a filter to the image that you drag into the project from this lesson. Print out files with the filters applied to them.

- Use a TextFormat object to format text that you drag into this application.

- Add a Camera object to the *workArea_mc* clip and include that in your printouts.

- Create AIR applications out of some of the other lesson projects that you've completed. Try creating AIR applications out of some of your own Flash projects.

Review questions

1 How is a Flash project turned into an AIR application?

2 What is the purpose of a digital signature in an AIR application?

3 What are the requirements for the four graphics files to be used as an AIR application's icons?

4 Which ActionScript 3.0 classes will work with AIR?

5 What native drag event is dispatched when a file is dragged onto an object in an AIR application? What event is dispatched when the file is dropped?

6 Which AIR-specific ActionScript classes are used to read and write files?

Review answers

1 An AIR application can be created from a Flash CS4 file by choosing Adobe AIR as the Player format in the Publish Settings dialog box (File > Publish Settings) for that file.

2 A digital signature in an AIR application is used to identify the publisher of the application, as a security measure for the end user.

3 The four graphics files to be used as an AIR application's icons must be PNG files. Their dimensions must be 128×128, 48×48, 32×32, and 16×16 pixels respectively.

4 All of the ActionScript 3.0 language works with Adobe AIR applications. In addition to the normal ActionScript classes, there are many ActionScript classes that are specific to AIR and will not work with SWF files. (These AIR-only classes are called out in the ActionScript 3.0 Language and Components Reference guide within Flash Help.)

5 The `NativeDragEvent.NATIVE_DRAG_ENTER` is dispatched when a file is dragged onto an object in an AIR application. `NativeDragEvent.NATIVE_DRAG_DROP` is dispatched when the file is dropped.

6 The `File` and `FileStream` classes are AIR-specific ActionScript classes used to read and write files.

INDEX

SYMBOLS

* (asterisks)
  in ActionScript, 75, 131
  to import classes, 277
_ (underscore), in ActionScript names, 31
{ } (curly braces)
  .as files and, 66–67, 68
  calling functions and, 35
  for loop and, 226
  setSongs() function and, 226
+ (plus sign), adding dynamic text fields
  and, 37
++ characters, variables and, 20
+= (plus equal), property values and, 48
< > (greater than and less than
  characters), XML tags and, 219
<!-- and --> characters, XML comments
  and, 219
= (single equal signs)
  changing MovieClip properties and,
    47
  language selection and, 39
  variables and, 19
== (double equal sign), language
  selection and, 39
: (colons)
  after variables, 19
  creating functions and, 31
  data types, setting and, 50, 60
. (dots), changing MovieClip properties
  and, 47
() (parentheses), creating functions and,
  31, 40, 171
"" (empty quotation marks), 199
../ (two dots and initial forward slash),
  201

NUMBERS

3.0 class files structure, 65–70
3D, rotating in, 137

A

access modifiers
  basics of, 156
  in Ellipse class, 67
Actions panel
  code and, 17
  coordinating with other panels, 15
  testing and, 57
  timeline and, 15
  wrapping and, 109
ActionScript
  3.0 vs. 1.0 and 2.0, 10–11
  AIR-specific, 333
  bones and, 273
  classes in files, 154
  control of FLVPlayback properties
    with, 247–250
  files, creating radio button quiz in. *See*
    radio button quiz, creating
  Flash and, 1, 9–10
  IK and, 272
  integrating with Flash video, 242
  naming rules in, 31
  new files, creating, 152–153
  prerequisites for using, 1–2
  resources, 4–5
  vs. timeline (Flash), 12–13
ActionScript, creating in external files,
  62–80
  ActionScript files, creating, 64–70

to control language, 38–41
more songs button function, 236–238
radio buttons, 156. *See also* radio
button quiz, creating
restart buttons, adding, 36–37
buttons for song selection, 200–205
chooseSong() function, 201–202
event listeners, adding, 200–201
Sound class instances, 202–203
Sound instances, loading, 203
SoundChannel and SoundTransform
instances, 203–205
updating, 237–238

C

calls, adding to setSongs() function, 231
Camera class, 285, 286, 290
cameras. *See* users' video cameras,
accessing
captions with FLVCaptioning
component, 254–257
case sensitivity
ActionScript and, 31
event names and, 30
naming functions and, 31
trace statements and, 130
casting, 252–253
CHANGE event listener, adding to List
component, 87
changeVid() function, creating, 261–264
Check Syntax function, 158
checkAnswer() function, 177–182
code to write, 178
functions, calling in timeline, 179–182
child elements (XML), 220
chooseSong() function, 201–203, 205,
231–233
class files
calling functions from, 179–182
conventions (ActionScript), 156
defined, 65
importing classes in, 277
instances of, creating. *See* instances of
class files (Flash), creating
properties in, 302
structure of, 65–70
Tween class, 55
variables and, 172
class variables, defined, 172

classes. *See also specific* classes
ActionScript, 65, 67, 333
AIR and, 333
dynamic, defined, 134
easing in ActionScript, 54–55
extending, 155
importing, 154
linkage properties to create new, 128
naming, 31
properties, setting, 302
wildcard (*) to import, 277
click.mp3, 283
ClipboardFormats (for AIR), 343–344
clips. *See* MovieClip properties;
MovieClips
code
ActionScript files and, 64
complex Flash projects and, 64
empty lines in, 35
code, placing on timeline, 17–24
conditional statements and, 22–24
labels, 17–18
looping playback, 18–21
colons (:)
after variables, 19
creating functions and, 31
data types, setting and, 50, 60
color
of ellipses, 75–77
email backgroundColor, 316
email textColor, 316
hexadecimal color, 70
color in videos, 250–254
casting to data types, 252
ColorPicker component, 250–251
skinBackgroundColor, 252–254
ColorPicker component, 250–251
comments, adding to files, 195–196
COMPLETE events
completeHandler() function, 110–111
to confirm loading external text,
92–93
distinguishing between, 261
listener for, 108
XML playlists and, 224–225
Component Inspector
creating button instances and, 33
FLVPlayback properties and, 244–245
List component and, 85
setting skins and, 246

Contributor

Chris Florio is an interactive media artist and teacher. He has been working with and teaching Flash and ActionScript since they existed. Chris is a faculty member of the New England Institute of Art's Web Design and Interactive Media Department. He teaches courses in ActionScript, AIR Development, Flash Video, Game Programming, and Interactive Performance. Students of the Interactive Performance class use ActionScript and other tools in a concerts with the Metrowest Symphony Orchestra, Hopkinton, Massachusetts.

Chris is also a composer and the director of Passion Records (www.passionrecords.com). He has released three CDs under his name and has composed music for many orchestras and ensembles. He lives in Ipswich, Massachusetts, with his wife Helen, dog Katy, and cat Esther. When not writing ActionScript or making music, he keeps sane by going for long walks with his wife and watching Jon Stewart while drinking good beer.

Dedication This book is dedicated to my wife Helen, who of course had to live through months of my ActionScript explorations and still seems to love me.

Acknowledgments Thanks to a terrific editorial team: Rebecca Freed, Robyn Thomas, Wendy Katz, Angela Nimer, and Matthew Newton, who were great to work with and saved me from embarrassing myself countless times. Thanks to many others who helped make the process successful and enjoyable, particularly Christine Yarrow, Chuck Toporak, Hannah Latham, Karen Reichstein, and Tracey Croom.

This book exists because of the amazing work of the Flash and ActionScript teams at Adobe. Thanks to them all. Special thanks for help on this book and support with the prerelease versions of Flash CS4 to Kevin Lynch, Justin Everett-Church, Mally Gardiner, Richard Galvan, Ashu Mittal, and Donna Dunn.

Thanks to the Web Design and Interactive Media Department (WDIM) at the New England Institute of Art (NEIA), whose faculty members provide an inspiring environment for creating and learning. Thanks in particular to WDIM chair Lauri Stevens, and all the administration at NEIA, for giving me the space to work on this book.

Appreciation to all my ActionScript students at NEIA, for inspiring me to dig deeper into ActionScript and for kicking my butt on a regular basis. Thanks to Max Jackson, Derek Tran, and Kyle Kellogg, students and serious ActionScripters who gave feedback and/or inspiration for the lessons.

It is due to the generous members of the Flash community that I and countless others stay abreast of the latest and coolest ActionScript techniques. Since there are too many to mention, I salute them all. Thanks to Keith Peters, Chris Allen, and Michelle Yaiser, who run the Boston Flash User Group and keep the standards high.

Special thanks to Passion Records, Jonathan Keezing, David Horton, Peter Cokkinias, Mimi Rabson, Thomas Sanger-Elnaes, Hiro Honshuko, and Mike Rivard for permission to use their music and performances in the audio and video files for the lessons.

Thanks to my mother Marianne Florio and all my family: I love you all.

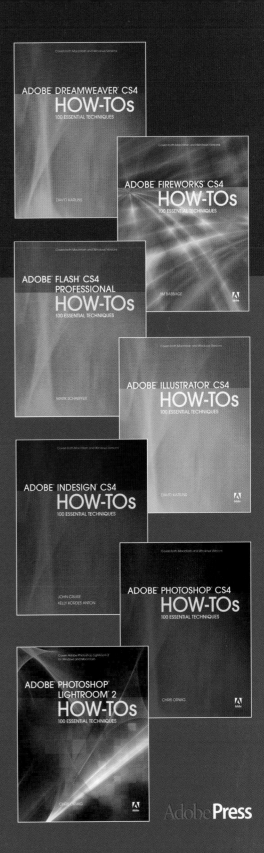

The fastest, easiest, most comprehensive way to learn
Adobe· Creative Suite· 4

Classroom in a Book®, the best-selling series of hands-on software training books, helps you learn the features of Adobe software quickly and easily.

The **Classroom in a Book** series offers what no other book or training program does—an official training series from Adobe Systems, developed with the support of Adobe product experts.

To see a complete list of our Adobe® Creative Suite® 4 titles go to www.peachpit.com/adobecs4

ActionScript 3.0 for Adobe Flash CS4 Professional Classroom in a Book
ISBN: 0-321-57921-6

Adobe After Effects CS4 Classroom in a Book
ISBN 0-321-57383-8

Adobe Creative Suite 4 Classroom in a Book
ISBN: 0-321-57391-9

Adobe Dreamweaver CS4 Classroom in a Book
ISBN 0-321-57381-1

Adobe Fireworks CS4 Classroom in a Book
ISBN 0-321-61219-1

Adobe Flash CS4 Professional Classroom in a Book
ISBN 0-321-57382-X

Adobe Illustrator CS4 Classroom in a Book
ISBN 0-321-57378-1

Adobe InDesign CS4 Classroom in a Book
ISBN 0-321-57380-3

Adobe Photoshop CS4 Classroom in a Book
ISBN 0-321-57379-X

Adobe Premiere Pro CS4 Classroom in a Book
ISBN 0-321-57385-4

Adobe**Press**